C000212186

The Anne Dialogues

Communications with the Ascended

A Channeled Work

By
Guy Steven Needler

For permission, serialization, condensation, adaptions, or for our catalog of other publications, write to Ozark Mountain Publishing, Inc., P.O. box 754, Huntsville, AR 72740, ATTN: Permissions Department.

Library of Congress Cataloging-in-Publication Data

Needler, Guy Steven – 1961 -

The Anne Dialogues by Guy Steven Needler

This is a behind the energetic scenes look at what happens in the incarnation process. You are taken each step of the way from the point of death to the decision to incarnate again and through the myriad of teachings in between.

1. Life After Death 2. Reincarnation 3. Metaphysics 4. Karma

I. Needler, Guy Steven, 1961- II. Life After Death III. Metaphysics IV. Title

Library of Congress Catalog Card Number: 2016951430

ISBN: 9781940265391

Cover Art and Layout: www.vril8.com

Book set in: Times New Roman, Marigold

Book Design: Tab Pillar

Published by:

PO Box 754, Huntsville, AR 72740

800-935-0045 or 479-738-2348; fax 479-738-2448

WWW.OZARKMT.COM

Printed in the United States of America

Table of Contents

Introduction

This was not a book I expected to write. Indeed, it came as a complete shock to me. I was within a year of finishing *The Origin Speaks* and was five months into being a widower. We, the UK that is, had been having some great weather for a change and I was making the most of it by taking my laptop outside, setting up a refreshment table and power cable, while wearing my Levi's shorts. I like a relaxed environment when conversing with any of the energetic entities, Source Entities, or The Origin I communicate with, and the more relaxed I am the better the link with them.

For some reason my mind wandered away from the dialogue I was having with The Origin and I began thinking of my late wife, Anne. I think about her every day and am fortunate enough to be able to communicate with her using the same methodology as that used in my previous work, so it came as no surprise that I heard her voice in my head, saying hello and letting me "know" that all was well and that I should "keep going." What was a surprise, though, was the intensity of the message she was about to deliver.

A: We have to write a book together.

And then The Origin added …

O: It will be called *The Anne Dialogues*.

Such was the intensity of the message that I almost fell off my chair. I laughed and cried at that thought and then wondered what the subject matter would be about.

A: It will be about the incarnation process.

As a result, over the last twelve months, I have been receiving some of the conceptual information that will be presented in this book (to whet my appetite I guess!). It plans to provide a leap forward in our understanding of the incarnation process and what happens behind the energetic scenes, dispelling a few myths and removing a few humanisms in the process. This, I thought, is worth doing as it will change the way we see ourselves, removing the human clothes from the current set of knowledge and deepening our understanding in the way that it should be understood. It would be done without metaphors and the limitations of the use of previous language/vocabulary.

In putting this to one side, I recall a very interesting event that took place in June of 2013. I was presenting one of my *Traversing the Frequencies* workshops at a very nice venue in Oxfordshire, UK. On the first day of the workshop one of my students, an extremely intuitive lady in her own right, said that she had a message from Anne for me, presumably to give me evidential proof of my communication with her from a completely different and independent source.

As if *I* needed proof!

This lady had never met Anne and neither had she communicated by telephone or the Internet. She said that she knew where I was to write a book with Anne, that it was to be on a bench with a green wall behind her and a bird table to her right or on the porch of a "log cabin." Both were places, she said, where Anne used to wait for me to come home from work or from a cycle ride. This was correct and that night I took some images of the area, presenting them to her the next day. She was excited and emphatic that these were the clairvoyant images she saw in her mind's eye. The green wall was a high evergreen hedge and the log cabin was our wooden summerhouse. The paneling looked like logs to the observer if seen from a distance but it was the same scene. Later that day this lady gave me another message from Anne.

A: Tell him he is going to Japan.

That was it. A flood of joy came over me and I had to hold back the tears. No one, certainly not of this group, knew that I was going to Japan to practice Aikido. I had only purchased the flights a few days before and made the decision to go a week or so before then. Moreover, no discussion was had with Anne about a Japanese trip before she returned to the energetic. Everything told me that this was a job that had to be done as soon as possible, and the previous plans for a book were put to one side in favor of this.

I have since been given another title for another book, *The Om: Dialogues with the Uncreated*, announced in the final pages of *The Origin Speaks*, making the number of "published/known" titles to equal seven. I will not bore you with yet another three unknown titles as they will be announced in due course. However, no more than five days ago (from writing this introduction) I was "told" that this "total" of ten books, five completed and five works in progress, is incorrect, and that two more would be necessary, making a total of twelve. "Now where have I heard that number before?" I thought with a smile.

A: Come on, you need to insert the eulogy you wrote for me before we can start proper. It's a nice summary of our/my life.

Some of the concepts, the chapter headings if you like, started to flood into my mind. This was going to be a very interesting and different direction to go in—certainly from my perspective.

I was going to enjoy this!

1

A Life Remembered

From the moment I met Anne, during an Aikido course in 1985, I knew we were to be together. Indeed I couldn't take my eyes off her while practicing with the other students! I was also a keen SCUBA diver and six months after asking her to a "Diving Club" BBQ I asked her to marry me. We had hit it off from the start and had in actual fact put a deposit on an engagement ring only two months into our relationship. I presented the ring to her on one knee on a canal bridge in the country near our parental homes. She was so excited, as was I.

Anne was to be our home hunter, and one night in 1987, after an Aikido class, I dashed over to the local phone box (no mobile telephones then) and asked her about the cottage she had seen in the paper. She was about to put an offer in. I asked her if she was sure. She said, "I love it, it can't get any cottager." We bought our cottage in August 1987 with a bridging loan and thankfully completed the purchase one day after the loan deadline of affordability. Anne loved it and called it her only home, never wanting to move. I remember having to repair the roof the day after we got the keys. Five slates were needed! The next six years were financially hard with the interest rate in the UK soaring to 15 percent and our combined salaries barely keeping up.

We worked on, though, building a front porch and a garage and enough internal decoration to make the cottage liveable, with the help of my father and a couple of short-term loans. Later, with a small inheritance from Anne's grandmother, we built an extension upstairs and gained an additional bedroom and a full-sized bathroom. We installed an AGA (cooker) in 1992. The year 1999 saw the last room redecorated and LPG central heating installed, with the final touch, a rear porch, being installed in 2003. In our cottage, Anne was in heaven.

Outside of home life Anne had a great affinity for the city of Birmingham, specifically adoring its university and multicultural roots, and very much felt the need to give something back to the city that had, in her mind, given her everything she had. Her desire to pay something back resulted in the creation of the "Friends of Birmingham Society" (FOBS). Helped with three other cofounders, the FOBS held its first multicultural concert in the City of Birmingham Symphony Hall in 2002. Anne raised £38,000 over ten years to support these events, the last one being in 2011. In 2005 the FOBS gained charity status and was awarded the rather rare number of 1110444.

Anne's career was in the biological sciences, which resulted in her gaining a PhD in 1991. She was a naturally adept scientist and found herself at the forefront of what was then a new area of research, to investigate the functions of programmed cell death, cell apoptosis. Scientists do not have it easy, though, and funding for grant-based research was starting to get difficult. As a result, in 1996 Anne traveled to Chicago for three months just to "keep working." Indeed, Anne never really gained a full grant from that date, and such was the nature of her resolve and excellent work, that she managed to continue to find work in Birmingham University on the residuals from other grants right up to the date of her (forced) retirement in 2008. Anne authored over thirty papers in her career.

Anne loved traveling and we had holidays all over Europe, America, the Far East, China, Japan, and Australia. We enjoyed Aikido, skiing, diving, cycling, and other activity holidays. This didn't include the visits to other cities resulting from university seminars or our city breaks. Anne loved the theater and enjoyed seeing Royal Shakespeare Company plays at Stratford and going to the ballet. She especially loved Christmas, and seeing the *Nutcracker* ballet with her goddaughter was one of the highlights of the year for her.

In the early 1990s we fell into a routine of going to a marina, "The Marina del Este," in Almunecar, Spain. In this era, from 1991 to 2001, we had many skiing (Sierra Nevada) and diving holidays as a result. Indeed, we wanted to buy a villa in Spain but it was just too expensive. However, on the flight back from a holiday in spring 2001 Anne saw an article stating that old properties in Crete were still affordable, and so she went to Crete to check out a few "plots" in July that same year.

In October 2001 we bought a derelict property at the very edge of a traditional Cretian village, and we had it renovated over the next eighteen months. Anne was enchanted by it and the nature around it. She called it her "secret garden." The garden was, in fact, part of the local mountain, and pine martins, owls, bats, praying mantis, and scorpions are to name but a few animals and insects we saw there, not to mention "her" feral cats.

Anne shared my appreciation of old British sports cars, specifically MG's, and in 2004 we drove an MG BGT I rebuilt to Crete—it's still there and works perfectly. It was our car in Crete!

Anne practiced Aikido with a passion for thirty-one years, gaining second dan along the way. She loved the community spirit surrounding national and international Aikido, seeing and wanting to take part in the work surrounding our organization. She was a past newsletter editor of the United Kingdom Aikikai newsletter and planned to be the treasurer of a new national governing body, the Joint Aikikai Council. She very much believed that we should all be one, a theme that permeates through our spiritual work.

Anne was (and still is!) an integral part of the workshops relating to my books, traveling with me during my attendance at the Ozark Mountain Publishing Transformation Conferences in 2011 and 2012, the US tour and the New Earth Cruise in 2012. She has seen the work go from strength to strength and was both amazed and proud of the interest, while also providing essential support. She graduated as a "Traversing the Frequencies" Level 3 Student in November 2012.

Retracing our steps a little to Anne's health, in September 2003, Anne had had a seizure, which was later diagnosed as being the result of a rather rare and diffuse brain tumor. A biopsy in January 2004 proved its morphology as being polyclonal, with one of the cell types being potentially aggressive.

January 2007 saw a de-bulking operation, removing a very large area of the tumor. Anne, in typical style, undertook this operation fully conscious, only taking a local anesthetic. The consultant surgeon was amazed at her resolve.

Daily life progressed and the tumor was monitored via MRI scan on a regular basis, but unfortunately the tumor was insidious and Anne suffered a major seizure and relapse in May 2009. After two months she was fully recovered but needed regular chemotherapy. The chemotherapy continued for eighteen months and during the Christmas/New Year of 2010/2011, Anne, feeling OK, took a therapy break. This break lasted through 2011 until she suffered another relapse in late December (two and a half years since the 2009 relapse). Recovering again she commenced therapy with a new series of drugs, one of which resulted in a reduction in liver function. This drug was removed from the regime during June 2012. Anne appeared to be OK, though, and a scan in August showed some improvement.

However, just before and during the Ozark Mountain Publishing New Earth Cruise, where I was working together with Dolores Cannon, we noticed a few, but increasingly progressive signs that the tumor was having an influence again. The latest scan showed massive infestation of the area where the tumor was. It was a complete and aggressive change to its function and resulted in Anne relapsing on 27 November 2012, spending three weeks in hospital. Although Anne initially responded to treatment, she continued to relapse and on 18 December was admitted into a hospice.

Sadly, one-half hour into Christmas Eve 2012, and with me holding her hand, Anne lost the battle and returned to the energetic.

Throughout this illness Anne was full of positive thoughts, actions, and resolve. She was, and is, an inspiration as a result.

We were married for almost twenty-five years and shared many wonderful experiences together. None the least, we both shared the recent excitement over the gradual, but accelerating, worldwide interest in my channeled writing, which was "our" work—we were, it seemed, finally "on plan."

Anne achieved much more than one can expect in a single lifetime. Indeed, we often conjectured that she was living two to three lives simultaneously. It is perhaps because of this that I feel that she had achieved that which she was destined to do. She had done her job, and now it was time to leave, mission accomplished, the tumor being the way out.

I am eternally grateful for her love, help, support, companionship, and advice. I of course miss her physical presence but because I am currently communicating with her, experiencing daily communication and gaining further insights as a result, I know that she has never really left me.

My love is with her—always and forever.

2

Communications with the Energetic Anne: The Start of a New Relationship

A: You should have put the poem at the front of the book, not at the back.

I felt the joy of hearing her voice in my head simultaneously with the realization that I was being reprimanded. I smiled.

ME: It didn't take you long to get stuck in. That being, kicking off our dialogues.

A: I have been here for ages waiting for you to finish The Origin Speaks.

ME: I thought time would not have been an issue for you now.

A: It isn't, matey. But I am doing my best to align myself to you so that it is easier to maintain the harmonic resonance necessary to complete this work in an efficient a way as possible. I had forgotten how low the frequencies are on Earth.

Anne called me "Matey" when she meant business. I was called other terms of endearment as well in more intimate circumstances—as you can imagine. I had the feeling that this series of dialogues was going to move in some interesting directions.

ME: The Sources and The Origin didn't seem to have this problem.

A: Of course not. They are the environment we are working within. Because of what we are, we reintegrate back into the True Energetic Self (TES) at a significantly faster rate than energetic mankind does when newly disincarnate. I have had to maintain myself, as an Aspect of our TES, in a reintegration holding pattern.

ME: For how long?

This was a new one on me. I was instantly interested and wanted to go down this investigative route straight away.

A: At least until I have finished my work here, which includes this book.

ME: How long will you be able to work with me? I mean, is it just for this book, or do you have other work to do?

A: I have been working with you/us for the last sixteen months, Earth Event Space, almost from the start of my ascension from the physical. I have been putting certain events, people, and actions in place to help with the dissemination of this new order of information you are currently working on. Feeding the flame, so to speak, maintaining the momentum. But in terms of what I will be doing beyond the collaborative work on this book, it is not yet fully decided.

ME: What do you mean, not yet fully decided?

7

A: You are aware that we are one and the same, that we are the Aspects of a single TES, one that is beloved of the Om?

ME: Yes. The Origin has ensured that I am aware of this information.

A: Then you should be aware of the fact that at some point this Aspect will NEED to reintegrate with the TES.

ME: Yes, I understand that as well.

A: Then understand that the maximum period for which I can stay in this frequential environment is governed by the amount of work I have to do to assist you in your work, your project, the amount of work that I still need to do on behalf of our TES, and the amount of work that you need to do to support that Aspect of work which you have taken on board on behalf of our TES.

ME: We have our own work and the work of our TES?

A: Yes.

ME: How does that work? I thought that we would only be working on that which we have been projected into the physical to perform on behalf of our TES and not anything that is associated with the individualization of the Aspect resulting from being in the incarnate state?

A: Normally this is correct because the Aspect of any TES is in fact only a method of the holographic processing of singular or multiple experiences. I use the word "holographic" because it would not have been descriptive enough to use the word "parallel."

ME: So what you are saying is that other Aspects, i.e. non-Om, only incarnate to experience that which their TES has decided it wishes to experience and nothing else.

A: That's right. You see, although autonomous while incarnate, the Aspect is responsible only for the experience/s that the TES has decided to work on using that specific Aspect. That Aspect is chosen due to the specialized functions it has accrued over the number of incarnations it has experienced,

8

and the genre of those experiences within which it has become specialized in.

If, for instance, the Aspect in working on this task decides it is better able to work on the task in a holographic sense in its own right, desiring to create a state of a holographic experience/s within a holographic experience, it can elect to create a number of Shards to help it experience the most important angles of the experience concurrently. But it has to decide on this before entering into the incarnate state itself. This, of course, also includes those fracturalized versions of the Shards and Aspects created by Event Space.

ME: As an Aspect of an Om TES then we have the capacity to work on our own projects as well, whereas the normal Aspects don't?

A: That's right. But also note this. We don't really have a TES in the pure sense of the TES.

ME: Explain.

A: We are pure sentience and elect to use a body of energy when it suits us. The entities created by Source Entity One, in general, have a body of energy (TES) assigned to them by their Source, which they can elect to move their sentience out and away from at some future point. Om are pure sentience "per se" and never really had a body of energy originally assigned to them, except in the first instance, but that was for the creation of a Source Entity and not an Om.

ME: So it was the sentience that separated itself out from The Source Entities and not the energies?

A: Yes, but only in the case of the Pure Om and in some rare cases the non-captive Om.

ME: So when you talked about reintegration you were talking about the reintegration of the sentience that is split between the incarnate vehicles that "was" Anne and "is" Guy?

A: Yes, except in this instance our sentience, our True Sentient Self (TSS) if you like, commandeered a body of energy (grouped energies together for a common purpose) to allow the incarnate process to take place. That being, we had to integrate with a body of energy to allow us to integrate into a gross physical incarnate vehicle. That body of energy our transient TES created by our TSS is only split between the two of us with a larger percentage of the body of energy remaining in the energetic. So in this case we reintegrate back and become one with the transient TES—later the TSS, with specialized Aspects of experience that create the Anne and the Guy functions of sentience or personalities within the TSS.

At this point I received an image in my mind's eye. It was like a banana, no a horseshoe with the two ends of the shoe projected into the gross physical, spirituo-physical, and energetic components of the construct that creates the human incarnate vehicle—most of it being external to the "vehicles"—that which was external being classified as the transient (temporary) TES.

I chuckled for a moment as I made a lateral link with the word "transient" and the word that the late Steve Jobs of Apple Computers used when he returned as chief executive officer (CEO) on a transient basis. He used the word "interim" with a lower case "I" calling himself the iCEO. He subsequently went on to use this acronym for the iPod, iPhone, and iPad. Would this mean I could use the same for the transient TES, calling it the iTes? I suspect I might get sued!

A: By the way, I like what you have done to the garden; you have kept it under control while maintaining its natural state. I approve, the trees approve, and the elementals approve.

I changed the focus of my eyes to that of the third eye and saw myself surrounded by elemental entities, The Source's maintenance entities, those who were here to maintain the functionality of the flora and fauna of the Earth in all its minute detail. Empathically I logged into them. If they would have adopted human form they would have appeared like small children lying on their stomachs, heads perched on the cups of their hands looking at me in wonder and admiration. It was an incredible feeling to know that they were also with me and were supporting me.

I had been receiving and typing up this information in the place within my/our garden where I was advised to be while working with the energetic Anne. The bench I was sitting on was not totally comfortable and my spine cracked as I sat up straight. My right leg had gone numb as well! If I had expected a rather cuddly start to this book I was grossly mistaken. We appeared to have jumped into the deep end straight away. And, the use of this bench was designed to keep me aware, awake, and alert, no doubt!

3

The Cats of Voulismeni: Anne's Influence with the Local Nature

As I stated at the end of the last chapter, I very much felt that we had jumped in to the deep end, and as a result I felt the need to start at the beginning of her transition from the incarnate to the energetic/sentient state that she was currently in. At this point I noted that I was using the feminine "she or her" to describe Anne in the third person, and being acutely aware that gender was not a consideration when energetic, I have decided to refer to Anne as "Anne," and not "she or her," using instead only the name, the label, that was given by Anne's birth parents.

Before I start on this, though, I have one final interesting story to tell about Anne prior to moving on to the subject of the next chapter title. I feel drawn to this because I don't always work on my books or other work while in the UK. Those who have read The History of God will know that we bought a property, a traditional Cretan cottage on Crete, Greece, during 2001, and will note that I made contact with other incarnate, but higher frequency, entities while meditating on the roof terrace of this property. Right now (April 2014) I am on the roof of this cottage and very much feel their presence. The activity of their coming and going is a wonder and delight to perceive. They acknowledge my presence by surrounding me in their love. Also note that all around me is the energy of nature, of our Source. It is largely pure and unspoilt and I hear the birdsong, hens clucking, and goats chewing the grasses. I also hear the meowing of a mother cat in the distance, calling to her kittens. It is the cats that are the focus of this short story, for the local feral cats were Anne's cats.

One of my oldest friends and his partner have lived in Crete for ten years now. They were not able to attend Anne's funeral service due to flight availability and so decided to hold a short service on the roof of our property at the same day and time as the service in the UK. They brought a photograph of Anne and the attendees lit a candle. As they started to assemble on the roof a very strange event was observed. A number of cats appeared from nowhere and walked in a processional line, in single file, making their way to the little wall that surrounded the roof. They then split up with each of them sitting on a corner of the roof, looking out toward the countryside. The cats stayed there until the end of the service and then regrouped, reversing the method that they appeared in as they exited the roof, dispersing once on the ground. The attendees were both amazed and delighted at what they "witnessed," stating that they all felt Anne's presence. I was not surprised to hear this story but was both delighted and overjoyed that Anne was making sure that we knew the truth of Anne's continued existence. The cats had saluted Anne's physical passing in the only way they could, by just "being there" in a way that would be noticed.

The Cretan cottage was and is Anne's Secret Garden; it is now named as such and will be the basis for further enlightenment, I feel. It has a role to play in the dissemination of my work.

A: I am pleased that "Little Momma" is still alive *[Little Momma was one of Anne's favorite cats. —GSN]*. Make sure she has plenty to eat while you are there.

ME: Yes, of course. She has just given birth—again!

A: Mmmm, that's nice, but hard work for her. You must "feed her up" as much as you can.

ME: I put food and milk out morning and night for them. In fact, I have noticed something interesting as well. I can get VERY close to these cats now.

No one could get anywhere near them before.

A: That's because I can use them as a vehicle for my sentience. You can only get near them now because I am with them. I can use them to be closer to you in the physical.

ME:This is a transient condition, I take it?

A: Yes. Their bodies, their incarnate vehicles, are not as easy to work with as the human body. Not that the human body is an easy vehicle to work with anyway, but I can use them to experience transient physicality when I want to. Why do you think that ChiKi cat *[one of our UK cats —GSN]* is more "Lovey Dovey" than she used to be! It's me getting close to you to give you company.

ME:I thought it was, and thank you for confirming that to me. This makes me want to ask a question.

A: Go ahead.

ME:Is it common place for disincarnate entities to experience physicality via the physical vehicles that the energy beings that incarnate as animals use?

A: Not from an incarnate perspective, not now. That being, not as much as it was. There was a time when the incarnate vehicle available on Earth was lighter, frequentially higher, and during this time the Aspect that occupied the human vehicle was still able to use certain functions that were associated with the purely energetic levels of existence. One of these functions was the ability to move the Aspect, or a portion of the Aspect, temporarily out of the human vehicle and into another vehicle, human or other, such as the animal. You can call this a type of "Walk-In," if you like, a temporary Walk-In.

ME:From the perspective of the disincarnate energetic being, though, this would be common place?

A: It happens, provided of course that there is an agreement between the entity that is occupying the animal vehicle and the entity wishing to "Walk-In" to the vehicle being used.

ME: They still need to have permission to "Walk-In" to an animal vehicle?

A: Yes, of course, but it is more easily obtainable because the incumbent entity is usually delighted to be of service in this way.

ME: Because it is only temporary.

A: Because it is only temporary and because the requesting entity is usually of a higher quality and evolutionary level.

ME: I already know the answer to this question but I will ask it anyway. Does energetic mankind incarnate into animal vehicles?

A: They can but they don't—primarily because it is generally not to their evolutionary advantage.

ME: So what about those religions that state that we regularly reincarnate as animals, plants, or insects, etc.?

A: That is based upon residual and now inaccurate racial memory of what energetic mankind used to do on a temporary "Walk-In" basis, and not on a full incarnate basis.

ME: Do you ask for permission to use animal bodies as a temporary physical vehicle?

A: Because of what I am, I don't need to. But I do anyway out of respect to the incumbent entity. It's only good manners to ask if you can borrow someone's car, isn't it?

ME: Yes, of course it is.

A: Right. It is time to move on now. We have to explain my experiences resulting from the demise of my last physical body.

I got the feeling that Anne was well and truly in the driving seat here.

4

The Demise Process

4.1

A Shocking Discovery about the
Use of Sedatives and Painkillers

I have to admit at this point that I appeared to be somewhat divorced from the demise process that Anne went through. It appeared, at least to me, that I needed to be as "normal" as possible when Anne was suffering from the effects of the brain tumor. I felt that Anne had realized that it was time to ascend beyond the physical but still had some resistance (a very human thing). If I was normal and optimistic of another reprieve, then so was Anne. If I was busy with everyday things while being with Anne, then all was well in Anne's mind.

In the flesh Anne was a sensitive soul while also being an incarnate master—Anne was and is a saint in every sense of the word. Being Anne's husband was a rare privilege and seeing the demise process, ultimately chosen as the exit route prior to incarnation, was so painful for me that ever since the initial diagnosis almost ten years prior, my emotions had shut down. In the hospital Anne knew very well that the administration of morphine and sedatives was not good news and made it known by quoting those immortal words "I am on my way out"—"I am not going to ascend" (this was on 18 December 2012, ascension was supposed to be 21 December 2012). She went on to further say, "You had better have my rings!" I retorted that of course she was not on her way out, that she would ascend, but not in the way Anne thought, and that I would not take her rings—comforting proof for Anne of my expectations, I thought.

In all of this I was being swayed by the human side of me, while my "knowledge" of the greater reality was keeping me on track. During the World Satsanga I held on 22 December 2012 at Anne's bedside at the hospice I conducted a metaconcert, a meditation designed to create a synergetic response based upon a multiple of the number of attendees, to give an energetic boost to help Anne move on ASAP. Anne's response of being uncomfortable told me that even under sedation Anne was able to hear what was being said and could respond in a limited way. Anne, I felt, was not too happy at me wanting the demise process to end. I felt guilty beyond belief. Two days later Anne left her body of almost fifty-six years, and me stunned—feeling very alone.

A: Ah, but you did me a favor.

ME: Sorry?

A: I moved on so quick, it was amazing. One moment I was incarnate, the next I was in the energetic.

ME: Please accept my most profound and humble apologies for wanting you to leave your body. Seeing you, my darling, suffer in this most undignified way was too much for me to handle so I shut down my emotions.

A: Yes, but you have them back now, in buckets.

Anne was right. I had been experiencing emotions on a level that were well beyond my previous experiences. I know it was something that I had signed up to before this incarnation as well. It was like I had inherited Anne's emotional content and empathy for other entities.

ME: You are right there. I have noticed a big change in me. I have even inherited your like of turbulence when flying!

A: It's there to help you with your travels and to show a side of you to the public that is in ultimate understanding of what people are experiencing while incarnate. It's designed to make you more accessible.

It's time to explain the demise process, the function of separation of the Aspect from the incarnate vehicle.

ME: Before we start, can I ask if this is a common process for all incarnate vehicles?

A: This is the process for those vehicles that operate in the same frequencies as the human vehicle—that being, the lowest frequencies of the physical universe and ultimately the multiverse created by Source Entity One.

ME: So it will be generic.

A: Yes and no. An Aspect has many ways to disassociate itself from the incarnate vehicle. My disassociation was both typical, and not typical because of the help you gave me. Because of this, my description will be based upon my own recent experience. I may explain other ways later on in this dialogue as this will provide a better level of understanding for all of those incarnate truth seekers while addressing a few inconsistencies.

ME: That's my girl! Removing the veil of mistrust created by different reports of the demise process is what I am ultimately looking for.

A: Don't forget that some of these differences are due to the lack of understanding, poor education, and existence in frequencies that are even lower than those currently experienced by incarnates. Incarnate mankind is now ready to experience a more profound level of knowledge. That's what WE are here for.

I felt Anne smile the smile of one who has access to ALL knowledge now. Having no inhibitions, no misconceptions, no beliefs—only knowledge based upon ultimate personal experience. It was time to get to the detail, detail of a level that is relative to incarnate mankind's new level of group ascension— its new level of incarnate evolution. We had graduated, I felt, to a level where we can now cleanse the knowledge-based system, moving away from hearsay and conjecture to raw knowledge. The incarnation process, I felt, was to be at the bedrock of this knowledge, for this is the starting point for many newly awakening incarnates and therefore, more than ever, needs to be accurate to give it credibility, and those new truth seekers the confidence to continue their quest for the truth without the need to question its validity.

A: Owww! It hurts, it hurts so much, can't you take the pain away? —HELP ME!

ME: What?

This is almost too much. I am in tears now. I remembered a rather intense moment when Anne suddenly woke up from sedation, looked at me directly in the eyes, and just said HELP! I instantly went to the nurse to increase the sedative and morphine pump throughput. By this time Anne had passed out—presumably the result of a protective device within the incarnate vehicle to spare the consciousness from the physical and mental discomfort.

A: That's what I was experiencing and thinking in those last few days. Brain tumors are painful things to have when they are in their last stages of development. The headaches are intense beyond belief when your poor brain is being squashed by a cancerous growth. Know this, the brain does have a sense of feeling, irrespective of what the neuroscientists tell you, and my brain was in pain—big time.

ME:I didn't expect you to relay what you were feeling pain wise as well.

A: It was part of what I was experiencing.

ME:OK. I understand. I will let you do the explaining in the way that you want to.

A: Good. In those last days I was not really associated with the energetic nor part of my incarnate vehicle. The sedatives put me in a state of limbo. I was not yet disincarnate, but I was also not conscious as an incarnate. I was under a very high level of sedation and so was unable to leave at will, which requires a conscious decision process only available while fully aware when incarnate.

ME:Are you suggesting the sedatives held you back?

A: Yes. If I was conscious, irrespective of the pain and the level of pain the morphine was able to remove, I would have been able to leave my body at will.

ME:How does that work?

A: There is a time during the demise of the incarnate vehicle when the bonds to the Aspect are loosened to the point of ineffectivity, that the Aspect is back in communication with its True Energetic Self (TES) and is aware enough of the greater reality to know how to move out of the incarnate vehicle before its demise. If the incarnate vehicle is sedated, the energetic function of the sedatives places this process in stasis because it relies on the removal of the ego, the transient personality created as a result of the incarnation, to allow the personality of the Aspect, a lower function of the TES, to take over. At the point the personality of the Aspect takes over, the decision to return to the energetic or wait to experience the full demise process is taken and the incarnate vehicle either lingers on (the incarnate Aspect sometimes departing mid-conversation) or demises straight away.

ME: So again, you are suggesting that the sedatives given by hospitals and hospices actually stop the Aspect from returning to the TES?

A: Yes.

ME: And that means that the supposed "help" that hospices give to those terminally ill patients are detrimental to them moving back to their TES and liberation from the diseased human vehicle.

A: Yes, it is.

ME: This information isn't going to be good news to many people who have "helped" their loved ones depart by easing their pain; in fact, I can see it causing a lot of confusion and concern.

A: Yes, I know. Incarnate mankind is like a child who is in the dark trying to operate the most complicated computer Earth has ever seen without any idea of what does what, let alone see the keyboard or command structure.

ME: I didn't know that you could use technology as an example?

A: *[Smile]* I picked it up from you. You did have some good points as my husband, don't you know.

ME: Well, thank you for that vote of confidence. *[I am also smiling here.]* Tell me. It's the energies or frequencies associated with the sedatives that create the stasis effect then?

A: Yes, it is. Unlike drugs like LSD, cocaine, or vast amounts of alcohol which crack open the auric layers, ejecting the Aspect from the human vehicle through severe disharmony, sedatives have the opposite effect. They actively reduce the frequencies of the human vehicle's energy field because they are low frequency themselves. They create a condition that makes the human vehicle energy field, the auric layers, act as a very effective barrier.

ME: Why is that?

A: Because they are so low in frequency they reduce the frequencies of the energy field, the auric layers, almost to the point of full physicality.

ME: But I thought that the Aspect, as an energetic condition, would be able to transcend the physical frequencies.

A: Of course it can, and ordinarily this is not a problem, but it's the frequencies of the sedatives themselves that create the barrier and not the frequencies of the gross physical Aspect of the human vehicle.

ME: Can you explain in some detail for me?

A: Yes. The frequencies of the sedatives blend in with the frequencies of the Aspect, the soul, and actively slow them down almost to the point of inactivity. Think of it like trying to swim in a swimming pool full of treacle.

ME: That would be impossible, it would be too sticky!

A: And that is what the frequencies of the sedatives do to the frequencies of the Aspect. They make the Aspect too sticky to move away from the frequencies of the gross physical, spirituo-physical, and energetic components of the human vehicle.

ME: But that's appalling.

A: You had better believe it. I was there!

ME: I am horrified that the sedatives would have made that much difference to your/an Aspect's ability to return to the TES.

A: What's more, it's compounded by the use of the morphine, which is a most effective painkiller.

ME: Carry on.

A: Morphine, on its own, is an effective painkiller, but if used in the correct quantities will cause the human vehicle to become ineffective, to pass out, or even cause its demise.

ME:I think this is well-known and recorded knowledge.

A: Yes, it is, but what is not known is the synergetic effects created by the use of morphine together with sedatives, especially powerful sedatives.

ME:Are you suggesting it creates another type of frequency, a hybrid frequency?

A: Not a hybrid frequency, a new frequency. Consider the periodic table and how it identifies how materials can change totally by the addition or subtraction of electrons, neutrons, or protons.

ME:OK.

A: Then consider how two separate materials added together will create another new material that has the best of the two parent materials.

ME:This would be called an alloy.

A: Agreed, but think again about the periodic table. It's the addition or subtraction of the electrons, neutrons, and protons that create the stand-alone material. This is at the subatomic level. Alloys are at the atomic level and above.

ME:Carry on.

A: Using this as an example we can look at frequency, a dominant frequency, in the same way. If we consider that the dominant frequency is the gross physical material in the example, the atomic and above, and the subfrequencies associated with the dominant frequency are the subatomic components, then the subfrequential Aspect of the dominant frequencies are at the subatomic level and therefore create a new frequency and not a hybrid or an alloy. It is this new frequency that acts as a major blockage to the Aspect and not the energetic or gross physical because it acts like frequential treacle.

ME: But we only see the physical Aspect and the subsequent results of the physical's response to physical applications, and …

A: … and not the energetic, let alone the frequential response!

ME: You took the words right out of my mouth.

A: Naturally.

ME: Mmmm! This is radical new information. It's going to cause quite a stir. It's going to frighten a few people.

A: The truth always hurts, and the truth always comes out.

The truth always comes out (the truth always outs) was a classic Anne response and it made me smile. Anne was clearly on form and eager to share every Aspect of her ascension, no matter what paradigms it shook!

ME: So what can we, that is, the rest of incarnate humanity, do in this instance? We can't just place a ban on the use of such drugs, can we? It brings a kind of peace to those who are going through the trauma of seeing their loved ones go through the process of physical demise, demise in some extreme circumstances as well. We believed up until now, and that included me, that you/they are being spared the pain and trauma of the process.

A: Well, it's time to wake up and smell the coffee, so to speak.

ME: Again, what can we do?

A: What you did.

ME: Sorry?

A: If they must help the physical vehicle and the ego, while it is still in existence, by sedating it using drugs to supposedly assist in the demise process, then they must research the effects that the drugs have at the frequential and subfrequential levels to ensure that they don't create a

25

synergetic effect that arrests the ability of the Aspect to leave the human vehicle.

ME: That makes the assumption that medical science or centers of palliative care want to believe this information.

A: There will come a time when they will understand and make the right moves to ensure that such drugs both assist in both the pain and anxiety and help to project the Aspect out of the energies associated with the human vehicle.

Alternatively they will recognize that certain individuals are adept energetically and frequentially, and can assist the Aspect's departure from the human vehicle, creating a fast-track route through the inhibiting frequential conditions created as a function of using such drugs individually or together. This is what you did for me. You created a rift in the treacle, so to speak. You tore it wide open while also pushing me up and out, back toward communion with my/our TES.

ME: But you aren't in communion with your/our TES right now, are you?

A: No, I stopped short of that. *[Smile]* I put the brakes on so that I could fulfill the rest of the work we agreed to do together, with me working from this side. You gave me quite a shove, you know. I almost couldn't stop the acceleration.

ME: Sorry! OK. Do you want to describe the process of your leaving your physical vehicle, the vehicle I knew as Anne in the physical?

A: Yes. Let's start right now.

4.2

The Light at the End of the Tunnel

I knew that this part of my dialogue with Anne was going to be traumatic. I could feel the energy associated with it already taking hold. It was a very emotional energy and one that I knew was absolutely necessary for me to enter into to remove my association with it. I had to feel the emotional energy to continue—not the sort of thing I was used to. In fact, I have no experience of any really deep emotions at all—not even when I first discovered that I had met my "wife to be," Anne, over twenty-seven years ago. This may seem like a strange position to be in from the perspective of the reader, but from my position it was a necessary hurdle to get over. This was another level of karma, association with the physical universe, that needed to be conquered.

I knew that I was not only going to experience the demise process from the position of Anne, and myself as a neutral observer, but that I was going to be catapulted back into those last moments of Anne's physical existence and actually experience "those" emotions that I was not able to experience at that point in time.

When they came they hit me like a sledgehammer. Able to traverse the frequencies of Source Entity One's multiverse, to rise to the challenge of moving through the voids—the distances between the twelve Source Entities and area of The Origin's polyomniscient self-awareness—I may be, and with relative ease, but when it comes to feeling emotions ... I am a raw beginner.

A: Don't let me go! I don't want to go, I want to be with you!!!!!

I see an image of the scene associated with this plea. I am sitting by her side, holding her hand in the hospice room Anne was assigned to, and I was summoning the energies required to allow Anne a fast, an unnaturally fast, exit from the human form. I felt that I was betraying her! I was feeling remorse (of helping Anne go quickly), betrayal (of Anne leaving me), and grief (of missing the only one incarnate on Earth who fully understood me).

A: I was scared for a moment. I had reentered my body to say goodbye in the physical and was feeling anxious, worried, and frightened beyond belief. I was experiencing the end of my physical life and had forgotten the preparation I had gone through over the previous couple of days.

ME: You had forgotten the preparation? What preparation?

A: How to disassociate myself from the energies of the physical and the "knowing" of what I truly was that came with it. Entering back into my physical form stripped away the knowledge of this functionality. It does that. My cry out, you could not hear it of course, was an automatic response that I was not in control of at that point in time. It surprised me just as much then as it surprised you now when you just heard it in your mind's ear. It was a very human response, one that is borne from the absence of no "real" knowledge.

ME: But, but the energies I felt were just immense. I felt horrible, lost, alone, helpless. From a human perspective I was losing the only person that understood me, who gave me incentive, who shared my vision, who was my vision.

Hearing you say that you didn't want to go just cut across everything that I/we knew was correct. It caused doubt!!!!

A: It would do. Especially when you are in a place of fragility, as we both were. Now we are communicating again, in a way that is most profound. The feeling of loss should diminish soon.

ME: Thank you, it is. So what happened after you made that automatic call for help? Did you go unconscious or were you conscious during the whole process?

A: I was conscious and it was wonderful, and it was so fast. Actually though, I bypassed the experience that most incarnates have.

ME: Go on.

A: Normally a "newly disincarnate" entity experiences a certain level of confusion overlaid with wonder at what they are experiencing. The confusion, really a state of disorientation, makes them observe what is happening as if they are watching a film at the cinema, that they are surrounded by a darkness that is all around them and that there is a light in the distance. Hence, the constant reports from near-death experiences that state that the person feels that they are moving through a tunnel.

ME: So they don't move through a tunnel then?

A: No. The darkness is a phenomenon that is created as a result of the lack of experiential knowledge of the frequencies that are an essential part of the human form, but that exist above the gross physical. The darkness is a result of the incarnate having no reference during their incarnate existence. Incarnate existence gives an entity a vocabulary, one that is not aligned to language, one that is aligned to their lifetime of experience within their physical form, one that is essentially limited to this existence and only this existence. Because the demise process is usually only experienced at the end of the life of the human vehicle, the ego of the incarnate entity has no prior knowledge of this experience, this process, and therefore has no means of understanding what it is experiencing. It has no reference point to work from. In this instance no images can be used as a form of translation, so a blank screen is returned. This screen is either black or white depending upon the levels of frequency being experienced. Simplistically put, the lower the frequencies, the darker the image returned; the higher the frequencies, the lighter the image returned.

ME: So the "tunnel effect" is the imagery received that results from the transition of the Aspect from the low frequencies of the gross physical to the high frequencies of the purely energetic. And, this is simply the result of the transient personality of the incarnate entity, the ego, having no memory of such an experience during its own limited existence.

A: Correct. What's more, there does come a time during the demise process when the feeling of being in a tunnel subsides and the feeling of expansion takes over.

ME: And the feeling of expansion is the result of the dissolution of the ego and the reintegration of the Aspect with the energies of the True Energetic Self, the TES.

A: And ... this is the light at the end of the tunnel, the light at the end of the darkness, the expansion from limitedness to omniscience.

ME: The expansion into omniscience provides too much simultaneous information for the ego to assimilate in the short time it has been in existence, and this results in the experience of seeing a blank screen, a light.

A: Yes, good, you are catching up—fast.

ME: There is talk of the disassociation from the human form taking three days. Is this how long it takes to get to the end of the tunnel?

A: Sort of. Although the individual experiencing it states that it happens very quickly, the actual disassociation of the Aspect from the energies of the human vehicle takes some time, especially when the Aspect is not exposed to the greater reality when incarnate. There is a sliding scale if you like, one that illustrates the speed of disassociation as a function of the level of knowledge of the greater reality while incarnate. It shows that the higher the knowledge, the faster the disassociation from the physical—the lower the knowledge, the slower the disassociation from the physical. The slowest takes three days, the fastest is instantaneous.

Most are slow, hence the unwritten rule that a newly demised vehicle should lie in state for at least three days.

ME: So, if this is what normally happens, what happened to you?

A: Simultaneous integration. This was a result of my own knowledge and your help. That is why I had to put the brakes on, so to speak.

Before I elaborate on my ascension process, which was akin to that experienced by adept yogis, I would like to add some more information to the "tunnel effect."

ME: Why?

A: Because there is another reason for an entity to experience the egress of the Aspect from the physical vehicle in terms of "being in a tunnel," one that is based upon knowledge of the process which therefore allows the entity to experience the truth and not a blank screen (black or white).

ME: Please explain. This may help with our understanding.

A: Think of the Aspect (soul) as being compressed into the lower frequencies as it is projected out from the TES. In this compressed state it has to associate itself with the human form, or other, it has decided to use as its vehicle on or off the earth. This can be considered as the Aspect being compressed to a point of focus, that focus being from the energetic to the spirituo-physical via a small energy vortex you call the **hara line**. The energies of the Aspect are positioned predominantly within the hara line as it descends the frequencies to the point of the highest frequency of the gross physical. At this point it balloons out from the tan tien and establishes energetic control of the incarnate vehicle by the use of the energetic system, which, although it is predominantly supported by the spirituo-physical (frequency levels 4, 5, 6, and 7), allows control of the gross physical (frequency levels 1, 2, and 3) and contact with the TES via the energetic Aspect (frequency levels 8, 9, and 10) of the incarnate vehicle. I will call this the point of absolute energetic control. This point of absolute energetic control is

31

via an area popularly called the **Core Star** and it is positioned very close to the tan tien. Another area close to the heart chakras, sometimes called the **Soul Seat**, is where the essence of the Aspect resides. It is the personality of what we, as a projected Aspect of our TES, are.

ME: I have just received an image of a balloon being squeezed through a straw and then inflated so that the balloon inflates from the opposite end of the straw that it was inserted into. The balloon then extends out and back on itself, engulfing the very straw it was inserted into and inflated via.

A: Good, you received the imagery OK.

ME: Yes, it was a very clear image and one that was very informative.

A: Thank you. If you consider the hara line as an energetic tube (vortex) then, a tube that assists the Aspect to be projected down into the frequencies of the physical universe, and that the Aspect has to go through it, you then have half of the imagery explained. It then makes sense to build upon this imagery by noting that it must return the same way when the Aspect withdraws back into the energetic and the location of the TES.

ME: I have just received the "knowledge" that the hara line acts as a form of protection from the effects of the lower frequencies of the physical universe for the line of energies that attach the Aspect to the TES. It allows rudimentary communications to be maintained.

A: Yes, it does. As you are aware, the lower down the frequencies an entity travels, the lower its energetic functionality. This rule affects the line of projection/ communication as well as the entity or projected Aspect. The hara line allows the basic communication necessary, via the projected energy within it, to ensure the Aspect stays in unison with the TES.

ME: And so as you just stated, it must withdraw via the same way it was projected into the lower frequencies of the physical universe, back through the hara line.

A: That's right. When the physical body demises, the energies that were inflated out from the tan tien, settling at the core star, disassociate themselves from the energetic network that is predominantly formed by the spirituo-physical, the chakras, and auric layers. The Aspect then deflates, so to speak, moving back through the hara line, back up the straw in your imagery, to the energies associated with the location of the TES. In your image the balloon would then be withdrawn from the straw, the air being released back into the atmosphere (the atmosphere representing the energies associated with the TES and/or its location).

ME: And in the case of the more spiritually aware incarnates, they experience the withdrawal of the Aspect through the hara line as moving through a tunnel, into the light.

A: The effect of the Aspect withdrawing would feel like the incarnate was imploding and then compressing to a level equal to its ability to contract back through the hara line. The imagery the incarnate Aspect experiences varies depending upon their spiritual education and level of connectivity with the TES just before the point of the demise of the physical body. Suffice to say, though, it would appear like the Aspect was traveling through a tunnel—that tunnel being the energies associated with the hara line, organized like a small vortex, which is also withdrawing itself from its association with the incarnate vehicle at the same time. The light at the end of the tunnel is when both the Aspect and the hara line are fully disassociated from the incarnate vehicle to a point where the hara line is no longer necessary. In this instance, the hara line dissolves and the Aspect is exposed to the energies associated with the TES and/or its location, which would initially be a bright light and would then be converted to any imagery the newly disincarnate Aspect expects to see. This imagery is a product of expectation based upon earthly education or actual real imagery based upon ultimate knowledge of the greater reality and a full acceptance of what it will be represented by.

ME: You just said that the imagery is or could be based upon what the newly disincarnate Aspect expects to see. Are you suggesting that the Aspect creates the imagery within the environment that is of the energies associated with the location of the TES?

A: Of course. Once back into the energetic the Aspect has access to all of its functionality, which includes creativity, but not all of its memory, so it creates what it expects to see, or not as the case may be, until it regains its full memory.

ME: What do you mean, "or not as the case may be?"

A: If a newly disincarnate Aspect expects to see a certain environmental image, an expectation resulting from its earthly education, it creates it. This environmental image is only dissolved once the Aspect recognizes that it is created by itself and is based upon false education while incarnate, i.e., it regains its memory. The Aspect is allowed to keep this "temporary" environment for as long as it needs it or until it recognizes where it is. This is part of the experiential process of being incarnate. This also includes those who expect nothing and therefore see nothing, or experience a nothingness—a limbo. Those incarnates who work with the higher knowledge will experience what is correct and true and will go straight into the review process.

We should talk about the post-demise process in the next chapter because right now I want to explain what happened to me, which is aligned to that experienced by those who work with higher knowledge.

4.3

How Anne Ascended

ME: So if the process you just described is a general process for separation from the physical form, how different to this was your own separation from your physical body?

A: It was a completely different method of separation. It was as if the rules associated with the connectivity of the Aspect with the physical form were not applied to me.

ME: Can you explain?

A: Of course I can. In the process I just described the Aspect has to be inserted into the physical via the hara line to allow it to integrate with the physical body and animate it via the tan tien and core star. The hara line acts as a level of protection against the loss of functionality resulting from being exposed to the low frequencies associated with the physical universe. During the demise of the physical the process of separation is required to be an exact reversal of the insertion process. That being, the Aspect's energies withdraw from the energetic network associated with the chakras and coalesce within the area assigned as the core star. Once in the core star the energies move back to the point of insertion, the tan tien, and then move back up to the TES via the hara line.

With me it was different.

Normally the energies gradually withdraw and coalesce at the core star over a number of days. This is the three-day rule. But when an advanced Aspect (soul) is fully aware of the process, this can be accelerated to the point where, when the physical body demises, the Aspect can leave instantaneously. This can only be achieved when the energies associated with the Aspect are withdrawn to the point of ineffectiveness in terms of animating the physical body prior to its demise.

35

ME: Would this be when the person who is dying appears to be asleep for most of time immediately before the demise of the physical body?

A: Yes, but not always. You see, in general and during demise based upon disease or plain old age, an Aspect enters into stasis before the actual separation. This means the body appears to be asleep while the Aspect enters the separation process, allowing the Aspect to leave as soon as the physical body ceases to function.

ME: Stasis can't be a general thing, though, because many die with knowledge of dying and others are alive one moment and dead the next, such as with heart attacks, strokes, and accidents to name but a few.

A: Clearly, some Aspects choose to be in control of the physical body right up until demise, but in these instances they are subject to the three-day rule.

Other advanced Aspects can leave the physical body at will, the so-called Maha Samadhi experienced by advanced Hindu yogis. But even in this instance the Aspect will have voluntarily withdrawn most of its energies prior to leaving the body. The Hindus know this and therefore recognize that they can dispose of the physical body before the three-day period is over. But in any event all of these methods require the reversal of the process of Aspect insertion into the physical body. It's just that the timing is different.

ME: OK, so how did you separate from your physical body?

A: I have already said it—with a whoosh!

Me: That's not very descriptive.

A: No, it's not. I am having some fun with you. As I stated earlier I needed to prepare, to place my body in a state of stasis, of infectivity but that was thwarted by the drugs. So I was a bit stuck. My body was sedated and so was my Aspect, if you know what I mean. On the night of my physical body's demise I was stuck in a dead body that would not let me go until the drugs became ineffective. That could have taken anything up to six or seven days.

ME: Almost doubling the three-day rule.

A: Exactly. The positive thing here, though, was that you were holding my hand, and you were willing me to go. A very noble act, I have to say. Because of this I had a physical coupling of energy from you and two powerful intentions for me to leave my body, mine and yours, and so I was catapulted out of the physical, rather than staying with it in a limbo state.

ME: What did this "catapulting" feel like?

A: It's not what it felt like, it's what it was. Not being able to withdraw my energies back to the core star and tan tien, I was stuck. OK, it was only a temporary paralysis that would extend the three-day rule to six or seven, but it was still paralysis. This meant that the connectivity of the hara line with the physical was starting to become unstable as it expected the gradual migration of "Aspect energy" back into it.

Noting that the hara line is a temporary construct only in use to place the Aspect into the energies associated with the spirituo-physical components of the physical body anyway, it ultimately dematerializes once the Aspect is back in the energies associated with location of the TES. It was this instability and the impending dematerialization of the hara that made my Aspect's association with it weak.

ME: So what are you suggesting here? That you bypassed the need to faithfully reverse the insertion process in your demise/ascension process?

A: Not me—us. Our energies and intentions, when coupled together, were so strong that the hara line was literally blown away and I was projected, "catapulted," back toward our TES. Like I said before, I quite literally had to put the brakes on, otherwise I would have reintegrated with our TES.

ME:There was no "tunnel" effect then?

A: Not in the slightest.

ME:And you bypassed the need to return through the hara line?

A: Yes. It was a quite amazing experience. All of a sudden I felt acceleration. Not in a speedy sense but in a frequential sense. I was going up the frequencies at an extremely rapid rate, one that gave me almost instantaneous expansion— expansion from every functional direction that is available. All of a sudden I was in an omniscient state of awareness, of memory, of observation, of beingness, of connectivity, and of love. I could go on. The list of what I experienced in an instantaneous moment was only limited by my recent human thought processes. It was like a sensory explosion of universe-creating proportions. Being in the human body is like being squeezed into a matchbox!

Everything that I was, I am, I will be, I can be, I could do, came back instantaneously. I knew where every galaxy was positioned in the physical universe, where all of the entities created by Source Entity One had incarnated and what they had done, where their TES's were located in the structure of the multiverse and how long and how much work it had taken them to achieve that position. I even knew what the other Source Entities were doing and how they were doing it. And, if I concentrated, I could "zoom in" to the detail of what their creations were doing and how they were doing it.

ME:I would expect that level of ability to be reserved to one of the Om.

A: Well, as we are both Aspects of the same Om TES that makes perfect sense.

ME:So why can't I access the level of detail you are experiencing now?

A: Simply because you are still incarnate, at a VERY low frequency and your physical vehicle could not possibly cope with the energies associated with such levels of connectivity.

Note this, though, what you are achieving while writing these books and teaching your workshops is phenomenal in comparison to what normal incarnates can achieve, so don't get jealous on me.

ME: I'm not, well, yes, I am, and that is a purely human and karmic trait. I suppose it's a good job I/we recognized it and nipped it in the bud when I/we did.

A: You bet it is.

ME: OK, you experienced explosive expansion and rapid ascension upon the demise of the physical.

A: Yes, but this was only achieved because we were working together.

ME: Yes, but what was it like to see your/our TES?

A: It was like nothing you can ever imagine. In fact, I will have difficulty describing it in human terms.

ME: I am used to that. Give it a try.

A: I talked about being expansive and regaining my memory set all at once. Well, the feeling of connectivity is the most amazing thing you will ever experience. Your ability to connect with any part of The Source, and in our case The Origin, is both instantaneous and multidimensional from a sensory-based perspective, so when you say what is it like to "see" your/our TES it is difficult to explain.

ME: Why?

A: Because we don't just "see" things, not in the human sense. Everything we experience is on so many different levels of sensory connectivity that the so-called visual Aspect of our senses simply pale into insignificance. However, I will put it in human terms for your readers.

When I became expansive I could see, perceive, feel, touch, taste, empathize, love, connect, sentiate, intelliate, and omniciate *[see the glossary —GSN]*. And this list is not exhaustive by the way. The so-called visual appearance of

39

the TES is like a ball of energy with lines of energy extending from it to all the Aspects that are projected from the TES and the Shards from the Aspect. The ball of energy that is the TES is not actually a ball, though; it is more like an amorphous mass that is nominally spherical in shape but that is dimensionally permeable. I would like to say that it has a color but that would not be entirely accurate as the color effect is a result of the energies associated with the TES. The energies (color) swirl around within and without the nominal spherical shape pulsating, rotating, irradiating, and dimensiating. The dimensiate condition is most interesting because you can see all the dimensions that the TES is being projected into. It's like you can see the localized content of all of the frequencies, subdimensional components and full dimensions that the TES is projecting Aspects into or that the Aspects are projecting Shards into. Sometimes it is mirror like. Other times it is, for example, like seeing the surface of Jupiter and the Sun together but in a sort of transparent intermingled condition. I prefer to think of it as being like quicksilver (mercury) or a chunk of sodium that has been dropped into a bowl of water.

ME: You can see where the other Aspects of our TES are projected into from a total environment and structural basis then?

A: Yes, but as you are the only other Aspect of our TES, it only goes to the first full dimension and the physical universe. If I were to look at other TES's that are projecting Aspects into the multiverse I can see a vast network of intertwining connectivity between the TES's and their Aspects and the Shards of the Aspects working within the multiversal structure they are working on or within. If I then focus on, say, one of them, I can see and experience everything that is being experienced and assimilated by the particular TES I am focusing on. What's more, I can see and experience any or all of the Event Spaces created by them as a result of their decision process/es. I also see where you go to when you are communicating with The Origin and other Source Entities, which of course includes all of the current and potential Event Spaces you create in the process.

ME:You can see, or should I say *experience*, all of this concurrently?

A: Yes, of course. You don't realize just how constrained you are when in the human form. It's as close to being nonexistent as an entity can get without actually being nonexistent.

ME:Mmmm. Don't you get information overload?

A: Not in the slightest. Everything that is presented to me, or that I focus on, is really already part of me anyway.

ME:And I guess that is because you/we are really just individualized units of The Origin anyway.

A: Sort of, yes. You see, when I focus on what a particular TES or group of TES's are experiencing, I expand exponentially until I reach a point where I have enough capacity to cope with the information being received. It's a bit like gaining access to more memory and processing power, but only for the duration of time that I need it.

ME:I somehow get the feeling that you are linking into The Origin in some way and becoming more like it.

A: Not quite. That's a higher function. What is happening is that, because I am still an individualized Aspect, I am using the resources of the TES.

ME:OK, but our TES is only so big. It must have an expansive capacity that it can't go beyond.

A: I don't see any limitations with our TES so far.

ME:Why is that?

A: Because two things come into play. The first is that it is Om and it is essentially working outside of the structure of the multiverse and the structural functionality of Source Entity One. The second is that another two things occur. The first is that our TES uses the residual expansive and functional capacity of the TES/TES's being focused upon, expanding into them, being them while remaining independent. The second is that it also uses the localized functional capacity of the structure of The Origin that is specific to the location of the TES. Once linked into the structure of The Origin, our TES becomes more than an Om TES, it becomes The Origin from the perspective of the location of the TES and the required expansion and subsequent functional capacity required to experience all that is being presented to the TES. There is a third thing that can come into play.

ME: And what is that?

A: That our TES, and any other TES for that matter, commandeers more energy to increase the, shall I say, the operational energetic "Mass" of the TES. From the perspective of an Om this is either the energies within The Source Entity they are working with/within or it's the energies of The Origin.

ME: But this is all expansion rather than actual TES capacity.

A: Of course. Generally, our TES is more than capable of coping with any level of informational experience, and usually it does not need to use these expansion methods.

ME: So our TES, a pure Om TES, is infinitely expansive.

A: Yes, as are non-captive Om. Captive Om do have limitations.

ME: And they are?

A: The point of capture. For example, the expansive capacity of The Source Entity they are captive within. But for all TES that are created by a Source Entity this is mirrored down the hierarchy, so to speak. So what I have described about our TES's functionality and how it interfaces with the functional structure of The Origin in this particular instance is also the functionality of a Source Entity TES, but with the TES connecting or expanding into the functional structure of The Source Entity that created the TES, and not The Origin.

ME: I would expect that a Source Entity can use the same methods to expand into The Origin, should they wish to do so?

A: Yes, but that is their functionality and not the functionality of their creations or those entities such as the captive Om, the Om that are unable to move unaided, outside the energetic boundary of their Source Entity.

ME: And you can see where our TES is now?

A: Yes, of course.

ME: And where exactly is our TES located frequentially?

A: You mention frequency. Frequency is relative to energy. It is not "located" energetically, it is more multilocated sentience.

ME: Explain.

A: It is both within the structure of Source Entity One and within the structure that exists between The Source Entities—the structure of The Origin that is its area of polyomniscient sentient self-awareness. There is also residual sentience that is still expressing your/our TES's sentience within the energetic boundaries of the other eleven Source Entities. This, my dear one, is how you move outside of the structure of the multiverse, and that which forms the greater part of Source Entity One, out into the wider structure of The Origin and its creations.

ME: And how exactly do I do that?

A: The same way as I do, by relocating the focus of your sentience, or should I say, that Aspect of our TES's sentience that has created the smaller individualized version of itself that is now occupying the human vehicle known as Guy Steven Needler.

ME: So the fact that our TES is outside the structure of Source Entity One is the main reason I can project my consciousness beyond its energetic boundary.

A: Yes and no. Yes, it helps, but, no, it is not a necessary requirement.

ME: Why not?

A: Because Pure Om can move anywhere and within and without any entity, whether created by The Origin or one of The Origin's creations.

ME: The Om appear to be **Om**-niscient, please excuse the pun here!

A: Good to see you are getting your sense of humor back. Yes, they are, especially when energetic or should I say, in the state of pure sentience.

5

Integration with the True Energetic Self

ME:Thank you. You just described what our TES looked like when you were ascending from your physical body. You also stated that you had to "put the brakes on" as a result of the help you had. This means that you are still individualized from our TES.

A: Yes, it does.

ME:Could you explain what it would be like to integrate with our TES.

A: Yes, I still have the knowledge from before our current incarnation. Although somewhat different energetically, the experience would be similar enough to that experienced by the Aspect of a Source Entity TES to be useful to you.

In essence, the Aspect of a TES is a specialized function of its overall sentience and the energies that the TES sentience has commandeered or been assigned to. When the Aspect ascends from the physical vehicle, it regains full connectivity from an energetic perspective and the individualized Aspect regains full functionality and memory. When, however, the Aspect reintegrates with its TES, the Aspect loses command of the energies that its individualized sentience was assigned to, and attains access to an area of energy within the TES that is assigned to it within the energetic boundary of the TES. The sentience that is the Aspect is then reintegrated with the overall sentience of the TES, which is distributed throughout the commandeered/assigned energies. The personality of the Aspect is maintained, though, because the sentience of that Aspect will have experienced different things in different ways to the other Aspects of the TES's sentience. That being, it has gained a specialism of series of specialisms.

ME: So the Aspect's sentience stays as an independent part of the overall TES sentience?

A: Yes and no. Although the sentience of the Aspect is distributed throughout the overall TES sentience, it has a personality, so to speak. The personality is the marker for all of the components that make up the Aspect's distributed sentience. These components, although divorced from each other, are also in communication from a functional and sentience-based level of communication. As a result, if the overall TES sentience wishes to call upon the specialism of the individualized sentience that is/was the Aspect, whatever its distributed state, it can communicate with it as if it was an individualized sentient entity.

ME: I am seeing a picture of a vast network of sentience, TES sentience. The sentience that is/was used to create specific Aspects are identified as components of that distributed sentience by a sentient label. That label is the product of the sum of the experiences registered by a particular Aspect of TES sentience. The sentience that is assigned as an individualized Aspect therefore has an experiential signature, one that allows the TES to reanimate that Aspect "of sentience" as an "individualized" sentience that can commandeer or be assigned to a body of energy, either from the energies used by the TES or those gathered from the environment that the Aspect will be working with.

To me it looks a bit like the files of a computer program that are distributed around its memory storage media, irrespective of whether it is a disk or solid-state memory. When the user of a computer wants to use a certain program he/she invokes the program by clicking on the launch icon. When the launch icon is selected, a launch program is initiated that collects all of the individualized files that are distributed around the storage media and assigns it to a temporary location in an area of Random Access Memory (RAM). When they are all together, they work together and operate as the program being invoked, including all of the peripheral functionality associated with it. In this way the individual program files, which are useless on their own, are brought together to create an individualized program that has the specific and/or desired functions that are part of the overall program. And so the program has individuality, function, and purpose. This is the same for the individualized experiences of the Aspect within the TES. The TES can be related to as the storage media and the experiences are the individualized components of the Aspect, the program files, which on their own are only experiences with no individual functionality. Put them all together and they operate as one, forming the overall experiential conditions that create the personality of the Aspect, the Aspect that worked on and within the experiences that ultimately created the Aspect as an individualized component, an Aspect of TES sentience.

A: And that is what we are when we reintegrate with our TES. Except, that is, for the fact that the personality associated with the collective experiences that create the Aspect is not lost when reintegration is achieved. It remains functional so long as all of the experiences are maintained within the TES or are assigned a body of energy in the same configuration outside of the TES for the purposes of collecting evolutionary content either through incarnation or other means that require the Aspect to remain in the energetic.

ME: What you are saying then is that the TES is full of components of sentience, experiential sentience, and that when all together in the TES they remain as a collective of individualized experiential sentience that creates a personality. Based upon this, the TES must be full of smaller separate personalities, personalities that were created as a result of it creating a smaller version of itself, an Aspect of itself, or as the result of an Aspect creating a Shard of itself, to experience some part of the multiverse it has an interest in, while it experiences something else, maybe something bigger.

A: Correct. And all of these personalities, when together, create the overall personality that is the TES.

ME:Ah, it is the overall personality then.

A: Yes, and if you refer to the Aspect in old speak and call it the "Soul," the TES would be called the overall soul, or the "Over Soul."

ME:OK! The penny is dropping on why certain nomenclature has been used in the past, or is being used now. It all refers to what we have been discussing now, but now we know why that nomenclature was used, whereas I doubt if we really understood what it meant.

A: I have no doubt that some people understood it.

ME:Agreed. I have one more thing to discuss about reintegration with the TES before we move on to the next subject, and that is the TES's use of, the borrowing of, the experiential sentience of known Aspects to create a new Aspect with a set of borrowed experiences.

A: Oh, you mean a composite Aspect (composite soul).

ME:OK, yes.

A: Yes, this is quite common. It is used when the TES desires to embark on a new individual experience or set of experiences that none of its existing Aspects have enough experiential sentience to enable them to work with while on their own. So with this being the case it fabricates an Aspect that will be able to work with this new set of experiences in a successful way.

ME:Does this not permanently create a new Aspect, though, making more than twelve?

48

A: Yes, it does. And when the composite Aspect reintegrates with the TES it also maintains its personality as well.

ME: And this doesn't result in the, shall I say, donating Aspects losing part of their experiential sentience?

A: No, because that sentience is then assigned to both the donating Aspect and the composite Aspect. It has a dual function. The full personality of the donating Aspect and the composite Aspect is maintained.

ME: OK, and this is true because the experiential sentience that was donated and now finds itself used in two Aspects is just like a shared file that can operate in two individual computer programs. For example, the "Spell Check" program files in a word processor and a spread sheet.

A: Correct. I do like it when you catch on quick.

ME: Thank you. I will take that as a compliment. I have another question, though. You said that the sentience of the composite Aspect is maintained. Does that mean that the personality created as a result of the use of a new and composite Aspect is maintained once its incarnate function is finalized?

A: Yes.

ME: But that means that a TES must have more than twelve Aspects associated with it.

A: Yes, it does.

ME: But I was under the impression that the maximum number of Aspects that can be projected into the multiverse by a TES was twelve.

A: And it still is twelve.

ME: Ah! So the TES can create any number of Aspects, but it can only project a maximum of twelve Aspects into the multiversal environment.

A: Correct. You've got it.

ME: OK, next question. Does this rule also work with the creation of Shards by the Aspect?

A: No. Shards are created and uncreated by the Aspect on a "need-to" basis. They are created to allow the Aspect to maximize its own evolutionary opportunities within the environment it finds itself within.

The personality of the Shard is not maintained once it reintegrates with the Aspect. The memory set, experience, and evolutionary content of the Shard's incarnate existence is transferred to the Aspect upon the demise of its physical vehicle, as is the potentially accrued specialization that the Shard may develop during its existence. The Aspect absorbs everything from its Shards.

ME: Wait a minute. This means that the personalities of those incarnate entities that are Shards disintegrate upon the demise of their physical vehicle. This could be very disturbing for some people because it means that in the case of an incarnate having a Shard as its animating "soul" or "sub-soul" it will lose its essence of self when its physical vehicle demises. This means it could be said to die with the physical and no longer exist.

A: That's correct.

ME: Then those incarnates whose soul is a Shard will experience true death. They will not experience immortality, the perpetuation of the personality, after the demise of the physical vehicle.

A: Correct again.

ME: This is going to be a real blow to those who find out they are Shards.

A: True but not true.

ME: What do you mean, true but not true?

A: What it means is that, yes, the personality that the Shard creates as a result of being incarnate is lost upon the demise of the physical vehicle, but, no, the total experiential and evolutionary content accrued during the existence of the Shard is not lost, and it never shall be. It is always integrated; it is always saved within the creating Aspect.

ME: So you are suggesting that the essence of what they are is not lost, just the personality that was generated by the ego is lost.

A: Yes. It is nothing to be feared.

ME: I can still see the fear in the eyes of some Shards, though.

A: Fear is always the product of lack of knowledge and experience.

ME: Yes, I understand. I have another question.

A: Fire away.

ME: We have discussed some of the process experienced by the Aspect when it is released from its incarnate vehicle and how the sentience is distributed throughout the TES when it is reintegrated with it. The question I have is, is this the same for a Shard, or does it follow an entirely different process?

A: A Shard experiences much the same process as an Aspect in relation to the retraction of its energies when the physical vehicle demises. The only difference, or should I say the main difference, is that it experiences dissolution of its individuality. The dissolution is experienced almost immediately after the demise of the physical vehicle. From the perspective of the Shard it would be like feeling and experiencing expansion and then almost immediately experiencing integration, where the integration results in the dissemination of the personality to the point where it no longer exists from an individual perspective. It would be like slowly falling into a cozy sleep.

ME: Why is it experienced immediately after the demise of the physical vehicle and not later, once the Shard has reviewed its existence? *[See later for the incarnate life review process. —GSN]*

A: Simply because a Shard does not go through the life review process. This is reserved for Aspect.

ME: Can you explain why?

A: Of course. A Shard is created by an Aspect to allow it to experience an extension to, or more detail within, its current agreed life plan, should it decide to experience more detail. Based upon this, the creation of the Shard is a result of the need or desire of the Aspect to augment a certain part of its experience and subsequent opportunity to increase its evolutionary content while it is in a state of "individuality."

ME: But isn't this the same for the Aspect in relation to the TES?

A: No.

ME: Why not? It seems pretty close to being the same thing to me.

A: Well, it's not. I will explain. The Aspect is created by the TES as a result of its need to enter into a known environment and a predetermined number of experiences that are relative to its specialization. In this respect, the Aspect is created as a fully functional "mini" version of the TES itself, having total autonomy from the TES when incarnate, which includes the time before the incarnation, hence its ability to create a Shard. The Aspect also needs to consider its options once the incarnation is over because it may decide, upon communication with the TES, to reincarnate again to experience similar environmental conditions with a view to perfecting its responses or addressing areas of non-response. This is described as the life review.

The Shard's existence is not subject to a life review because its experiences, its incarnation, is/are a result of the Aspect wanting to augment or duplicate its experience while it itself is in a certain area or genre of experiential environment. As a result, the experiences of the Shard are integrated into the Aspect upon its reintegration and are reviewed by the Aspect when it itself is newly disincarnate.

ME: So what you are saying is that the life of the Shard is counted as part of the life of the Aspect, that it is not sentience that is individualized as a result of the Aspect projecting it into a physical vehicle, like the Aspect is sentience that is individualized from the TES.

A: Not quite. The Shard is individualized from its Aspect, but only on a one-off basis. It has to be individualized to make the incarnation work effectively—whereas the Aspect is individualized from its TES on a multiple/continuous basis as a fully functional Aspect of its wider personality, experience, and evolutionary content.

ME: So to summarize, a Shard really is a temporary state of sentience that only exists as a function of the Aspect to support its desire/need to investigate an evolutionary opportunity while it itself is in the incarnate state.

And, based upon this, the Aspect is a semipermanent or permanent state of individualized sentience that exists both in the individualized state and within the integrated state as part of the overall TES sentience. It is employed over and over again as a result of its specialism—the specialism being developed as a result of being exposed to similar or same experiences within differing environments and/or circumstances.

The TES itself is autonomous of The Source in every way, including the need to incarnate in a holistic sense because it can, in effect, evolve while in the energetic. Incarnation is therefore a function used to accelerate evolutionary content in a gradual way by only exposing a certain percentage of itself to the lower frequencies of the multiverse, thereby ensuring it does not succumb to karma in totality.

A: Correct. Note this, though; the sum of the total parts of the TES that are incarnate can never be more than 30 percent of the total TES energies.

ME: Why is that?

A: Because it is a function of the structure of the TES that it must have 70 percent of its total energetic mass, so to speak, within its dominant evolutionary frequency.

ME: And what is the dominant evolutionary frequency?

A: That frequency where the TES has evolved to within the structure of the multiverse, that frequency where all Aspects the TES projects must ultimately return to. Once, that is, they have reviewed their incarnation and feel the need to reintegrate with the TES.

6

The Life Review

ME: We have talked a couple of times about the life review and it is mentioned and described by many spiritual authors and leaders, but what actually is it? I mean, it all seems very human to me, too human.

A: The descriptions are humanized to help with understanding the whole point of incarnation. Look, as an incarnate entity mankind is but an infant working out what causes pleasure or pain, let alone understanding what the environment is that it finds itself within.

ME: Touché. Alright, tell me what the life review is and why it is done.

A: The life review is more than just looking at a group of pictures or events that took place within the entities, the Aspect's, incarnate existence. It is also more than looking at what went well and what went not so well when comparing the life plan against the performance of the Aspect as an incarnate entity.

ME: Well, you have just described the subject headings that most people would expect to cover in a life plan. You say that this is not it, though?

A: I said that it is more than this, which means that the subject headings I just stated are included within it. It's just that these limited subjects are all that mankind could understand, until, that is, now.

ME:OK, fill me in with the detail.

A: The life review is conducted in a number of ways.

These are:

Against the life plan from a holistic perspective. This is the most popular level of review, and it is the one that most spiritually aware incarnates recognize. In this review the Aspect takes an overall perspective of the incarnation against the overall expectations of the life plan. This is used to see if the general objectives of the incarnation have been achieved and to what level of achievement it can be categorized as. This is the ultimate decision point and is the acid test that dictates whether or not the Aspect needs to undertake an incarnate existence that is identical in environmental and circumstantial nature.

Against the life plan from a detailed perspective. This review goes into the absolute detail of the life plan versus the performance of the incarnating Aspect. It looks at the opportunities for experiential and evolutionary progression presented to the Aspect and the ways in which it responded to those opportunities. This review looks into the ways the Aspect responded to its challenges and those challenges that were repeated if the response was not appropriately taken. It also identifies the different ways the guide and helpers employed to assist the incarnate Aspect in times of poor or lacking response to get the Aspect back on track.

From the evolutionary content gained. Simply put, this is a measure of the Aspect's incarnate efficiency. It is its ability to experience, learn, and evolve in as short a time as possible, allowing the incarnate to evolve in a maximal way while it is within the lower frequencies. It is a measure of the Aspect's ability to maximize its opportunity, while incarnate, thereby exceeding the evolutionary expectations agreed upon in the overall life plan during the planning stage of the incarnation.

From the number of local Event Spaces created to support the generation of evolutionary content. This is a metric, a function, of the effectiveness of the decision process used by the incarnate in terms of how it works with the guidance from its guide and helpers. That being, how it works with the information sent to it to assist in the decision processes that are presented to it in order to change its direction in order to experience a known set of experiences or make a change in its thought processes. These decisions can also affect the incarnate's ability to finalize or complete a karmic circle or sever a karmic link.

This metric is also used to determine how effective the methods used by the guide and helpers were to attract the attention of the incarnate in order to make a change in direction or thought process. In some respects, this is also covered in the next performance check.

From the number of Event Spaces that were unnecessarily created. Unnecessarily created Event Spaces are those which attract no evolutionary content. No evolutionary content is accrued when an experience does not result in learning. If a state of learning is involved, no matter how small, evolutionary content is accrued and the Event Space is deemed of benefit to the incarnate and therefore necessary.

This is therefore a method of checking the magnitude of error in judgment in its decision-making process. The magnitude being the number of fractal branches and subsequent Event Spaces (localized personal universes) created as a result of an incorrect decision at the point of the root or nexus of a decision point. The root or nexus of a decision is one that takes the incarnate away from the mainstream direction of the life plan. Clearly, there is an accepted and desired tolerance in respect to the number of Event Spaces created because some of them are expected and therefore form part of the overall picture of the life plan, adding to the evolutionary content accrued.

The positive effect of the incarnate on the evolution of others. In essence, this is a measure of how well the incarnate interfaces with other incarnates in terms of being a positive role model. Being a role model can be actioned by actively or passively educating other incarnates in how to act or behave or think while incarnate. The measure of this is identified in how much of this education is absorbed and used in daily incarnate existence and how the accrual of evolutionary content is affected as a result. In this instance a "with" and "without" education scenario is viewed in the evolutionary section of the Akashic records.

The negative effect of the incarnate on the evolution of others. This is a measure of the way an incarnate is both affected by low-frequency behaviors and thoughts, and how the incarnate influences the thoughts, behaviors, and actions of those incarnates they interface with in a negative way— the negative influence in this case being if those incarnates actively change their thoughts, behaviors, and actions from being a higher level to one of a lower level, removing any chance of their gaining evolutionary content.

We cannot evolve negatively in Source Entity One's multiverse, but we can reduce our evolutionary expectations of an incarnation if we choose to take a path that results in lower frequency existence. The incarnate that actively influences the thoughts, behaviors, and actions of another to the point at which its evolutionary content falls short of expectations will experience no personal evolutionary growth as a result.

The effect of the incarnate on the global evolutionary stage. This is not a metric that is applied to every incarnate because it is specific to those incarnates who decide to work for the benefit of others on the world or global stage. It is a supplementary function and as such is a parallel life plan. Again, this is a metric based upon the incarnate's ability to work within the agreed plan. The level of success is based upon how close to the plan the incarnate's world work is upon the demise of the human vehicle used and its projected longevity once the incarnate is away from physical influence.

If an incarnate does not meet the expectations of the plan, there is no need for them to reincarnate to finish the work because this is not based upon a karmic link. Additionally, it is recognized that this is based upon the incarnate's ability to remember its world life plan to the extent necessary to allow it to be activated and work with the direction of the guide and helpers in a way that is parallel to the personal life plan.

Any level of positive influence, irrespective of how close to the world life plan the work is, attracts evolutionary content. In the event that the incarnate exceeds expectations, a proportion of the evolutionary content accrued by those influenced by the incarnate is bestowed upon the incarnate. This is not taken from those influenced but is a function of the wider effect of triangulation from an evolutionary perspective.

The opportunities taken to be of unselfish service to others. These opportunities are interspaced within the life plan of the incarnate and are located in Event Spaces where the incarnate may, should they choose to do so, move into, knowing that they will be working for the benefit of others and not themselves. This also means that they are aware that they will not be rewarded, will not actively seek reward, or will not feel that they should be rewarded for the service they commit to. Being of unselfish service to others allows the incarnate to accrue additional evolutionary content as a result of their work, but they are not aware of this.

There are a known number of opportunities and the guide and helpers are only allowed to influence the incarnate in ways that are consistent with the personal life plan. The level of success is simply based upon the number of opportunities taken versus those missed. Analysis in terms of the depth of service given is also used to determine the level of "unselfish application" of the service.

The opportunities missed to be of unselfish service to others. This is the inverse of the opportunities taken insomuch as it is analyzed in terms of understanding both the number of opportunities missed and "why" the incarnate missed the opportunities. It is also analyzed in terms of what was done, or not done, by the guide and helpers to bring the incarnate into "recognition distance" of the opportunity/ies to be of service.

Whether or not the incarnate Aspect recognized the bigger picture, the greater reality. This is not a measure of whether the incarnate worked with the greater reality. It is simply a point of reference to note the level of recognition of the greater reality the incarnate was aware of, and as a result, that it "knew" that there is a reality which is beyond the physical universal environment and that it could potentially work with/within it.

Whether, once recognizing the bigger picture, the incarnate Aspect chooses to work with the greater reality, being in the physical but not of the physical, or remain human-centric. This is a review of the decision points presented to the incarnate that could have resulted in significant personal growth and evolutionary content, or not as the case may be, and the reasons for the decisions taken. The decisions for both remaining in a human-centric state of mind and working with the greater reality are analyzed, understood, and recorded in the Akashic for the benefit of other incarnates to review. The object of this is to educate those using incarnation as an evolutionary fast track of the possible ways in which an incarnate can go off track as a result of karmic influences, even when working with the greater reality is to all intents and purposes assured.

The level of karma accrued/removed. This review speaks for itself from a high level but at the working level is easily misunderstood. This analysis is not specifically a review of the number of karmic links made or broken but what genres of karma have been created or broken. Karma can be, and is, graded in terms of difficulty of removal and ease of attraction. Based upon this, some genres of karma can be difficult to attract but easy to remove as well as easy to attract and difficult to remove. They can also be easy to attract and easy to remove as well as difficult to attract and difficult to remove. This analysis is therefore focused upon not only what karma was accrued or removed but the ease at which it was accrued or removed relative to its genre and grade.

The performance of the Aspect as a result of its autonomy while incarnate. This is a measure of how well the incarnate works with the Aspect of its life plan that is integrated within the energies associated with the incarnate vehicle it occupies. What's more, it is a metric that identifies how well the incarnate recognizes this in-built life plan guidance and works with it. In most instances, and from the human perspective, this is a function of how well the incarnate feels an overwhelming desire to have a certain career or specialism and acts upon that desire. In this instance, although the incarnate works with the life plan in ignorance of the greater reality, it may still be drawn into, and work with, its potential world work, fueled by a feeling of wanting to put back into the world something to compensate for what the world and its inhabitants has given it.

From the spiritual perspective this is a measure of how well the incarnate feels and works with the recognition of being an energetic being, relating to it as a function of its True Energetic Self, and not the incarnate vehicle it occupies. In this instance, the incarnate will know that it has a three-fold responsibility and will endeavor to work with these responsibilities. These three-fold responsibilities are: to work in the physical but not be of the physical, satisfying its commitments to family, friends, and work colleagues; to be of service to others where possible, thereby satisfying its commitments to its world work; to progress on a personal basis, thereby satisfying its commitments to its spiritual work.

The performance of the Aspect as a result of its guidance while incarnate. Based upon the autonomous function, this is a measure of how well the incarnate's performance was augmented by the work of the guide and helpers in variance to receiving no help or guidance.

The performance of the guide. This is a function of how well the guide performs while in the role of the guide, illustrating how it "grew" within the role, accruing its own evolutionary content as a result. One of the main functions observed here is the creative ability of the guide and how it employs this ability in attracting the attention of the incarnate under its care, ensuring that it remains on track with its life and world plan.

The effectiveness of the relationship between the incarnate Aspect and the guide. In a lot of respects this is covered by the performance of the guide and its creativity. However, this metric also takes into account the additional function of the longevity of the relationship between the guide and incarnate Aspect resulting from past incarnations, together with how the relationship develops during the term of the current incarnation.

The performance of the guide's helpers. This is a function of how well the helpers perform while in the role of being a helper. In variance to the performance of the guide and how it works with the incarnate directly, this metric identifies how well the helpers work with the guide and helpers of other incarnates.

This metric is ultimately used to identify the effect on the accrual of evolutionary content of the incarnate under their care as a direct result of their work with the guide and helpers of other incarnates. Included within this is the effect on the accrual of evolutionary content of the interfacing incarnates as a result of the interfacing work with their guide and helpers required to support the incarnate they are responsible for. In some respects, this is a measure of the overall evolutionary synergy created between the guide and helpers of the incarnate and all those incarnates it will work with during its physical existence.

The effectiveness of the relationship between the helpers and the guide. This analysis is designed to establish the strengths and weaknesses of the guide and helpers in the configuration used to support the incarnation. It looks at:

- The numbers of helpers chosen by the guide. This can be variable during the period of incarnation.
- The skill set of the helper/s chosen by the guide.
- Which/how many helpers are changed/rotated/ introduced during the incarnation.
- The times the guide and helpers have worked with the incarnate in previous incarnations.
- The skills they have accrued in those incarnations and which are used to support the incarnate in this incarnation.
- The skills they accrue in this incarnation.
- How well the guide orchestrates the work of the helpers.
- How well the helpers respond individually and collectively to the orchestration of the guide.

The effectiveness of the relationship between the incarnate Aspect, the guide, and helpers as a total team. This is a single summary-based response given to the TES's of the incarnate, guide, and helpers as a result of their self-assessment. This is a product of the analysis of the results of all the previous areas of sub-analysis giving an overall picture of performance. It identifies the level of success of the incarnation, what content should be in the next incarnation, and which guide and helpers should be employed.

In all of these areas the Aspect then finally reviews the incarnation with both the TES and the Aspect chosen by the TES to act as the main guide or initiator of directional change. The guide can be another Aspect of the TES or an Aspect of another TES that both the TES and the Aspect have elected to share experiential and evolutionary content with.

ME: I have a question. All of this is in human terms, or so it seems to me. I expected it to be more energetic in its description.

A: It is energetic. Most people expect it to be a life review in a "hall of memories" surrounded by a guide/s and helpers. This is a review that, although its description is in an analytical form that is readily understandable by incarnate mankind, it is "generally" performed in our natural energetic form.

ME: Why generally? Why not all of the time?

A: There are some Aspects (souls) that continue to think in terms of being incarnate when their physical body demises. They have difficulty making the transition back to being totally independent of the physical vehicle and its demands.

ME: Why is this?

A: Because they relate to themselves as being in the same form, irrespective of their incarnate state. This is a function of them being stuck in the physical and not evolving, while incarnate, to a state of being where they question their environment.

ME: But surely they recognize that they are no longer in their physical vehicle, the human body?

A: Some recognize that they are released from the physical but use the "form factor" of the human vehicle because they either prefer it or they have difficulty disassociating themselves from the thought process that everything is aligned to a human form. Others still actively think they are alive and are in a dream of one form or another. These Aspects, these poor souls, need to be coached back into the thought process, the knowledge, that they are pure individualized Source Entity sentience, sentient beings with a body of energy.

ME: How do they keep up the illusion of being incarnate?

A: We are masters of creativity and we create our surroundings and anything else we want or need. These poor Aspects need to experience incarnate existence and so they create the illusion that they are still incarnate and overlay this creativity on everything and everyone so that even when presented with an entity in its true energetic form they clothe it in the human form.

Don't get me wrong, this is not just an issue with those Aspects who incarnate in the human form. This is also an issue with some of those Aspects who incarnate in other low-frequency forms as well, those that are not specifically bipedal or breathe a gas.

ME: And this slows down their ascension to integration with their TES?

A: Yes, it does. And it can take what you call seconds to years of Earth clock time to assist them into making the change in thinking necessary to allow them to move into the totally energetic condition that they are.

ME: Well, I certainly don't want to go down that route when I leave this human form.

A: You won't. No matter what you do thought-wise, you won't. You will ascend the physical fully conscious of it.

ME: Thank you for those words of future knowledge. Event Space must be easy to access and manipulate from where you are?

A: Yes, it is.

ME: OK, so if most quickly accept and work with their true energetic/sentient condition, how does the life review take place or look to the outsider?

A: It doesn't appear to take place or even look like a life review from the perspective of human knowledge, even though the analysis looks as if it is something incarnate mankind could understand.

ME: Why?

A: It's just not visible to the outsider; it is all done within the energies of the TES.

ME: Can you explain in a little more detail.

A: Of course. The review of the incarnate existence is analyzed as I previously advised you. One does not need to be human to be able to be analytical. It's just that the way in which the actual life is reviewed is not as you would understand it.

ME: Can you explain?

A: Certainly. Every part of the incarnate existence is reviewed by the TES, the Aspect, the guide, and the helpers in a concurrent way. They enter into an area of energy, extended from the TES who "projected" the Aspect into individuality for incarnate purposes, allowing them to engage in a communion-based state of being. In this way each and every one of them can and does experience the incarnation in a "holistic sense."

ME: What do you mean, *holistic sense*?

A: Basically put, they all experience the incarnate existence as if they were the incarnating Aspect themselves—that being, the guide, every one of the helpers, and the TES receiving the information. In this way they can all see where the work they did was effective, efficient, ineffective, or inefficient, and the varying levels of success that this means. They see how the incarnate Aspect responded to their promptings, when it was working autonomously, how it would have responded when the guide or even one of the helpers delivered the prompting, or if the method of prompting was changed by the guide or given by another helper. Every entity involved in the guidance of the incarnate Aspect, including temporary helpers, experiences every possible scenario that was made available to the incarnate Aspect.

ME: Are you saying that they all relive the incarnate Aspect's life as if it was their own?

A: Yes, they all experience the life in exactly the same way as the Aspect in the same "real time way"—except that is, there is no such thing as "real time" in the energetic.

ME: And does this include all of the parallel conditions created by Event Space?

A: Yes, of course—how else would they be able to analyze the incarnation properly!

ME: Wow. So, based upon this, they may actually be experiencing every conceivable possibility that the incarnate Aspect experiences or could have experienced in another Event Space and the fractal multiplications of those Event Spaces.

A: Yes. You're getting it.

ME: But that means that they could experience more lives than the incarnating Aspect themselves experiences!

A: No.

ME: Why?

A: Because the Aspect itself also experiences all of the possibilities, the possible possibilities, the possibility of possible possibilities, and the possibility of the possibility of possible possibilities.

ME: But ... This seems laborious ... no, ludicrous!

A: I do have to agree to your thoughts that this level of post-incarnation analysis would negate most entities' desire to incarnate. But it doesn't. It is done in this way because it allows the true understanding of the actions and reactions experienced in this low-frequency environment in a very efficient way. The many can experience the work of the one by being the one and the many.

ME: I am glad I am deciding not to come back.

A: That's what you said last time!

ME: Mmmm.

67

A: Actually, and relatively speaking, the several thousand or more lives that the incarnate Aspect experiences, as a result of the effect of Event Space, is experienced very quickly here in the energetic, even though it is experienced "real time."

ME: And I guess this is what persuaded me to come back this one more time.

A: You've got it.

7

After the Life Review: The Time before Reintegration with the True Energetic Self

So far I was both amazed and delighted that I was being given the pleasure and honor to be able to communicate with Anne in this way. To be able to communicate with a loved one who had ascended the physical was one thing, but to be able to ask questions about the incarnation process was another. I know that there are many texts in the public domain that have pertained to describe, in some way, a little of what happens to the Aspect (soul) upon the demise of the physical body, but the information I was receiving from Anne was starting to deliver a whole new level of information. I knew that my readers would expect this given my previous track record, but I was still humbled by the ability to receive information at such a level and honored to be in a position to be able to broadcast it in the way I do. To be honest I expected to experience a spiritual block due to Anne being so close to me, but thankfully this was not happening.

Having just finished a dialogue with Anne on the detail behind the life review, I was interested to know what the Aspect does in the "in-between" time, that time where the Aspect has completed the life review and then can choose to either reintegrate with the TES or seek the opportunity to reincarnate again. The process of incarnation is chosen therefore as a result of the desire to experience the physical and evolve (seeking incarnation for evolutionary progression), experience the sensations of the physical (as a result of some form of addiction to the physical), and/or the need to dissolve a karmic link (or a number of karmic links). Of course there are many other reasons to incarnate, but I consider the three reasons above the main ones, other than of course the desire to incarnate to just be of service to others or to provide some form of spiritual leadership. Intrigued and inspired to know what we do in this "in-between" time, I contacted Anne to see what she is doing herself and what the other Aspects (souls) or Shards (sub-souls) do or are doing.

A: Morning!

ME:Yes, it is a good morning.

A: You are looking tired.

ME:I feel tired. I get the impression that I am doing a lot of extra work while my physical body is sleeping.

A: More than you could possibly know or imagine. We are doing a lot of work together. We are preparing for the future of incarnate mankind.

ME:Now you have my full attention. What are we doing for the future of mankind?

A: We are helping to give incarnate mankind a frequential boost before we leave.

ME:Where are we going?

A: Back to our TES and back to the Om. You have achieved what you wanted to achieve and are now in overtime, so to speak. You knew that you were here to see if you could do it all over again, just one more time. And now it's time to concentrate on the final pieces of work. We don't have much time; we don't have much Event Space to work with.

ME:But, I don't feel that I have finished yet. I mean, I know that I have another six books to write after this one and I have a feeling that I need to set up a foundation to allow the continuation of the Traversing the Frequencies *[TTF, see my website www.beyondthesource.org. —GSN]* workshops, teaching people to project their consciousness into the greater reality after I leave this planet.

A: They, and that, will happen in the fullness of Event Space. There is no need to get stressed about it. You always did want to do things "Now."

Know this. Although these are very early days, you and I have started a revolution in the spiritual world with the work you/we are doing. We have created a paradigm shift, a new level of understanding of the greater reality. To make this work we, together with myriad others, are injecting energy into the Earth and the incarnate population—lifting their frequencies and their thought processes as a result. Have you noticed the number of people who are coming to you now, where you feel the need to open their third eye?

ME: Yes. I recently felt the need to open the third eyes of all of my students in a *Traversing the Frequencies* (TTF) workshop. It was a very strange feeling and one that I followed up in class. I noticed that I could open the third eyes of all of the students at the same time. It's like there are NO LIMITATIONS.

A: There are no limitations. There never were. The opening of people's third eyes is one of the things you are doing at night as well.

ME: Why don't I remember this?

A: Because it would distract you from the work you are doing in the daytime.

ME: Oh! I think you might be right.

A: We should get on with the material that supports this chapter heading.

ME: Yes, you are right. It is nice, though, to be able to just chat about a random subject with you, even when it is about us and the spiritual work. Cutting to the chase, though, just what do we do after the life review?

A: As you previously stated, the Aspect has the choice of reintegration with the TES or reincarnate into the physical.

ME: But there must be things that the Aspect or Shard does before committing to incarnation or integration?

A: There are lots of things. I will explain a few of them. Some of them are rather important because they involve the rehabilitation of the Aspect.

7.1

Rehabilitation

ME: Rehabilitation? Why would an Aspect or Shard require rehabilitation?

A: Addictions, specifically if the Aspect has had a drug or alcohol addiction. Treatments by the use of chemotherapy also cause a problem. We have already discussed the use of morphine and sedatives and how that affects the energies used by the Aspect in its ability to leave the human form, but there is still a problem to solve once the Aspect has departed. In short, the state of the energies that are used to create the human form at the end of its existence can and do effect the energies of the Aspect or Shard. And, if not treated in the appropriate way, they can affect the TES itself.

ME: How could the TES be affected by the energies experienced by the Aspect or Shard?

A: The TES is affected because the Aspect and/or Shard are, simply put, extensions of the TES.

ME: So what affects the Aspect or Shard must, by definition, affect the TES.

A: I always thought that you were a quick learner.

ME: I see that sarcasm is still a useful communication medium in the energetic.

A: No, we don't use it here, but I find it useful when communicating with my incarnate husband and fellow Aspect of an Om TES. I also use it because of the sense of humor you have adopted in this incarnation.

ME: It is appreciated. It keeps me on my toes and helps in my calibration of the information being received as being true.

For the reader of this dialogue, I calibrate what I am receiving in a number of ways; by the tone of voice in my mind's ear, by the inflection of language used in delivering the information, and by my own knowledge. If none of these is considered to be not my own, in any way, I then know that the information is genuine. Doubts arising from any of these calibration methods result in the information being discarded. This is a strict rule that I follow at all times because I don't want to bring my own thoughts into play as information, not that any of us truly has our own "human" thoughts, because I have a personal and professional need to broadcast only genuine information. And what's more, this information must not be made-up information. It must be either new or leading toward new information about the greater reality and not something taken from someone else's information and clothed in my method of dialogue. I do have to say, though, that I find it quite amazing that it has taken me almost six books to make this statement.

A: I thought I would interject here.

ME: Please do.

A: I want to address the readers myself.

ME: Please do.

A: Know this, dear reader. This information that I give is true but is modulated toward your ability, your level of understanding, or your ability to be stretched. That being, stretched in terms of your ability to take on board new levels of understanding and use them as a basis for further "stretching."

ME: Thank you for that clarification. It was almost as if it was necessary. I wanted to say it myself, but never did.

A: Well, I have said it now instead of you.

ME: And I thank you for it. Now, what about this rehabilitation? Can you explain more?

A: Any projection a TES makes into the lowest frequencies of this, or any other Source Entity's environment, which are of course the lowest frequencies of the multiverse, has the ability to be attracted to those frequencies. More importantly, though, they all have the ability to be contaminated to the point where they affect the TES itself, hence the need for rehabilitation. This means that those parts of the TES that are attracted to, or are affected by, some part of the attributes of the lower frequencies that it has been exposed to need to be quarantined in some way before reintegration can be allowed.

ME: And I take it that rehabilitation is the removal of the attraction to the lower frequencies?

A: More than that. It is the energies associated with these lower frequencies that cause the problem. I will explain further.

The TES needs to operate in a way that is independent frequentially, and energetically, from any of the environments that it projects Aspects, or the Aspect projects Shards into. It must be totally separate from the functions associated with being "in" these low frequencies. Although, in reality it can never be separated because both the Aspect and Shard are parts of it, it still needs to have its autonomy in this respect.

As a result of this, the Aspect and/or the Shard are moved into an area where they can be either disassociated with the frequencies or energies of the multiverse, or can be quarantined for a period long enough for them to go through the review process and then be reeducated to the level necessary to allow them to participate in the incarnation process again.

ME: Are you suggesting that the Aspects are kept in separation from the TES and the Shards are kept in separation from the Aspect?

A: In short, yes. You see, the TES cannot allow itself to be affected by the attractions, addictions, or preferences that its projections or the projections of its projections are exposed to.

ME: Even though they are exposed to those environments and experiences by the TES for its own evolutionary progression?

A: Yes. The TES is happy for its overall "self" to be in evolutionary stasis, creating evolutionary tension, as a result of its desire to progress by entering into the incarnate cycle, and it is happy to donate part of itself to establish and complete this. But, it is not happy with the potential for the greater part of itself to be affected by the results of this exposure, hence the need for these parts to be quarantined.

ME: Even though ultimately it is affected as a result of those projected parts holding its own evolutionary progression back?

A: Yes. I will say again that the TES needs to be autonomous from the actions or addictions of its projections.

ME: Even though it experiences everything that the projected Aspects or Shards experience?

A: Of course. I will explain in another way. The TES always experiences what its Aspects or the Shards of its Aspects experience. It does it to experience, learn, and evolve in a parallel way. That is the whole point of it projecting parts of itself into the lower frequencies and other frequencies of the multiverse, to do things in a parallel way. All of this includes the parallel conditions created by Event Space. But, within all of this it needs to be in control of the greater part of itself. It needs to be able to separate the effects of the experiences of its Aspects and the Shards of its Aspects from the experiences themselves. It does this by assigning the effects to the Aspects and the Shards of the Aspects while maintaining the experiences, learning, and evolutionary content within itself, even though it is in evolutionary stasis as a result of projecting parts of itself into the lowest frequencies of the multiverse. In this way the Aspects and Shards, but predominately the Aspects, work out the "effects" in a way that is both individual and isolated from the TES. This is done while also allowing the TES to experience, learn, and evolve from the actions of the Aspect or Shard to alleviate the attractive and/or addictive functions of such exposure, exposure to the karmic functions of the physical universe.

ME: Hold on, you have just said that the TES is in evolutionary stasis and that it also evolves. Which is true?

A: Both. You see, the TES evolves even though it is in evolutionary stasis.

ME: And this is through the function of evolutionary tension?

A: Correct. Evolutionary tension is the way in which the TES still evolves while parts of itself are locked in the incarnate and/or karmic cycle that is associated with incarnation within the physical universe.

ME: I thought that evolutionary tension was created as a result of not being able to evolve, but while the TES was still experiencing multiple existences.

A: Yes, it is. The TES still evolves, though; it's just that those parts of itself that are projected into the lowest frequencies of the multiverse remain in and around those frequencies until they break the karmic cycle that they are working with, thereby negating the need to incarnate. In essence, the TES evolves in the same way that it would have done had it worked purely within the energetic environments of the multiverse. But when the last of the ties to the lowest frequencies is removed, when the last Aspect disassociates itself from the karmic functions, the evolutionary status of the TES is catapulted beyond its normal "energetically accrued" evolutionary level.

ME: So what is evolutionary stasis then if the TES actually continues to evolve in the normal way, because I thought it was arrested, full stop!

A: Evolutionary stasis is the arrest of, the stopping of, instantaneously accrued evolution.

ME: Now I am confused.

A: If you could see your face *[I see a smile on Anne's face in my mind's eye, it was the smile of one who knew the answer to everything while me being here "incarnate" knew nothing relatively speaking. —GSN]*. I will explain further. Although the TES is in evolutionary stasis it is, in effect, still evolving in another Event Space, one where the TES elected not to project any part of itself into the lowest frequencies of the multiverse.

ME: Ah! So the TES is affected by Event Space and can therefore take evolutionary advantage of being affected by Event Space?

A: Correct.

ME: And to continue its evolutionary progression and create this evolutionary tension it needs to remain separate from the effects of the lower frequencies that its Aspects and the Shards of its Aspects are exposed to.

A: Bingo!

ME:Getting back to quarantine and rehabilitation then how does that affect the Aspect or Shard's ability to reintegrate with the Aspect or TES at a future point in Event Space?

A: The projections from the TES are affected in two ways. Firstly, from the point of view of the Aspect who projects a Shard—secondly, from the point of view of the TES. To do this, though, I will need to explain the difference between the functions of the Shard in relation to the Aspect, and then the function of the Aspect in relation to the TES from a karmic perspective.

A Shard is not autonomous from the Aspect; it is part of the Aspect. Of course the Aspect is part of the TES, but the Aspect has the gift of autonomy while projected from the TES. The Shard does not. This means that the Shard must reintegrate with the Aspect after the incarnation the Shard was associated with has finished. The problem here, though, is that the attractions, the addictions to the environment the Shard was projected into as an incarnate "sub-soul," the karma therefore accrued by the Shard, is passed on to the Aspect if reintegration occurs directly after the incarnation, so this needs to be "stripped off" in the energetic before the Shard can be reintegrated.

ME:So you are saying that the Aspect does not accrue karma from its Shards?

A: If dealt with properly, no.

ME:And if immediately reintegrated after an incarnation it would do?

A: Yes.

ME:So how are the addictions, attractions, or karma stripped off? How does rehabilitation work?

A: In the case of the Shard, and while in the energetic, the Aspect reviews the ways in which the Shard accrued the addictions, the attractions, the karma, and sees where existing experience can be used to break the links to the physical that the addictions, etc., create.

ME: How does it achieve this?

A: By going through the life review process and identifying where and how the links were made, and by using the useful function of Event Space, going back into the area of the life to change the outcome while still maintaining the learning and evolutionary growth.

ME: And I would guess it has to consider all of the possible Event Spaces that the Shard had created as a result of its decision process?

A: Yes, but it can do that by pulling in all of the Event Spaces that were created and experiencing them simultaneously, so it's not as laborious as you may think. This part just deals with the attractions, the karmic functions. It does not deal with the addictions, the energetic affects that the Shard may have accrued as a function of being exposed to drugs or alcohol.

ME: There is a separate process required for these then?

A: Yes, and it is an essential one because when the Shard, or even the Aspect itself—we will talk about this later—is exposed to the energies associated with drugs or alcohol abuse the Shard itself is energetically damaged.

ME: It's not just the physical vehicle that is damaged then?

A: No. Just as we have talked about the energies associated with drugs used in palliative care causing a problem with the "body of energies" used by the sentience that is the essence of the Aspect (and TES), so do those energies of the Shard become affected. In effect the frequencies of the energies of the Shard are contaminated by drug or alcohol abuse. The frequencies of the energies become disharmonious and cannot be accepted back by the Aspect, they cannot be reintegrated, until they are back in harmony with those of the Aspect.

ME: So how are they brought back into harmony?

A: It's a simple process of extraction. The disharmony is caused by the energies and their frequencies being "attracted" to the energies of the Shard through "intentional association." This intentional association allows low-frequency energy to "stick" to the higher frequency energies of the Shard creating the overall disharmony. Once the Shard has been quarantined the low-frequency energies associated with the intentional association, the drugs or alcohol, are extracted by a "protected" Shard of the Aspect, one created specifically to work with the extraction process. It literally picks out and recycles, within the greater energies of The Source Entity, those low-frequency energies that are not inherently part of the body of energies the Aspect used to create the Shard in the first place.

Once the Shard's energies and the associated frequencies are harmonious again the Shard is taken out of quarantine and reintegrated with the Aspect. Only when all Shards have gone through such a process, and have been reintegrated with the Aspect, can the Aspect itself go through its own review and cleansing process, which I will now describe.

So secondly, the Aspect also has to be cleansed before it can be accepted back for reintegration into the TES. This process of cleaning is the same whether the Aspect has projected Shards, and needed them cleansing before reintegration, or not.

ME: You are saying that some Aspects don't project Shards then.

A: Correct. Not all Aspects project Shards into the low frequencies associated with the physical universe. Just to answer your question before you ask it, this is because Shards are only projected by an Aspect when the Aspect considers that the use of them would be of benefit while it itself is destined to be incarnate—that being, there is a significant opportunity for evolutionary growth that would not be available as a singular Aspect.

ME: Wouldn't that always be the case, though?

A: No, not in the slightest. Many Aspects choose very complicated incarnations and these provide the evolutionary growth, the evolutionary content, desired and or expected from a particular incarnation. Others feel that they can benefit more by sharing the load, so to speak, by dividing up the level of complication by the number of Shards required, and because the level of incarnate complication is divided up, each Shard can experience a deeper level of incarnate experience, augmenting the overall evolutionary growth, the evolutionary content accrued.

ME: So using Shards acts as a method of simplifying the incarnation of both the Aspect and the Shard.

A: Yes, but the Aspect is the primary beneficiary because it is the creating entity and the Shards work for the Aspect. So, in this instance, the Aspect, through the use of Shards, is allowed to have a less complicated incarnation while accruing a potentially higher level of evolutionary content.

ME: Well, I still feel that it would be of benefit to all Aspects to project Shards, especially if it means we get an easier incarnation.

A: It does from the perspective of the incarnation but it creates downstream complications due to the karmic affects, the addictions to that which is only available at the lowest frequencies of the multiverse. It is these downstream complications, such as the need to cleanse and reintegrate all Shards before it itself can reintegrate with the TES, and then having to go through the whole process of the life review from the perspective of all the Shards projected, together with the potential need to cleanse the Aspect itself and then go through a life review before reintegration with the TES that makes a lot of Aspects remain singular. In essence, the evolutionary benefits are great but the workload to support it is significant and that is why many Aspects don't use the opportunity of projecting Shards. Also note this: Aspects that are highly evolved openly resist the use of Shards because of the potential "remote" karmic attractivity that it can be subjected to.

ME: I have heard that some incarnates are protected from karma, even when they are clearly acting in a way that attracts it.

A: Yes, they are. We will discuss the need for karmic protection later, in the next chapter if you like, as there is a reason for it.

ME: Yes, I would like that, and I very much feel that the readers would like it as well.

A: OK, we have digressed enough and need to explain the cleansing process that the Aspect goes through before it can reintegrate with the TES.

ME: I agree, please carry on.

A: The cleansing process addresses two main areas. The many things associated with the energies of the substances used by the Aspect while incarnate, and the karmic influences associated with being attracted to low-frequency behavior/ thought patterns and actions.

I will identify them individually for you.

Oh! By the way! If I haven't already mentioned it, the process being described first, the clearing of the energies associated with substance abuse, etc., is the same process used to remove the same addictive content from the Shard.

So with reference to attractions/addictions to substances only—we need to work on:

The connectivity of the energies associated with the substance. This is the first thing to be actioned. In the first instance the energies are attracted to the Aspect by the Aspect's intention to experience the effects of being incarnate and exposing the incarnate vehicle to the substance desired. This attractivity creates a level of energetic connectivity that is not normally possible due to the incompatibility, the lack of harmony with the frequencies associated with the energies and the Aspect's own body of energies. Think of it in this way: that the Aspect's energies are normally too fine to connect to, it's just like food being cooked cannot stick to the Teflon coating on the inside surface of a saucepan. The Aspect's desire to experience the sensations of the substance while incarnate also create a local level of harmony with them, allowing them to connect with the body of energies that the Aspect is using. In terms of the Teflon saucepan used in my illustration, this is akin to damaging the surface of the Teflon coating to the point where the base metal of the saucepan is exposed allowing the food that is being cooked to adhere to it. The food needs to be scrubbed or scraped off the area of damage within the saucepan as a result. It also needs to be scrubbed or scraped off so that the area can be cleaned and recoated with Teflon, ensuring that more food cannot stick to the area of damage. So back to the Aspect, the intention for experience of a substance needs to be removed from the area of the body of energies being used by the Aspect to experience it so that the energies cannot adhere to its energies. This means that the low-frequency energies that have attached themselves to the area of local and intentional attractivity associated with the substance addiction the Aspect has gained need to be removed, and then, the intention itself needs to be removed from the psycho-spiritual area of the Aspect's sentience. This is achieved by injecting higher frequencies that are energetically neutral into the adhering energies so that they are transposed to a level equal to that of the Aspect and safely integrated with the energies of the Aspect. The intention is removed by relocating the thought processes associated with the intention, and the intention itself, into an area outside of the Aspect where it can be dissipated by the TES. The TES can dissipate this intention and its associated thought processes because it is, in effect, above such addictions—even though its Aspects, and their Shards, are not.

The effect of the substance on the Aspect's ability to evolve—the anchor effect. The physical effect is not as marked as the energetic effect of the substance, even though the physical effect is more visible to the incarnate. As I have previously stated, the energies of the substance are not in harmony frequentially with the energies of the incarnate vehicle and so energies of the vehicle are at odds with the energies of the substance. As a result the Aspect also becomes out of harmony with the incarnate vehicle and the substance that it has taken. The response is that the Aspect has to temporarily depart the vehicle until the substance has been diluted by the metabolic functions of the gross physical part of the incarnate vehicle. One would think that once the frequencies of the incarnate vehicle were corrected as a result of metabolic dilution that the energies of the Aspect, which were forced to depart the vehicle, would be unaffected. This is not the case; the Aspect, the soul, experiences desire, the desire to experience the physical effects of the substance taken while in an incarnate vehicle. This desire stays with the Aspect both when it is incarnate and when it is disincarnate. When incarnate the desire becomes addiction, an addiction to the sensations resulting from the effects of the substance on the incarnate vehicle and therefore the Aspect itself. When disincarnate the Aspect retains this desire or addiction and either chooses to stay close to the frequencies associated with incarnate existence, or waits for an opportunity to share a similar experience with another addict by temporarily using their incarnate vehicle when the addict's Aspect leaves its own incarnate vehicle due to the energetic disharmony created by the substance being taken.

For the disincarnate Aspect this desire or addiction creates a more powerful condition, one of intention—the intention to stay in the lowest frequencies of the multiverse. This intention creates a sort of anchor effect when the Aspect cannot ascend the frequencies due to the intention to experience low-frequency sensations. As the Aspect is simply a projection from the TES this intention affects the

TES by default, ultimately holding the evolutionary ascension of the TES in a form of stasis, one that creates evolutionary tension. In this way the addicted Aspect becomes the anchor that holds the evolution of the TES back. Because addiction to low-frequency stimulus can affect the TES in a most profound way, the TES places the addicted Aspect in quarantine, an energetic quarantine so that the addiction, the intention to experience low-frequency stimulus, is not passed on.

Before the TES can allow the Aspect to reintegrate with it, it therefore needs to work with the Aspect to remove its addiction/s to low-frequency sensations/stimulus. This is because if the Aspect is reintegrated with the TES without being free of its addictions it will suffer a loss of evolutionary and frequential integrity equal to its total evolutionary and frequential level minus the difference in the level of integrity of the Aspect before and after the addictive state. It may appear to be a small reduction but when a TES is striving for an increase in its evolutionary level, any reduction, no matter how small, is not something that it will accept.

And this is where karma comes into it. Karma is attraction to low-frequency thoughts, behaviors, actions, and stimulus or sensations (the addictions to disharmonious substances), and any Aspect that has any level of karma is held in quarantine until it is worked out.

In order to remove this evolutionary anchor effect on the TES the Aspect is coached by those Aspects that have elected to be helpers or guides either by the TES itself or the projections from other TES over an undetermined number of incarnations to work out the intention, the desire, the addiction, until exposure to such substances no longer cause an addiction and therefore a desire to consume them.

Clearly, while this is happening, other levels of work are being done on the Aspect, like injecting higher frequency energies into the body of energy the sentience of the Aspect is assigned to and reassigning the low frequencies that the naturally higher frequencies of the Aspect are attracted to back to the environment they represent.

The overall qualitative effect of the energies of the substances with the energies the TES used to create the body of energies used by the Aspect. In some respects, this is dealt with within the last subject heading, but this is especially relative to the base frequency of the Aspect's body of energies. Essentially I just stated that the TES will not reintegrate an Aspect that has not been normalized to a condition that was at least equal in frequency to that which it was before it was used as a projection into the lower frequencies of the multiverse, those associated with the physical universe, and this is true. However, this piece of work is relative to the TES and its understanding of the quality of the Aspect's body of energy. It looks at not only the frequential losses and how the Aspect's body of energy is affected but also how the, shall I say, "Morphology," of those energies is affected. That being, have the energies of the Aspect been affected in a way that changes them into an energy that is no longer capable of supporting sentience? If you remember from your work with The Origin, in *The Origin Speaks*, an energy or energies must be of a certain quality before it can sustain or create a level of intelligence. As this level of quality increases so does the ability to support higher levels of intelligence which lead to creativity and sentience. So, in this instance, even though the energies of the Aspect may be of the correct frequential level, the quality of the energies may have been affected by the substances taken to the point where they cannot support "effectively" the sentience of the Aspect. In this instance, those energies are removed and replaced by energies that are capable of supporting its sentience at the same level as those energies that are unaffected.

The effect on the Aspect with reference to the desire to experience the physical sensations of the substance—addiction. Again, to some extent this has been dealt with in an earlier dialogue, but the thoughts, behaviors, and actions associated with low-frequency existence, an Aspect's karma, are cleansed by isolating them with the help of the guide and helpers.

Addictions are powerful and difficult to remove in any frequential condition and so the Aspect is coached and subjected to similar or same addictive conditions until it can experience them without creating the "desire function" of addiction. As I stated before, desire is a function of intention and energetic desire creates a natural and automatic attraction to the energies and their frequencies that create the addiction. As a result, the Aspect finds itself being energetically drawn, like iron filings to a magnet, to those energies and frequencies whose sensations and stimuli it desires. The Aspect is drawn in this way because of the sympathetic relationship created between parts of its energies and the energies of the substance, the sensory stimulus. This "automatic gravitational effect" on the energies of the Aspect add to the evolutionary anchor effect that creates evolutionary tension experienced by the TES. In extreme circumstances the sympathetic relationship can be negated by the TES removing the affected energies within the Aspect's body of energies in the same way as described for those energies that have a low quality and can no longer support sentience, replacing them with unaffected energies of the correct quality. This, however, is a last resort as the whole point of incarnation is to experience the physical but not be of the physical, and the Aspect, and therefore the TES, gains more evolutionary content if its addictions, its karma, is "worked" out by the Aspect rather than "saved" by the TES in this way.

ME: This is a lot of work for the Aspect to go through before it can be allowed to incarnate.

A: It is, but it is a necessary requirement for the Aspect to go through before it can be allowed to move on to its next task. The Aspect must be neutralized of its addictions and attractions, within certain parameters, before it can be allowed to incarnate again; otherwise, neither the Aspect nor

TES will gain from the opportunity to incarnate again. The TES's who used the incarnate human vehicle the first time learnt a lot from allowing contamination to continue, as was explained in the text within *The History of God*, and the current rehabilitation work required of the Aspect "post" incarnation is a direct result of their findings.

ME: It all seems very human to me, all of it. Is this information described in a way that the readers would understand for a reason?

A: Yes. Although the information is correct, it does have a human slant on it. It needs to because the information is at a greater depth than that previously exposed, and, more importantly, incarnation and the processes surrounding it is a VERY popular subject. As such this will be a bridging book crossing many levels of reader understanding and expansiveness.

7.2

Suicide

Although it was part of the overall plan I hadn't expected to tackle the rather thorny subject of suicide in this book quite yet. I have personally known three people who committed suicide and knew of two others who had one of their children depart in the same fashion. However, because recently an increasing number of my readers were asking the question, I decided to wait no longer and ask Anne about the processes that surrounded the Aspect who had returned to the energetic via this route.

A: This is going to be a big subject to discuss.

ME: In what way, dialogue or impact?

A: Impact. This is going to be relevant to areas that are not considered suicide, and as a result it will open a few people's eyes. Basically put, suicide is a huge spiritual crime. The use of the human vehicle must be maintained as long as possible. This is why you all have a strong instinct for survival, for self-preservation. You all buy into this upon being given the opportunity to incarnate.

ME: Why is it a crime?

A: Because it is terminating the use of the human vehicle and the possibility for evolutionary growth too early. Suicide is NEVER an acceptable way of returning to the energetic. In real terms, the number of human vehicles is minute in comparison to the number of Aspects/Shards that line up to become incarnate. To defile one in this way is to break a sacred contract, one that states that each and every Aspect or Shard will do their very best when granted the honor to evolve in this rare and accelerated way.

ME: Why is it never accepted? *[I knew of one possible exception and my publisher, Dolores Cannon, had also discovered one during one of her regressions. —GSN].*

A: There are not normally any exemptions from this. The examples you are thinking of were extremely special cases, and required a lot of planning to make it work, not to mention permission from the Aspect's guide and helper and the TES of the Aspect. We will discuss the detail behind gaining permission later but suffice to say the planning behind such an agreement is massive and horrendous.

ME: OK, can you list those areas and we can use them as a point of discussion as we proceed.

A: I would be delighted to. OK, here we go. These also include the areas that are considered the same as suicide from the energetic side of things.

- Personal suicide—self-termination of the human vehicle. Used in cases of depression.

- Assisted suicide—asking another to terminate your human vehicle when able bodied. Also used in cases of depression.

- Euthanasia—asking another to help you terminate your human vehicle. Used in cases of terminal illness or disability.

- Killing another—resulting from war, argument, crime, mental disorder, or judicially administered death sentence.

- Euthanasia of an animal—resulting from terminal illness, bodily damage, or aggressive action to a human.

ME: Hold on. You're saying that killing another, whether it is an animal or human, is also considered in the same light as suicide.

A: Yes. And what's more the killer has to answer for the crime of terminating the human or animal vehicle in the same way as if it were committing personal suicide.

ME: Why is this?

A: Because of the downstream activities. I wasn't going to go into this yet, but I think it is important to state the problems associated with the early demise of the human vehicle through any of the routes just stated.

As you are aware, there is a team of helpers managed by a main guide assigned to each incarnate. This team ensures that we are in the right place at the right time, experiencing the things that we identified in our life plan, and that these things include the right people. All of these things help us experience, learn, and evolve in as efficient a way as possible. The downstream function of this is that all of those people we interface with also experience, learn, and evolve as a result of working with us. This is a huge logistical effort, and as such it requires constant attention with all of the guides and helpers of all of the incarnates on this planet, including other locations within the physical universe who interact with each other, planning when and where we should meet, and what we will experience together. Our whole incarnate life is mapped out, and the effect we have on others, and those effecting us from the interface with others, is largely known and in place to a certain extent. This certain extent, of course, is governed by how well we are in tune with our guide and helpers and therefore make the right decisions when prompted. If one of us causes the demise of the human vehicle by personally terminating it early, then all of the downstream functions resulting from us being incarnate are lost, causing a massive logistical issue for those who are still incarnate.

ME: Based upon this then, the so-called crime committed by those who commit suicide is not just against defiling the honor we have in being allowed to incarnate, but is also against the commitments we have made to work with other incarnates and the downstream effects it has on the incarnates that interface with the ones we interface with.

A: Correct. It is a real problem.

ME: So what happens when we do commit suicide? What happens to the work all the downstream incarnates have committed to?

A: Simply put, it has to be replanned. What happens is this. Firstly, the Aspect that committed suicide is quarantined. That being, it is not allowed to go through the process associated with the life review.

ME: Why is this?

A: The guide, helpers, and TES of the Aspect need to understand the circumstances surrounding the suicide and establish what went wrong. Secondly, the guides and helpers of all those affected make an emergency meeting to ascertain the changes necessary to reduce the downstream impact of the experiential, learning, and evolutionary content that was lost as a result of the suicide.

ME:This sounds like a mammoth task!

A: It is, and there are Aspects whose service to others is based upon their ability to work with the "what if" scenario functionality of the Akashic records. They are specialized in understanding the important junctures that were lost and how to resolve the opportunities they created.

ME:How do they do that? It almost feels like they would create an Akashic overlay, one with suicide and one without, and compare and contrast them, overlaying with a third that shows the corrections made to resolve the issues created.

A: Very good. It sounds simple but it is a very large and complicated task to undertake. Not only that, it is a dynamic and constantly changing piece of work. Consider this: the Aspects who are specialized in working with the Akashic in this way are constantly employed.

ME:Of course they are. Thinking about it, there must be hundreds of suicides a year to cope with!

A: You had better believe it. The Aspects that specialize in working with "what if" scenario functionality of the Akashic are constantly reviewing, organizing, and manipulating the various scenarios that present themselves as incarnates succeed or fail in their actions. The guide and helpers of each incarnate constantly work with the Aspects who work with the Akashic to introduce or reintroduce experiential opportunities and the environments and incarnates that support it. This is normality; it's just that the odd suicide puts a spanner in the works, so to speak.

ME:But if suicides are happening all the time, the guide and helpers of an Aspect that returns to the energetic via suicide must be able to see the signs, act, and guide their incarnate accordingly.

A: You would think so, but this is not always the case. This is why the Aspect is quarantined. The guide, helpers, and TES of the Aspect that commits suicide need to work out what went wrong, how they missed the possibility of suicide.

ME:OK, if the guide and helpers are constantly using the Akashic to review the progress of their incarnate, how could they miss the possibility of suicide?

A: That is the whole point of the review, because experienced guides and helpers can see these things ahead of time by the use of Event Space within the use of the Akashic, so if they miss it it's a big deal. I told you a moment ago that the work behind the analysis is difficult, but the work behind the guidance of the incarnate is just as difficult. Let me give you an image of what the Akashic feels like when performing this analysis.

I then gained an image; call it a holographic image if you like, one where I was part of the image. I was surrounded by a whole universe of events, bubbles of activities that were relative to individual Aspects that were incarnate. This, I knew, was just the part of The Source Entity's energetic memory that was assigned to the incarnate vehicles we call the Human Body. No other incarnate vehicle was taken into account here. That part of The Source Entity's energetic memory that was assigned to other incarnate vehicle form factors that were available in the physical universe was something else, something different, something separate. Of course, I felt, they could all be overlaid together, and The Source Entity sees all of these as one energetic memory set ultimately; it's just that it would not be relevant or useful for me to experience this level of functionality. I don't doubt that it would be too much for me to cope with. This felt like it was stretching me, and it was. Anne of course had no problem in her energetic state, and I heard her chuckle as I tried to focus on what was being presented to me.

A: It's nice to see you struggle, Guy! I never saw that side of you too much while incarnate. I can see how it humbles you from here.

ME: Thank you for those words of concern. Actually I struggle a lot without you being incarnate, but that's a conversation we can have privately.

A: We can. Please continue with your narration.

The bubbles of activity, the events, duplicated and disseminated as the various possibilities of duality, triality, and quadruality became apparent, creating links with the bubbles of activity relative to the incarnates that they affected or were affected by. As I witnessed the dances of all these bubbles, some converged again and moved to another location. This, I thought, was when an Event Space became no longer relevant and therefore re-converged with the "main" Event Space of the incarnate and the activities that supported it. I was then exposed to additional imagery; I could see lines between the bubbles of activity. These lines showed where the bubbles were going and which other bubbles they were to interface with, that being, where incarnates work together for some common evolutionary cause, disseminate or reintegrate. They disappeared within and without each other, and reappeared within and without each other. It appeared as a huge living and undulating multispatial, multifrequential network of interactivity. It was alive and alight. Suddenly I saw a huge sector of the connectivity between the bubbles disappear. It was like someone had turned the lights out on the lines of connectivity that were between the bubbles. No, the lines had gone and the bubbles that were previously connected now hung unconnected, drifting free in whatever space they were in. Then I saw new lines being created and the whole dynamic of the network changed. Bubbles of activity changed direction, converged, or disseminated. The change in the "pattern" created by the network was either dramatic or unaffected with varying degrees in between.

A: I see that you have already guessed what was happening, but what you have just witnessed is the effect on the interconnectivity of the bubbles of activity and the various

Event Spaces relative to those Aspects who are incarnate when an Aspect terminates the existence of the incarnate vehicle early. Whole sectors of downstream activity are lost as a result. The new lines and the changes in the way the bubbles of activity interface with each other or disseminate/re-converge are a result of the corrective work of the Aspects specialized in working with the Akashic and the guides and helpers of the incarnate Aspects affected.

ME: It looked like everything was rerouted.

A: That is in essence what happened.

ME: It's quick!

A: It appeared to be quick, but there was a significant amount of work done to achieve this level of change—specifically if it was going to be a robust change, and one that would operate within the tolerances, the certain levels of uncertainty expected when one is working "incarnate." In essence, there was a long period of Event Space used to formulate a plan, test it, modify it, test it again, and then administer it. Everything was achieved "outside of time," so to speak. Realizing of course that time doesn't exist, I would like to rephrase it as being "outside of Event Space," that being the main volume of Event Space used by incarnate mankind.

ME: How often does this happen?

A: It is constantly happening. Remember, there are hundreds of people who commit suicide every year. In fact, it may well be a figure that is in its thousands.

ME: I guess this keeps you all very busy then?

A: VERY BUSY! As you can imagine, the work we are doing to put things on track as a result of one incarnate person committing suicide is immense, even with all of our enhanced functionality while in the energetic. So, when we have a number of multiple suicides either as a number of unrelated suicides or, in rare cases, a cult mass suicide and even suicide bombers, we have a lot of downstream work to do.

It's at this point that we need to add some additional categories because we are about to embark upon the details surrounding the quarantining of those who commit suicide.

The additional categories would be:

Participation in a mass suicide is where the incarnate entity has, through the requirements of the life plan, allowed themselves to be coerced to the point where they are convinced that the early demise of the incarnate vehicle is desirable. The life plan, in these instances, though, is not designed to allow the incarnate entity to create an early demise of the incarnate vehicle, more to allow the entity to experience extreme coercion and steer themselves away from it. This is extreme work, as it involves a high level of synergy resulting from group coercion, and removing oneself from the synergetic effects of group coercion is difficult at best. Final participation in such an act requires the entity to be quarantined to remove the association with the group members and more importantly with the instigator, as this can accentuate karmic links and subsequent participation in future incarnations that end in the same way. Individual coercion that results in the demise of the incarnate vehicle at the orchestration of the instigator that is not part of the life plan needs to be analyzed for errors in the work of the guide, helpers, and incarnate entity. The incarnate entity therefore needs to be quarantined to allow the underlying reasons for the entity's decision process to be understood in isolation from the directional work guide and helpers. For example, what made the entity ignore the directions of the guide and helpers, and what made the directions of the instigator overrule the directions of the guide and helpers— why were they so compelling?

The instigator/s of a mass or small group suicide need/s to be quarantined because of a complex energetic condition that makes the ego of the incarnate fully believe that they are bringing all of the members of the group that it is responsible for back to The Source, on behalf of The Source. Clearly, they are being brought back to the energetic, which is ultimately The Source, but the reasons surrounding the desire to bring them back to The Source are not pure. Firstly, because many instigators do not commit suicide themselves, this is therefore called mass murder and is classified differently, and those that do, have a strong coercive link with the group members that can affect them even in the energetic. Secondly, those that are coerced are naturally attracted to the instigator, even in the energetic, and so will be drawn toward them during the life-planning phase of the next incarnation, which could result in the incarnate being easily coerced again. The instigator is also analyzed for misdirected leadership skills or deviation from a life plan where they are to be of significant spiritual influence.

Suicide for the use of terrorism and the death of others is when the incarnate entity is again coerced by an instigator to allow it to be used for the early demise of the incarnate vehicle and, more critically, the demise of those who have been targeted for politico-religious means. In this instance, the incarnate entity causes both the early demise of their incarnate vehicle and the early demise (murder) of other incarnate vehicles. Although this is very similar to the two categories just discussed, this has the added complication that the incarnate entity itself is actually responsible for the early demise of the incarnate vehicle of others through allowing itself to be coerced.

ME: And this would be the same for those who commit suicide for martyrdom?

A: Yes, it's exactly the same.

7.2.1

The Function of Quarantining the
Aspect Who Commits Suicide

I could see that this was going to get complicated. Not only that, it was a very sensitive subject both personally and religiously. I am lucky that I gain spiritual information without any religious contexts, at least none that I could allude to, which makes it universally acceptable. Note the fact that the dialogue above related to the individuals and instigators and not the underlying motives of a particular religion. An incarnate entity can be fanatical about anything, and as such it can be seen in all walks of life, so attributing the energies associated with fanaticism to a particular product would not be useful to the reader. Based upon this, it seems that the ability of the entity to coerce and/or be coerced to operate in this way is more important as a function of analysis than to focus on religion as a motivator.

A: I am glad you said that.

ME:Why?

A: Because it's true. Religion has no bearing on the analysis of an entity who commits suicide in any of the contexts discussed. It may add to the confusion, but it has no influence in how the entity is helped to recover from involvement in suicide, either as instigator, coerced participant, or individual.

ME:We have talked about quarantining an entity who has committed suicide for some time now. We have even discussed some of the methods of normal post-incarnation rehabilitation, so how is this different from the normal post-incarnation analysis/rehabilitation?

A: The energies surrounding an incarnate that has returned to the energetic or caused the return of other incarnates in this way are intoxicating.

ME: Why are they intoxicating?

A: Because of the intention surrounding the need to depart the incarnation. They are not intoxicating in the way you are thinking of, such as they are addictive, although they can be. They are low frequency, they are heavy, so to speak, and as such they pull everything and everyone (entity/Aspect) down around them through triangulation.

ME: So what you are saying is that these "intoxicating" energies need to be removed before any other work with the Aspect can be initiated?

A: Yes. The Aspect has to be put in a bubble of energy that is neutral to all effects of the energies associated with the suicide. The biggest intoxicating energy is the acceptability of returning to the energetic in this way. As we have discussed before, ending the life plan through the self-inflicted early demise of the human/incarnate vehicle before it is finalized, or at least is as close to being finalized as the Aspect can get to in the current incarnation, is not acceptable. If it were acceptable, every Aspect that experiences difficulty in their incarnation would be tempted to remove themselves from incarnation through it being "too hard." If this were allowed to happen the whole point of using incarnation as an evolutionary accelerator would be negated because Aspects would "bail out" at the earliest opportunity. Incarnation is hard, and we all signed up in full knowledge, with our spiritual eyes wide open, so to speak, of its difficulty, and as such we need to fulfill our commitment. This energy is the sort of energy that makes the early demise of the incarnate vehicle acceptable, in the mind of the Aspect that is, and it is the energy surrounding the acceptability that needs to be placed into quarantine as it can act like a virus, spreading throughout the energies of the TES and the area of The Source Entity we know as the multiverse.

ME: So you are suggesting that the energies surrounding an Aspect that committed suicide are contagious?

A: In essence, yes. Do you remember the chapter in *The History of God* where incarnate mankind had its links removed between every incarnate Aspect so that they could only incarnate in a linear fashion and not in a multiple fashion? That they could not jump from one incarnate vehicle to another due to the ability to pass on disharmonious conditions from one vehicle to another, and by the newly incumbent Aspect picking up this disharmony and taking it with them to the next incarnate vehicle they inhabit?

ME: Yes, I do.

A: Well, this is the same thing, albeit from a different angle. Let me show you.

At this point I saw an image of a group of energies. They were all in order, interfacing with one another in a logical and repeatable way.

A: This is a representation of energies that are in harmony with each other because they are working in the way they are supposed to work while under the direction of the sentience of an Aspect that is using them in the way they should be used as well. Look again.

I did, and saw something rather insidious. The energies that were used correctly, that being, correctly in terms of their frequency, function, and interconnectivity, were being changed. Rather than being organized in a logical and regular interconnecting pattern, there were energies that were connecting with energies that they were not supposed to connect with. As a collection of energies they appeared to work correctly, but when asked to perform a specific task they never finished it, even though through interrogation, they gave all the messages to the interrogator to suggest that they had in fact completed their task, and within the expected level of functionality.

100

ME: This is like a cancer. It fools the rest of the body (energies) into thinking that it is a fully functioning organ (group of energies), when in fact it isn't, causing the rest of the body (group of energies) to fail without warning that it is going to fail.

A: Yes. The simple process of going against our programming, our commitment to undertake a full and fruitful incarnation, irrespective of how long the planned existence is, creates a fundamentally critical disharmonious condition that rewires the connectivity of the energies that are used to create the Aspect. As this is essentially the same energies that are used to house the sentience of the True Energetic Self, the chances of this disharmony spreading to the TES are 100 percent. This would be catastrophic to the TES as it would have to essentially evacuate its sentience from the "body of energies" it is using, and these energies in totality would then need to be quarantined. Ultimately speaking, if this disharmony was allowed to spread from the Aspect to the TES and then from the TES to The Source, The Source could then also, in time, become contaminated in this way.

Now that we have the background information on why this is necessary, I will give you a high-level description of the quarantine process.

The energy of the Aspect is, as previously described, placed in a bubble of energy that neutralizes the effects of the disharmony. The energies are then disentangled and the new connections removed. They are then separated out into their singular formats and again quarantined. Once in their own isolated environment they cannot affect those other energies around them, because the energies that make up the quarantine are modified so that no other energies can connect to them. They are independent of any other energy. Once isolated in this way, any residual sentience is removed from them, specifically the sentience behind the intention to go against the commitment, which in this instance is to terminate the incarnation before the agreed end date. Additionally, the sentience itself is cleansed by eradicating the processes behind the intention that created the thought processes. In essence, this is "resetting" the sentience that is assigned to the energies that became dysfunctional through incorrectly applied intention. The effect of resetting the sentience is created by deleting any "personality" that the sentience has accrued, leaving it as pure, unapplied sentience. This process resets the functionality of the energies as well, leaving them and the sentience in a new and "unused" state. Once this level of, shall I say, "sentient reprograming" is achieved, the energies are reabsorbed back into the TES as part of its bulk energetic and sentient condition. They are not used with the intention to create an Aspect again, though, as those energies that are to be used to create Aspects will have already been assigned to an Aspect. The personality of the sentience needs to be deleted because it is this "personality" that created the desire to go against the commitment in the first place.

ME: So the Aspect loses some of its energies, its sentience, and its personality.

A: Yes.

ME: That's a bit like a sentient lobotomy.

A: You could think of it in that way, but it is a necessary procedure to administer, to ensure the overall function of the Aspect and TES are unaffected by this level of disharmony.

There is a down side of this, though, and that is that the Aspect has a reduced level of ability to experience, learn, and evolve.

ME: How does the Aspect get over this?

A: It doesn't. The TES accepts that this particular Aspect is reduced energetically and sentiently. As I just stated, the overall energies and sentience are not lost to the TES, who projects the energies and sentience that is the Aspect, it's just that they are no longer associated with the Aspect of the TES that committed suicide.

ME: And I would guess that the reduction in the Aspect's energy and sentience is one of the major reasons why committing suicide is a problem?

A: Yes. But it is not the only problem an Aspect faces.

7.2.2

The Price We Pay for Committing Suicide

ME: You mean that there are more things to consider. I mean, we have gone over quite a lot of reasons why suicide is a problem in the identification of the need to quarantine the Aspect—the removal of the energies and the sentience associated with the thought process, and intention, to end the incarnation early, being one of them. Not to mention gaining a glimpse of the necessary downstream work that the guide and helpers need to perform to ensure that the experiential and evolutionary paths of those other Aspects the Aspect was destined (planned) to affect directly and indirectly are maintained in some way that is consistent with The Original plan. Oh, and I almost forgot the work the guide and helpers have to perform. They need to understand how and why they either missed the signs of an impending suicide, or if they were aware, why the work they did to stop the Aspect from going down the route of suicide failed. All of this being additional to the normal, shall I say, debriefing that an Aspect and its guide and helpers attend after incarnate existence.

A: Correct. You see, contrary to popular belief, an Aspect that commits suicide does not return into incarnation immediately after it has terminated the incarnation so that it can finish off what it had in the previous life plan. Once the Aspect and the guide and helpers have finished all of the quarantine-based analysis, cleansing, and corrective downstream interactions, the Aspect needs to be educated and the opportunities for future incarnations renegotiated.

ME: Educated? Renegotiated? In what way?

A: The Aspect needs to experience the whole incarnate existence that led up to the point of the suicide from the perspective of the passive observer. This is achieved "real time," so to speak, so that the Aspect can be truly absorbed in the incarnation it terminated, but, without experiencing the emotions and other incarnate sensory experiences that created the desire and intention to go down the road of an incarnation that leads to suicide in this instance. It also needs to see, in full experience, how the termination of the incarnation affected those Aspects downstream of its own incarnation from both the direct and indirect interactive functions.

ME: This sounds like a lot of work, especially as it is on top of the existing work.

A: It is, and it is very painful for the Aspect. Not emotionally painful as you would expect from a human perspective, but from the fact that the Aspect, in its desire to relinquish its evolutionary responsibilities through "evasion," created by the suicide, causes so much downstream chaos that it requires the help of thousands of Aspects, guides, and helpers to put right. The Aspect has not only let itself down but it has let down those other Aspects that it agreed to work with when planning its incarnate existence and when using the Akashic simulations ("what if" scenarios), to help them experience, learn, and evolve.

Being allowed to incarnate is a rare honor, by the way, and maintaining the incarnate vehicle to the best of its abilities while incarnate is a sacred commitment. Additionally, when an Aspect is allowed to, or chosen to, use a certain incarnate vehicle (human body) many others are denied the use in preference to the successful Aspect.

Demising it early is therefore a serious break of this commitment because when an Aspect subsequently decides to finish the incarnation through the use of suicide, the Aspect has denied those other Aspects who failed to justify their use of the human body concerned the opportunity to have a whole and complete incarnation, and therefore maximize the human body's existence. So, the Aspect who commits suicide has also created a sin. A sin is described as the following: it is when an Aspect has denied the evolution of another's in preference of itself when in fact they have not met or completed their own agreed commitments.

ME: So the Aspect who commits suicide also commits a sin in relation to those other Aspects, who were, in essence, in negotiation for the use of the human body, as an incarnate evolutionary vehicle.

A: You've got it.

ME: They must feel terrible then when they return and remember enough to see the results of their actions while incarnate.

A: Correct. And this is a huge weight for an Aspect to bear. In actuality it is almost too big a weight to bear.

ME: And realization of how we have affected the evolutionary progression of other Aspects is the price we have to pay for committing suicide?

A: It is, and it is a very heavy weight to bear.

ME: So what can an Aspect do to alleviate this weight, this, what I will call "evolutionary debt," a debt to all those Aspects affected by its decision to terminate its incarnation early?

A: Firstly, and bearing in mind that the Aspect has had many desires that could create the intention to commit suicide in future incarnations removed, it has to commit to helping those that its suicide affected in a direct and indirect downstream interactive way to recover their missing evolutionary content. Secondly, it has to agree to undertake significant levels of energetic interrogation, so to speak, to ensure that it is capable of being able to complete the level of commitment required to enter into the incarnation process—again.

ME: Because?

A: Because it has broken the confidence bestowed upon it. As I loosely stated a moment ago, there are a limited, a finite number of, incarnate vehicles available to allow the accelerated evolutionary conditions that are available "only" in the physical universe to be taken advantage of. And those that are assigned to the Earth are even more finite (rare). So, being allowed to incarnate into the Earth environment, a unique environment that supports fully individualized free will, instead of individualized but collective free will, is a rare opportunity. Because they, the incarnate vehicle, are only generally made available to those who can illustrate a life plan that shows significant evolutionary progression, progression which maximizes the use of the incarnate vehicle, the human form or body, for its maximum operational period, an Aspect must be fully capable of not only committing to agree to the tasks it set itself as part of its life plan, but to the downstream function of its incarnate existence as well. These commitments are expected to last the agreed duration of the incarnate vehicle as well. As a result, any Aspect that illustrates the potential to deviate from this plan is placed back in quarantine and worked on again. Any signs of deviation therefore result in the Aspect needing to undertake the whole post-incarnate process again and again until the correct response is noted.

ME: So they have to prove that they have the ability to incarnate all over again then?

A: Yes.

ME: So, based upon this, stories of Aspects that commit suicide coming back to Earth almost immediately after the forced demise of the human form are not true then?

A: Not in the sense of a "back-to-back" incarnation where the Aspect can jump straight into another incarnate vehicle either as a newborn or a Walk-In, no.

ME: Why would we have these stories then if they are not true?

A: Because from the limited perception of the Aspect while being incarnate it can seem to be this way.

ME: Oh, I get it, it is a function of Event Space. The incarnation has the appearance of incarnating straight away but in actual fact a lot of work has been done over a long period of time, so to speak, and the Aspect is "cleared" for incarnate existence again.

A: Correct. The Aspect who commits suicide needs to go back into a similar or same environment, an Event Space, which created the initial desire to end the incarnation early and continue with the life plan that was in place at that time rather than demise it.

ME: And does this help with the downstream interactions and evolutionary content that was lost?

A: It helps but it does not solve the problem in totality.

ME: Why?

A: Because any evolutionary opportunity that is lost, especially one that was planned for and agreed to be worked on by the TES, Aspect, or Shard, needs to be recovered. This includes all of the downstream evolutionary content that was lost or that did not meet the expected level of evolution due to the sudden loss of the initiating Aspect at a specific evolutionary juncture and the attempts to recover it by rerouting the downstream interactions through the use of other incarnate Aspects.

7.2.3

The Multiversal Law of Evolutionary Recovery

ME: So evolution, or should I say, certain levels of evolutionary progression, is planned for, is expected, so to speak.

A: Yes. This is the whole point of our existence—to accrue evolutionary content, so what is lost MUST be recovered.

ME: Hold on, you said "MUST" be recovered, with an emphasis on the "MUST." Does that mean the Aspect has to recover what is lost and continue to evolve in the normal way?

A: If you mean, is this a sort of "evolutionary overtime" the Aspect has to put in, the answer is yes. This is another of the prices that an Aspect that commits suicide has to pay. It's called being responsible for the results of your actions and repaying the evolutionary debt created. This is a multiversal law and one that cannot be circumnavigated.

Every Aspect that incurs evolutionary debt through unplanned and self-imposed demise, of any classification, has a care of duty to recover the evolutionary potential it announced as part of its justification for being allowed to incarnate, which includes that which was lost by other incarnates in the subsequent lack of downstream interaction.

The multiversal law of evolutionary recovery is one that is taken most seriously because neither an Aspect, nor its TES, can move forward until that debt is repaid. This incentive, major as it is, is the only incentive an Aspect has to repay the debt. But it is significant because if it is not repaid then the whole point of the Aspect (that part of the TES that owes the debt) being in existence is negated. In some instances, an Aspect that has found itself in significant debt, and unable to recover that debt, has been reintegrated to the TES early and a more capable, and sometimes hybrid, Aspect is projected in its stead. That being, to work with the incarnations, experiences, lessons, direct interactions and downstream interactions, and evolutionary opportunities required to clear the debt by the TES whose Aspect accrued it.

ME: So what you are ultimately saying is that it is the responsibility of the TES who projected the Aspect in the first instance to clear the evolutionary debt of its Aspect?

A: Yes, but in all cases the default is to allow the Aspect the opportunity to clear it itself, because in this way it also accrues evolutionary content by going through this process.

ME: An Aspect can actually create evolutionary content by going through this process? I find that quite a bizarre twist!

A: Ah, it gets more interesting as well.

ME: Tell me why.

7.2.4

The Only Exception/s to the Rule

A: So yes, there is a slight twist to this requirement because the very experience of being in this position creates evolutionary content in its own right, and so an Aspect, if it is experienced, can recover the lost evolution while surpassing the expectations of the evolutionary debt within a minimum number of incarnations.

ME: I have just had a rather interesting thought come into my head, one that is rather radical.

A: And that is that some advanced Aspects would enter into evolutionary debt via the suicide route merely as a way of accruing more evolution than would be normally accrued via incarnation, accelerated though it is.

ME: You took the words right out of my brain.

A: Of course, dear one. Who do you think put them there in the first place?

109

I then saw an image of Anne smiling. She was enjoying this dialogue and was clearly having some fun with me at the same time.

ME: So they actually do this; some Aspects actually commit suicide while incarnate to experience all of the cleansing processes and pressures of evolutionary debt as a method of accelerating their evolutionary level.

A: And the evolutionary level of those involved in the downstream functions, yes.

ME: But what you are saying here is that suicide is acceptable.

A: No, I am not saying that. What I am saying is that some advanced Aspects are allowed to go down this route. In this instance, the suicide is agreed up front and in an understood method. Its effect is calculated, and the work involved by the Aspects, guide, and helpers affected in the downstream function of its suicide are agreeable to the subsequent dilemma. This of course also involves the resulting evolutionary effects when the Aspect who committed suicide is allowed to incarnate again and recovers the lost evolutionary content, and in the process succeeds, creating the additional evolutionary content accrued as a result of using this method.

ME: This seems very dangerous to me. I mean, the Aspect could fail again and again, resulting in serious evolutionary debt.

A: Correct. That is why it is only the VERY advanced Aspects that are allowed to use this method, and even then it has to be justified and authorized at TES level first.

Let me tell you this. Ever since the work that the Aspect you call Lucifer resulted in the drop in frequencies of the Earth and its incarnate vehicles, this extreme route to evolutionary acceleration is tested in the Akashic in all possible angles in all possible Event Spaces, with all TES and Aspects involved in the analysis. As a result, its acceptance is a rare occurrence indeed. Indeed, if I had a hand I could count the number of times it has been authorized on two fingers.

ME: Only twice?

A: Yes, only twice before. So difficult is such an undertaking that it is generally refused.

ME: And I would guess the risk is far too high as well.

A: The risk being the level of evolutionary debt that an Aspect can find itself in as well. Not to mention the level of downstream work that the guides and helpers have to commit to in order to correct the situation. Note this. Not even Aspects that you could classify as ascended masters have seriously contemplated such action other than in joke, so to speak, for they fully recognize the level of work required and the Event Space it would take to complete.

ME: OK, just how long would it take to complete such an undertaking?

A: Hold on, I will need to ask our TES how best to answer this question. Mmmm, let's just say that those two Aspects that entered into this type of commitment are still working on recovering the lost evolutionary content.

ME: And how long have they been working on recovering it?

A: Relatively speaking they have only just started.

ME: Only just started? What does that mean?

A: Well, to put it into your human terms, over three hundred thousand million years.

ME: WHAT! But, from my limited knowledge the human form has not been in existence that long!

A: Who said the human form was the only incarnate form where an Aspect could end the incarnation via suicide?

ME: Oh! Of course! But, that means that other Aspects that incarnate in other incarnate vehicles in the physical universe choose to end their incarnation via suicide as well?

A: Yes, they do. Note, though, that they usually existed in the same or similar frequential space/s within the physical universe—that being the third and fourth frequency levels.

ME: Hold on again. You just said, usually existed!

A: Yes, I did.

ME: That means that the incarnate vehicle they were using no longer exists in the physical universe.

A: Correct.

ME: And, I also have a bit of a problem here, because if human kind is the only one where incarnate Aspects have individualized free will, how could another form allow individualized suicide?

A: Because the level of collective authority assigned to the forms that were allowed to work in this way are also working on recovering the lost evolutionary content.

ME: So it wasn't one individual incarnate Aspect that was allowed to work in this rare and difficult way prior to incarnation, it was a whole group?

A: No, it was the singular Aspect/s that were allowed to work in this way. It's just that the responsibility for the recovery of the evolutionary content was shared between component Aspects of the collective. Let me explain. The groups concerned are contained within a single TES, actually two TES's.

ME: Now you are confusing me.

A: OK, in order for the individualization to work within a collective condition the collective needs to be under the creative authority of a single TES. This means that a single Aspect can work in an individualized way while still working within the functionality of a collective. This can only work when the TES is in full projection of its primary Aspects, all twelve and without Shards, and they are in the same frequencies in the same Event Space in the same

112

incarnate vehicles concurrently when the act of the pre-agreed suicide is actioned.

ME:And this is how the two Aspects were allowed to work in this way?

A: Yes, because at the time of suicide the use of individualized free will was not being used. It was still being investigated.

ME:I have another question. I sort of know in human terms how long ago the suicides started, but I get the impression that they were actually close to each other temporally.

A: Relatively speaking they were because the same incarnate form was used.

ME:The same one? Why was it the same one?

A: Because at the time of agreement this form was the only one that could achieve the desired outcome without being capable of fully individualized free will.

Just as the human form is an experiment in individualized free will, and as such is in a quarantined section of the physical universe, frequentially and event spatially, so was the environment that these two Aspects were allowed to work in a temporary condition.

ME:They are in quarantine?

A: No, it was an experiment.

ME:Oh, OK.

A: And it was one that took a lot of negotiation between those Aspects that suggested it and their TES's, together with the agreement of all eleven remaining Aspects of their TES's to work out the evolutionary debt. By the way, temporally, the Aspects were within a couple of thousand years of each other in their acts of suicide.

ME:I can feel the complication behind this specific direction. It makes me shudder. I am glad I/we didn't choose this route for evolutionary progression.

A: You/I have other things to do that are not associated with this Source Entity's multiversal environment, and so could not contemplate such a limited set of actions resulting from such a narrow band decision. You can see, though, why only two Aspects have been allowed to actively demise their incarnate vehicles in this premeditated way.

ME:Yes, I can. I have one more question, though, before we move on.

A: Carry on.

ME:If three hundred thousand million years of human, shall I say, "clock time," have gone by, how many Event Spaces does this involve?

A: Currently or in the downstream condition where the maximum numbers of Event Spaces are invoked?

ME:Can I be greedy?

A: Yes.

ME:Both!

A: Currently there is only one overall Event Space being used because of the need to contain the results of the downstream actions.

ME:So it is quarantined!

A: No, it isn't. It is quite common for an overall Event Space to be created as a result of a series of downstream actions that have a common origin. This overall Event Space houses all of the Event Spaces that are created by the dualistic, trilistic, and quadrulistic decisions of those incarnates affected by the downstream interactions that didn't happen. As you are aware, Event Space/s is/are a fractal condition both in creation and dissolution. This overall Event Space is created because of a single existential condition—that there is an end or a final outcome to the downstream actions that are derived from the common origin.

ME:Ah! And so it becomes self-contained as a result.

A: Yes. So, to answer your question there are three Event Space conditions to consider and not two. The first is that there is an overall Event Space created because there is a final outcome. Within this overall Event Space there are currently a little over 62 trillion local Event Spaces created to support the level of downstream activities currently expressed. The maximum number of Event Spaces that will be created are in excess of 342 billion quadrillion before dissolution begins and the number of Event Spaces created starts to collapse due to their being unnecessary. Note, though, that is only an approximate figure because the actual creation of Event Space is fluid.

ME: Thank you. It makes a little more sense now.

A: There is one more exception to the rule, though!

7.2.5

The Other Exception to the Rule

ME: Mmmm, I saw this coming. I just felt that I wasn't being allowed to move on quite yet.

A: This is a difficult and complicated subject and one that needs to be treated with respect. As a result, this "last" part is one that also needs to be broadcast.

ME: OK, I am all spiritual ears.

A: This last part is relative to when an Aspect is of a naturally high frequency and is one that normally, or more frequently, incarnates within the highest frequencies of the physical universe, rather than those associated with the location of the Earth. They generally, but not always, incarnate with a passive role, one where they are here to help lift the base frequencies of the Earth without embarking upon actively creating a spiritual direction or service. They are, by and large, covert in their spiritual interactions, with many having no knowledge of spirituality or displaying signs of self-awareness/realization. Generally, these Aspects are both seemingly innocent and immature in relation to other "incarnates," lacking interpersonal skills and a desire to interact as a result. In these instances, the Aspect is unprepared for the difficulties experienced with working within the Earth realm, has significant difficulty relating to those around it, and more importantly, their energies and action profiles. They can appear meek, timid, confused, bipolar, and suffer from constant but varying levels of depression.

When one of these Aspects decides they can no longer operate in the frequencies associated with the Earth, they seek help in finding an early end to their incarnation. This help is ALWAYS achieved within the energetic by the Aspect concerned discussing and negotiating the early end of the incarnation in a way that is acceptable to the guide, helper, and TES.

As you are aware from our previous dialogues on the subject of suicide, there is significant amount of work achieved downstream by both the Aspect itself and those interfacing with the Aspect and the fractal downstream interactive opportunities that could or may occur. Based upon this, the guide, helpers, and TES of the Aspect work hard to find an acceptable solution to the desire of an Aspect to terminate its incarnation early, if it is "struggling" with the energies surrounding the incarnate state or commitments made prior to incarnation. Remember, the human form is a rare commodity, so the first opportunity to be considered is one where the human form is maintained.

ME: A Walk-In, the first thing to be considered is a Walk-In!

A: My, you are on the ball, and I am very pleased that you have actually managed to do what you have been thinking of doing for a number of years—writing in the olive grove.

I have to break off for a moment to explain.

I am currently in Crete, and ever since we purchased a small olive grove that is linked to the land attached to the cottage we bought in 2001 I have been meaning to, or should I say have had the intention/desire to, sit under an olive tree and do my work. For some reason today (18 October 2014) I had been feeling Anne's presence very strongly and the desire to get off my backside and do just that was more than compelling. I had been very emotional all day—very human and it was like I was shoe-horned into place. So here I am under an ancient olive tree. It is full to bursting with olives and is providing me with shade from the sun and protection from the dominant northwesterly breeze we have in Crete. I decided that I will do my daily meditation here tomorrow and not on the cottage roof as normal.

The Aliens I discovered here are suddenly around me. I also feel Anne's energy in front of me. The Aliens tell me that I am, while in this position, connected with the basic natural energies of the Earth. I focus my third/spiritual eye on my surroundings and notice that twelve of the trees close to me are connected to me by an energetic link. I have the same link to my heart chakra from the energetic Anne. It is one of the most blissful states I have been in outside of being directly connected to a Source Entity or The Origin itself. My body tingles all over and I am in tears.

I suddenly see my plans in my mind's eye. This cottage and the land surrounding it will be part of the "Beyond The Source" foundation that I am told I will create. It is going to be an ashram in the future, a sacred area where I will teach my teachers—those "Traversing the Frequencies" Level 3 students who show a desire to be of service to incarnate mankind and help other truth seekers gain a direct, permanent, and robust communicative link with The Source. These teachers will carry on and expand "the work" when I ascend beyond the physical.

Each of these olive trees will have a small area created beneath them for personal meditation practice, and the one I am under now, I have just been told, is the one I will use in the future for years to come. It all feels very Indian as well. "Mmmm," I thought. "I wonder which of my very small number of

117

incarnations is linked to this state of beingness in India?" "But that," I thought, "is for another book!" I need to get back to Anne now and complete the content of this dialogue.

A: Let's get back to the Walk-In bit shall we.

ME: Yes, of course.

A: As you quite rightly suggested, the first route considered is to exchange Aspects, to create an opportunity for a Walk-In. Although this is a simple solution in thought, it is not so simple in actualization and the search for a suitable Aspect can take some time to complete.

ME: Why? I would have thought that many Aspects would be knocking the door down to Walk-In to a mature incarnate vehicle with a known life plan and path of downstream activity?

A: Yes, there are and they do, but many of them have already put into place their own life plan and have agreed the downstream activities with those incarnate Aspects that they planned to work with. They have to negotiate robustly to gain agreement to change their direction from the incarnation that they agreed on, and become a Walk-In candidate.

ME: So what you are suggesting is that a Walk-In is hard to initiate?

A: With those who have already established an agreed incarnate existence yes, but with those who have not there is a chance. Again, this is not easy, though, because those Aspects that are not currently incarnate and who are acceptable, that being, they have similar energetic characteristics and experiential incarnate knowledge to the current incumbent Aspect, have to work hard and fast to catch up on the demands of the life plan and the downstream expectations resulting from that plan.

ME: OK, so if a suitable Aspect is available and works hard enough to catch up on the plan, the existing Aspect is allowed to end the incarnation by walking-out, thereby swapping the incarnate form with the Aspect that is walking-in?

A: Yes.

ME: And the Aspect that walks-out has no penalties attached to its walking-out of an incarnation?

A: Not if all the downstream interactions are maintained—no.

ME: What then if a suitable Aspect for a Walk-In cannot be found?

A: Then other routes need to be found that are acceptable and within the normal incarnate regime.

ME: What do you mean "within the normal incarnate regime?"

A: Every incarnation has a number of termination junctures; they are sort of "bail-out" opportunities. These termination junctures are chosen exit points where the Aspect can leave the incarnation in a pre-agreed way at known and accounted for junctures in the duration of the incarnation. Before you ask the next question I will answer it for you. The Walk-In is always preferred to the termination juncture because the Walk-In preserves the human form so that it can benefit another Aspect. It is only when this route is exhausted as an opportunity that the termination junctures are considered.

ME: How many termination junctures are available to an incarnate Aspect?

A: No more than five but no less than three.

ME: Can you explain what they may be?

A: Yes. They are demise by accident, illness, or murder.

ME: That just about sums up the higher level descriptions of how most incarnates leave their incarnations.

119

A: Yes, it does, but of course they offer myriad opportunities. For example, you have already gone past your termination junctures. You had five, all accidents. Four of them included demise by drowning in water, one, the fourth as it so happens, involved a motorcar. The last and fifth ...

ME: Was when I got momentarily disorientated in a "night dive" in Spain where I found myself in a cave with limited exit points.

A: That's right. You were suddenly on the point of panic and could have made the wrong decision. As it happens it was not necessary for you to terminate the incarnation at this final juncture as everything was in place for the rest of your incarnate existence. So, you didn't panic and you retraced your steps, making your way quickly and safely out of the cave. There was no way you could fail from this juncture onward, and so the incarnation was preserved. I, on the other hand, had fulfilled all of the expectations of my incarnation and did not need to continue. In fact, I had to leave my incarnation at its agreed "final" termination juncture through disease (brain tumor), because I have a job of work to do here in the energetic, which is in support of the work we started together and the work you will continue with until your own "final" termination juncture swings into place.

ME: OK, so, as with all the rest of the opportunities discussed for leaving the incarnate vehicle, the opportunities for using the termination junctures have to be discussed at guide, helper, Aspect, and TES level, along with all those other Aspects, guides, helpers, and TES's who are affected in the downstream activities?

A: No, the downstream activities are not included because they are part of the plan and terminate naturally if a certain termination juncture is used. It only needs to be discussed at the guide and helper level.

ME: Because it is already baked into the life plan.

A: Correct.

ME: So using a termination juncture is an easy option.

A: Yes, in some respects.

ME: Why in some respects?

A: Because if the Aspect is in between termination junctures all the guide and helpers have to do is steer the Aspect toward the next juncture. The only issue here is the Event Space, the time between them. If the Aspect can wait and work with the guide and helpers, then the demise of the incarnate vehicle at the termination juncture will be a successful one.

   If the Aspect cannot wait then it may affect a suicide, which includes all of the downstream implications we have already discussed between the point of suicide and the termination juncture to be used. Additionally, if the Aspect has gone past all of its termination junctures and it wishes to leave the incarnation and secure an early demise of the incarnate vehicle, then we are back in the suicide scenario.

ME: Which gets me to the chapter heading, "The Other Exception to the Rule." What is it?

A: If, and ONLY IF, an Aspect can no longer tolerate incarnate existence AND IT HAS ACTIVELY AND DILIGENTLY sought energetic assistance, guidance, and direction from its guide, helpers, and TES, and it transpires that none of the opportunities just described are available, then the Aspect is given permission, it is given authority, to demise the incarnate vehicle via suicide.

   BUT, and I say BUT, this is a VERY, VERY rare decision, one that is avoided at all opportunity.

ME: And in this instance the Aspect is not affected by the penalties attached to it by evolutionary debt, etc.?

A: No, because there is a significant amount of downstream work agreed upon by the Aspect's guide, helpers, and TES, and the guides, helpers, and TES's of those incarnates that the Aspect would have interacted with in those downstream interactions when this condition is experienced and authorized.

BUT, I say AGAIN, this is a VERY, VERY rare decision. This knowledge MUST NOT be used as an excuse for justifying suicide!

The depth of effect surrounding suicide had taken me both by surprise and had a strange ring to it, that of old and ancient truth. The whole feel of the energy surrounding the subject was one that told me that, if we are of this mind, the need to resist the self or assisted early demise of the human vehicle was one of the most important things we should be concentrating on. Not just for our own sakes but for the sakes of others, an indeterminable number of others.

8

The Rest Period

I suddenly felt myself needing to move on to another common subject found in spiritual texts that broadcast the truth surrounding energetic existence post-physical demise—that of the so-called rest period. As I thought about this subject, a little voice in my head quite clearly stated that "there is no such thing as a rest period, per se; there is only continued progression." I knew instantly that this was not multiversal knowledge but that it was Anne grabbing my attention.

A: It's me!

The voice in my head felt and sounded almost like the way that Anne introduced herself when she was calling me on the telephone back in the days of being incarnate. It brought a tear to my eye, and it was comforting, to say the least.

ME: It's you!

My typical response.

A: We are going to talk about the rest period now, aren't we? That period in between one incarnation and another?

ME: Yes, we are, except that something is telling me that there is no such thing as a rest period.

A: Well, it depends upon how you look at it. If you consider it from the point of view of the Aspect who has just returned from an incarnation then the answer is yes, it is a rest. If you are talking about the period in between the debrief and reintegration with the TES then no, there is some work to be done.

ME: OK, let's talk about the period "just" before the debriefings.

A: This is a time for contemplation. The Aspect is still working and thinking in a purely individualized way at this point and has much to consider before undertaking the level of work required before reintegration with the TES. More importantly, it is time for the Aspect to disassociate itself from the form factor, the incarnate vehicle, used in its incarnation. This takes some "time," shall I say, and the Aspect has to come to terms with the fact that it no longer needs to hold on to this "now" mental "form" in its own way and at its own speed.

ME: Are you suggesting that an Aspect holds onto the form factor of the incarnate vehicle post demise?

A: Some do, some don't. This is the reason we have a "rest period." You see, it all depends upon the level of integration the Aspect has with the incarnate vehicle and the level of energetic connectivity the Aspect has while incarnate. That being, the level of understanding of spiritual matters it has and how this helps the Aspect disassociate itself from its incarnate vehicle post demise. Integration in this context means the level of immersion into the association with the physicality the Aspect finds itself in. Or, to put it more succinctly, whether the Aspect feels and believes that it is the incarnate vehicle and not the sentient energies that are animating it. Remember, an Aspect is a master creator and can create anything once in the energetic—irrespective of its level of disassociation/immersion.

ME: The picture I am getting here then is that there is a whole area of space within the multiverse that is created to look like the environment that a disincarnate Aspect used to have when incarnate.

A: Correct, but this is only local to the Aspects and the frequencies they find themselves in due to the evolutionary level of their TES. What I mean here is that each frequency level that a TES exists within which requires its use of incarnation to accelerate its evolutionary progression has a similar environment. The interesting thing here is, though, that although within a specific frequency level, this same space is used by all Aspects, it has multiple representations. I will elaborate. If an Aspect is so immersed in the form factor and environment of its last incarnation, it will see and experience its reestablished energetic existence as being the same.

ME: I have just received an image here that suggests that an Aspect that is, for example, from an environment that is based upon an arachnid form factor will create a new environment around itself that is based upon its previous environment, and every one of the Aspects that it perceives will have the same form factor created around them. It will give them an arachnid form, even if they are disassociated or immersed.

A: Correct, but note that this form factor is only in the perception of the creating Aspect. Other Aspects with similar levels of immersion will create other environments and form factors that reflect those that they existed in when incarnate in the myriad other form factors that are available in the frequencies associated with the physical universe.

ME: I have just received another image, one that the fully disassociated Aspect would perceive. It would see all of the other Aspects in the frequential environment that it, and their TES, is in. It would perceive them as they truly are. If, however, the disassociated Aspect focuses upon the "local" environment created by an Aspect that it is still immersed in, it would perceive its incarnate form factor and the environment that was relative to it. And, if the disassociated Aspect then performed this function on all of the immersed Aspects simultaneously, it would see a mosaic of all the form factors and environments overlaid upon each other.

A: Correct and well done. This period of time, this "rest period" if you like, is required to give the Aspect "time" to disassociate itself with its last incarnation and operate as a sentient energetic Aspect of its True Energetic Self within its true state, within the energies associated within the frequencies that its TES exists.

8.1

The Period in between Physical Demise and the Debrief/Life Review

ME: How long does a rest period last for?

A: It depends upon the evolutionary level of the TES that has been allowed to be part of the Aspect's sentience content.

ME: Sorry, are you saying that an Aspect does not automatically assume the evolutionary level of the TES while incarnate, or disincarnate?

A: No, this is all part of the life plan. This is how a TES accelerates its evolutionary content. It does it by part of itself, the projected Aspect, entering into an incarnation "cold," so to speak, so that it can experience the physical universe at the Earth level in the way it is supposed to be experienced, in an isolated, or almost isolated, way. Do note, though, that those Aspects that incarnate in the higher frequencies of the multiverse, those that are still associated with the physical universe, naturally enjoy higher levels of connectivity with their TES and The Source, and so although they are more connected, they do not experience the levels of evolutionary acceleration experienced by incarnation into the lowest frequencies of the multiverse.

ME:So why do some Aspects have more connectivity with their TES and The Source then?

A: Because they have a specific spiritual job to do, one that is either personal, or global and personal. An Aspect needs to work on its personal progression first before it can work on the global.

ME:OK, let me get back to the Aspects that are still immersed in their past incarnate state then. Just what do these Aspects do in this rest period? How or what do they do to become awakened to their true energetic state as an Aspect of a TES or a Shard of an Aspect?

A: They simply exist as they would have done while incarnate. They go to work, go home, enjoy recreation, sleep, eat, drink, and drive a vehicle—everything that they would have done had they still been incarnate. As I have just stated, they can do this because they create the environment they left behind as an incarnate being around them. Although they have to break free of this self-created illusion by themselves, their guide and helpers do their best to offer "continuity errors" so that the Aspect recognizes, at some point, that something is not quite right.

ME:How do they make the continuity errors? Why not just tell them that they are now disincarnate and have done with it?

A: Because the Aspect has it do it itself, that's all part of the life plan and part of the route to energetic self-realization—even though it is just a change in their state of consciousness— their awareness. They help the "immersed" Aspect by changing things in a subtle way, a way that allows them to work it out for themselves. Eventually they see the errors in continuity and start to see/perceive the reality around them for what it is—pure energy.

ME: They see "what," for instance, that allows them to realize there is an issue with their environment?

A: One example is that people that had returned to the energetic before them are now part of their life again.

ME: This is created by their guide and helpers?

A: In some instances, the guide and helpers enlist the help of an Aspect or Aspects that were "known" by the "immersed" Aspect to help provide the continuity error. They suddenly become part of the scenery of the "immersed" Aspect, and the "immersed" Aspect, recognizing them energetically, gives them the appearance of the incarnate vehicle (body) they had when incarnate. At some point the "immersed" Aspect starts to recognize the continuity error when they remember that that person/Aspect demised, returned to the energetic, before them.

ME: What happens then?

A: They start to question their environment and themselves—specifically as they start to remember that they had a certain disease and no longer have that disease or the pain from the disease, or they remember the events leading up to an accident and realize that they could never have survived it.

My mind wandered back to a rather nasty car accident I had in May 1991. I wondered for a moment whether I had actually died. The ambulance drivers said that it was a miracle that I had survived the type of accident I had. Was I experiencing, have I been experiencing, an environment I had created around me in the energetic for the last twenty-three years?

A: No way, José! I can solidly confirm that you are still on Earth. That accident was a nightmare for me. And what's more those Aspects that create an environment around themselves paint a very bright picture, not one where strife and struggling is experienced. As an example I refer to the nine years I had after my brain tumor diagnosis and the uncertainty surrounding it that we both experienced. No, you are most definitely still on Earth and still working on your spiritual mission. Sorry, mate!

ME: Thanks for that. It was an interesting thought process, though.

A: Mmmm. Not for long, I might add. I soon nipped it in the bud! Let's get back to the task at hand.

Once the continuity errors are noted, and considered, the Aspect starts to see more and more errors, and continues to see more and more until the environment they created around them dissolves and the "bodies" woven around the Aspects that the "immersed" Aspect recognizes energetically are also dissolved, leaving only the pure energetic state of the surrounding environment and the Aspects recognized.

ME: And at this point I guess the Aspect is freed from the constraints of the previous incarnation and is free to progress on to the debrief stage.

A: Yes, it is. But this doesn't happen straight away, though.

ME: Why not?

A: Because the Aspect then has to sit on its own, so to speak, and contemplate the incarnation, remembering it in all of its detail before it can enter into the long debrief process that we discussed previously. Within this the Aspect also has to remember the work done prior to the incarnation and recognize the guide and helpers that it is in partnership with.

ME: Ah! This is remembering the whole incarnate life, it's before the life review.

A: Yes, it is. Although we have tackled this subject somewhat out of synchronization with the detail behind the life review and subsequent debrief, the rest of this chapter will detail the work the Aspect goes through after the debrief, the life review.

8.2

The Period in between the Debrief Period and
Reintegration with the TES

ME: What could an Aspect, a soul, possibly need to do once it has gone through the rest period, established what it really is, and then endured the debrief, other than reintegrate with its TES?

A: It can decide to socialize.

ME: Socialize?

A: Yes, socialize.

ME: I don't understand.

A: So I see. It's not socialization as you know and understand it, it's about commitments that have been made before the incarnation and during the incarnation.

ME: Such as helping those who are still incarnate, for instance?

A: Yes, together with other things agreed in the life plan.

ME: What are you suggesting? That the life plan still exists even when we return to the energetic?

A: Yes, of course it does. What do you think we are doing now?

ME: Writing a book together, one that I didn't have on my personal list of things to do.

A: Well, I would like to advise you that this book was very much on the list of things to do before we incarnated. And my working with you while you are still incarnate, opening so many doors for you, so to speak, was/is part of that life plan.

ME: OK, so this is socializing.

A: Yes and no. I will explain. I expect that I will cover this again later on in this dialogue but I will go over it now as well. As I alluded to a moment ago, we have commitments that we make prior to incarnation and those that we make during

130

incarnation. The commitments made prior to incarnation are part of the life plan and involve working on those parts that involve working partnerships with other incarnates, whether it be in marriage, friendship, or working for the better good with incarnates of like mind. This means that the Aspect needs to stay close to the frequencies associated with the physical universe to continue to work on the rest of the plan and the incarnates that are part of it. In this instance, the Aspect works behind the scenes to ensure that the guides and helpers of the incarnates it is working with, including those who are downstream, are continuing to work on the part of the plan that they are responsible for or are affected by. They can also offer guidance or directional change above and beyond that offered by the guide and helpers of an incarnate in the, shall I say, "first line" of communication, or those incarnates that the Aspect was physically interacting with while incarnate.

From the perspective of the commitments made while incarnate, the Aspect may well have decided to offer comfort to a partner or close relative/friend who is left behind, who is still incarnate. This is achieved by leaving a sign that only the incarnate that the sign is destined for would receive and understand as being evidence of the continued existence of the Aspect after the demise of the incarnate vehicle. This is designed to help remove, in some way, the feeling of loss, reducing the effect of the emotion behind the bereavement process you feel while on Earth. I gave you a sign and I had great fun both doing it and seeing your response. It was also interesting to see how hard it is to manipulate gross physical frequencies while in the higher frequencies. It takes a LOT of energy. Giving a sign is one of the most common things that married couples give each other at the point of the demise of the incarnate vehicle, and it is the most common reason that a newly released (from incarnation) Aspect likes to stay close to the frequencies associated with the physical universe.

ME:Does everyone have a life plan that involves continuing to work with incarnates after the demise of their incarnate vehicle?

A: No. It's not uncommon to have Aspects leave their incarnate vehicle and not give a sign or need to continue to be associated with another incarnate's life plan. In this instance, they go through the rest period, debrief, and then straight to reintegration with their TES.

ME:OK. One thing is bugging me, though, and that is the length of time taken for the Aspect to recover from the incarnation, to re-associate itself with its true energetic state and TES and go through the debriefing process, and then give a sign and/or continue to work with other incarnates.

A: Why, it is all done instantaneously from your perspective!

ME:Ah! Yes, I was forgetting about the use of Event Space.

A: Yes, you were. All of the work behind the rest period and the debrief is achieved in another Event Space. This ensures that there is not a gap in the continuity of contact between the release of the Aspect from the incarnate vehicle after its demise, the giving of a sign and continuing the work with those incarnates that its life plan was part of.

You will notice that there was a gap in between the demise of my incarnate vehicle and me giving you a sign to indicate my continued existence.

ME:Yes, I did notice the gap. I thought this was strange because of your/our level of experiential knowledge. I expected to receive the sign in your hospice bedroom.

A: Yes, well, the gap was due to where I went. As you can recall from a previous dialogue, I almost reintegrated with our TES, such was the inertia associated with your energetic help. I had to almost reverse the reintegration process and then check myself out. I didn't need the rest period, but I did need the debrief, which by the way was directly administered by our TES. This in itself didn't cause a temporal gap, but it did make me think about what to do to attract your attention. Even with your level of connectivity and knowledge the association with the gross physical at this time caused energetic problems in contacting you. In losing my physicality you were stunned. You were stunned to lose me, a part of yourself, as you are part of me, and your love for me was augmented beyond any previous levels that I had experienced while incarnate, even at the start of our physical relationship. You were closing down emotionally but your love for me shone through. When I experienced this, I felt that there was only one thing to do—bask in its light. It was wonderful. Then you shouted at me to give you a sign, and I found the electronic bottle opener I gave you as a Christmas present five years before. It was next to your side of the bed so I activated it. I was pleased it worked because the battery was low.

ME: These are personal examples, though, and we are still working on the plan, what is now my life plan.

A: Actually it's my life plan as well; it's just that I am this side of the frequencies of the physical universe now and not your side.

ME: Now we have an example, a personal example, what about the length of time you will be working with me for? Is it to the end of my incarnate existence?

A: Yes, and I will be there for you when your incarnate vehicle demises as well, for this is another of the commitments that an Aspect can make either at the planning stage of the life plan or while incarnate.

ME: And does being met, helped, to pass over by a friend or loved one accelerate the recognition of the true self during the rest period?

A: Yes, but it can also confuse the newly demised Aspect, especially if an earthly appearance is used in the initial contact. We won't need me to use an earthly appearance when your incarnate vehicle demises. But if I/we chose this route it won't slow the recognition of your true self either.

I believe that this information is quite common, so I would now like to move on to the process of reintegration of the Aspect with the TES as this is not so well known.

9

Integration with the TES

This part of the dialogue is one that I was very much looking forward to. And, to my knowledge, it was one that was not well understood, if at all. I was aware that the Hindu Vedas talked about the God Head and that the soul was an Aspect of the God Head, but that was about as far as my personal information went. I found this a relief as I am very much aware that it would be easy to read some information on this subject and have it stay hidden in the subconscious, only to be regurgitated later, The Original source of the information being forgotten. I am fastidious in the use of the process I employ when desiring and receiving new and detailed information, and it continues to serve me well. I may have mentioned this personal constraint before, but I very much feel that it is one that needs repeating as it would be easy for the reader to think that a spiritual author can become complacent when looking for new material to broadcast. However, I am also aware of the need to reference information that is already known to act as a datum, an area of familiarity for the reader, without becoming the core text. I was excited at the prospect that the dialogue I was about to have on this subject would slot into the category of both new and unique.

A: Excited, are you? I thought you would be more excited about talking with me again.

ME: Of course, I am. It is always a delight to be able to communicate with you in this way. It makes the fact that you are no longer incarnate easier to work with.

A: That's nice.

ME: It's the truth.

A: Again, that's nice. Let's move on to the information you desire now—what happens when the Aspect integrates with the TES.

ME: Yes, please.

A: Fine. This is quite a simple subject actually, for it is achieved almost automatically when the Aspect has finally been through all of the work it has to do after the demise of its incarnate vehicle.

ME: Just a thought. Doesn't the Aspect get a choice in the matter of integration with the TES, though? What if it doesn't want to reintegrate?

A: There are those Aspects that decide to wait a while or not reintegrate with their TES. These are either Aspects whose TES has created them to act as guides or helpers for those Aspects whose TES has formally chosen to enter into the incarnate cycle as a means of accelerating the accrual of their evolutionary content, or they wish to help other Aspects whose incarnate vehicles have just demised. In the second case it is merely a delay factor.

There are other Aspects that choose to stay separate from their TES as well. These are those Aspects that have been chosen by their TES for the route of undertaking "back-to-back" incarnations. Others are created by their TES to be part of the group of entities that maintain the evolutionary integrity of the structure of the overall multiversal environment, which of course includes the physical universe. The Aspects whose TES created them for the "back-to-back" route do not reintegrate with their TES until the planned series of incarnations and the subsequent life reviews and debriefings have all been completed.

ME:How many incarnations can be achieved in a back-to-back plan?

A: Thousands. And, there are a lot of TES's that plan the incarnations their Aspects undertake in this way. This is why there is a queue of Aspects that are waiting to incarnate that have not yet incarnated. They are waiting in line, so to speak. This is why many spiritual people feel that the Aspect, the soul or spirit, is an individual condition and not a component of a small collective state of sentient consciousness, the TES. It is also why most of the spiritual information to date addresses disincarnate existence in the individual tense and not the collective.

ME:And that is because?

A: Most sensitives or mediums contact individualized Aspects and not the TES. Sensitives and mediums are incarnate and therefore refer to the human state of thinking. This thinking, at best, refers to itself as the human body which is animated by the Aspect or soul. At worst the thinking is that the human body is the individual and not the Aspect that animates it as a component of the TES. It is this thought process that limits the thinking process that in turn limits the level at which they can contact those entities that are energetic; that being, they only attract the attention of the individualized Aspects and not the TES, or those integrated Aspects of the TES that have been given individualized but integrated sentience.

ME:OK, so some, a large proportion it would seem, are Aspects that are "in transit," so to speak, "in transit" being that period in between incarnation and reintegration—a smaller proportion being employed as guides, helpers, or "multiversal" maintenance entities.

A: That would be a good summary, yes.

ME:And furthermore, this state of transit, along with the underlying thought process of the sensitive or medium, is why most communications with Aspects that are not associated with an incarnate vehicle is with the Aspect's themselves and not their TES.

A: Yes, correct.

ME:And this is why we have a skewed understanding of what we really are when disincarnate.

A: Bingo!

ME:This is actually very interesting as it clarifies a lot in my mind, and I would guess it will clarify a lot in the minds of those truth seekers who read this text later.

A: It will. This will act as a bridge. It will cross the knowledge gap incarnate humankind has in understanding how we as incarnate human beings can be singular, with so-called spiritual proof that we are singular, when in fact the reality is that we are individualized units of sentience within the TES that has been given a body of energy to allow it to animate a denser body of energy, the incarnate vehicle.

ME:Great. Now we have clarified this part of the subject matter we can continue working on the subject of the Aspect's reintegration with the TES.

Well, right now I am here in singularity as well.

ME:This isn't Anne? Who is it?

A: It's Dolores! The Aspect that incarnated as Dolores Cannon! This is wonderful.

ME:More than that, it's amazing!

D: Not so amazing as probable.

Dear readers, this is not on the agenda for this book or subject matter. It is a complete surprise. For those who don't know, Dolores Cannon ascended beyond incarnate existence on 18 October 2014. I was VERY fortunate and humbled to be allowed to attend the private side of the funeral service and celebrations that the Cannon family had organized. Indeed, I was the only author present. The only other external participants were the UK and Chinese agents for Ozark Mountain Publishing, the couple of dedicated Quantum Hypnosis Healing Technique (QHHT) practitioners who run the forum, and a QHHT practitioner from Japan who attended the more "open" aspect of the service the following day.

D: I am only here for a few short moments because I have something to say to you. You, like I was in the start of my work, are working in the forefront of metaphysical knowledge, of *Spiritual Physics, Spiritual Science*, and will get persecuted on a regular basis. This is because people in authority like to back each other up, even when wrong. They like to justify their own paradigms. They have made their careers on it after all. Keep on going, don't stop. Eventually people will question the existing metaphysical paradigm and will look further afield for the truth. It will be hard, it will be exhausting, but you will succeed—eventually. Just look at the problems that Galileo had! Remember the truth will always come out and this is the truth.

Send my love to them all. Tell Julia to take the time she needs to adjust to her new role, she will be better off for it.

Well, it's time to go now; I have work to do before I consider reintegration. I am so glad you bridged this gap.

Be diligent, be firm, and be humble.

ME: Thank you.

A: Yes, thank you. If I could cry tears of joy, I would.

D: It's a pleasure to be of some little service in this way.

139

A: Oh, she's gone.

ME: Yes, she has. She has moved on.

To say that I was emotional while channeling this unexpected knowledge and encouragement would be an understatement, as I was starting to lose certain people around me. People who I thought were with me energetically are now dropping by the wayside. The beauty of this, though, is that I am being exposed to new people who are able to cope with the associated energies, understand the new knowledge being presented to incarnate mankind, and are enthusiastic about it.

A: How wonderful.

ME: Yes, how wonderful. Phew!

A: Shall we carry on?

ME: Yes, please do. Let me settle down for a moment first ...

OK, let's carry on.

A: Right, let's get on with it. First, though, I want to make a point of demarcation—that being, the integration of the Shard with the Aspect, because this follows a different direction and is therefore an isolated case. The Shard is a "Subincarnation" and not a "Secondary Incarnation" from the Aspect. I will go into the detail of these descriptions later in our dialogues. Suffice to say, there is a significant difference because a secondary incarnation involves the Aspect "In Totality," the Aspect leaving its "Primary Incarnation" in a condition of stasis, whereas, the subincarnation involves a "Smaller Aspect" of the Aspect, with the Aspect maintaining its primary incarnation as well. As with the TES when it integrates with The Source Entity, the Aspect has two choices to make. One is to integrate in "Full Communion" with the TES, becoming one with the TES and surrendering the individuality of the TES sentience with The Source; or two, entering into "Partial Communion" with the TES, that being one with the TES but remaining as individualized but fully connected sentience within the TES. Think of these as being either a line of code in a computer program, or an essential cog in its works, versus a subroutine or individualized program within an overall program in a computer. In the case of the Shard, it has no choice and all its experiential data and individualized sentience is reintegrated into a state of full communion with the Aspect. When an Aspect projects Shards to create subincarnations and maximize its experiential and evolutionary content while incarnate, it has to wait until all of its Shards have reintegrated with it before it itself can reintegrate with its TES.

When the Aspect has reintegrated any Shards it may have projected into an incarnate state, it then makes its decision about which integration route to take.

ME: I would have thought that this decision would have been made by the TES and not the Aspect itself?

A: Agreed, but the TES, in creating the Aspect, bestows upon it a certain level of free will, of individual choice. Some Aspects, as I recently stated, are left in the "Projected" or "Individualized" state because of the overall incarnate or service plan.

ME: So an Aspect has a third choice, to not reintegrate?

A: Yes, but this is usually only a temporary condition, for eventually all Aspects choose either full or partial reintegration. There is a further complication, though, and that is that the TES may have decided to reintegrate an Aspect or Aspects itself, overriding the decision process of the Aspect or Aspects.

ME: Does the TES override the decision process of an Aspect often?

A: Yes, quite often, especially when an Aspect resists reintegration.

ME: An Aspect can resist reintegration?

A: Yes, but this is rare and occurs when the Aspect retains an element of human fear, the fear of loss of self, which of course never really happens, even in full communion, because the individualization blends into the background of the overall sentience of the TES, becoming the overall sentience. Based upon this information, I will split the description of reintegration with the TES into two: full communion and partial communion.

9.1

Full Communion

When either the Aspect chooses full communion as its condition of reintegration with the TES, or the TES recalls it, the sentience and the body of energy that the sentience is assigned to merge together with the larger sentience and the body of energy that is the TES. The body of energy, simply being a vehicle for the sentience to associate itself with gains or regains its bulk volume—just like pouring more water into a jug of water. The reintegration of the sentience follows a different path, though. The sentience itself is individualized for the period of the work before the incarnation—the planning, the incarnation itself, and the period of work after the incarnation—the life review and the debrief. In all of these instances, an Aspect of TES sentience is separated out, fully individualized, and assigned to a body of energy. This individualization creates two things: a memory set and a personality. Ultimately both the memory set and the personality are created as a function of the integration of the sentient body of energy with the incarnate vehicle—the ego. However, there are small Aspects of both that are aligned to the period prior to incarnation. This gives the incarnate Aspect a feeling that there is "more" to incarnate existence and a desire, if this feeling is strong enough and the incarnate Aspect has not fully associated itself with the incarnate vehicle to creating a "solid" ego, to know more about itself and the wider environment that is not physically experienced. This makes the process of integration easier to conduct.

ME: Why would it be easier to conduct?

A: In the case of the Aspect that is being recalled into full communion by the TES, the Aspect may not wish to accept such loss of individuality. But in the case of the Aspect that is aware of the reality of what it is, it will accept the loss of the small level of individuality it has for the greater level of presence it will have as a fully integrated Aspect of TES sentience.

When the Aspect experiences full integration, the personality that is associated with the incarnation, the ego, is stripped away, leaving only a clean set of experiential memories, memories that become part of the overall memory set that is the TES. In essence, though, there are two sets of memories that result from incarnation.

The TES already has the memories of the incarnate Aspect prior to its reintegration with it because they are transferred to the TES at the point of experience. However, this does not contain the sentience that experienced it. Hence the need to reintegrate the sentience assigned to the Aspect. When the TES reintegrates the Aspect's sentience the experiential memories associated with it also include the resultant evolutionary content.

ME: That means that the TES does not accrue the evolutionary content in parallel with the experiential memory.

A: Correct. It stays aligned with the sentience that experienced it, hence the ultimate need to reintegrate all Aspects projected into the physical and other universal environments within the multiverse.

From the perspective of the TES this integration creates a sudden "high-definition" effect on the memory set, giving the TES significant detail over those memories that it accrued in parallel to the Aspect experiencing them.

From the perspective of the Aspect, it is a gradual awakening to a greater memory set which results in a merging of those memories and a loss of individuality. The loss of individuality results from the sheer magnitude of memories that are the TES versus the finitude of those memories that were accrued by the Aspect. It is like a single drop of water being introduced into the world's oceans, the individuality of the drop of water being dissolved in the greater magnitude of the water. Initially the Aspect experiences greatness, which is then replaced by oneness and loss of individuality.

9.2

Partial Communion

A: Partial communion is the most common form of reintegration of the Aspect with the TES. It is the state of continued individualized beingness while still being integrated with the TES.

ME: Why is it the most common form of integration, of communion?

A: Simply put, because it is the most useful configuration for the TES to operate with.

ME: Mmmm. How many Aspects are in this state of integration normally?

A: There can be no more than twelve of course, but there are many TES that have all twelve Aspects in this state of integration, and there are others that have a smaller number.

Some TES on the other hand have no Aspects in the state of individualized integration at all.

ME: Why the variation in integration? I would have thought that there would have only been full communion as a state of integration?

A: The level or state of integration is of course a product of how the TES ultimately wants to experience its environment and its own existence within that environment. There are no hard and fast rules here, except that everything is acceptable. It all adds to the overall diversity of evolutionary experience forwarded on to The Source (our Source, SE1) and The Origin.

ME: OK, we have two versions of partial communion to work with then. The first is fully partial; the second is partial with Aspects of full communion, true full communion being explained in the last section.

A: That's correct. If we take the last section as an example of how an Aspect would integrate into full communion as being identical for the function of partial communion with Aspects of both full and partial communion, then we don't need to describe it again. Except for, that is, the reason why an Aspect would allow or use this mixture of communion.

ME: Let's answer that part first then. Why does a TES choose partial communion as a state of being for its Aspects?

A: It's not so much for the Aspects but for the TES itself. You see, a TES needs to be unique in its application of experience and subsequent accrual of evolutionary content, so they choose to work in a way that both suits them and/or supports the level of uniqueness they want to apply. In the case of the TES who has a number of Aspects that are in partial communion, each of the Aspects has two specific specialisms. The first being a way of working based upon its own experiential knowledge base and skill set derived from working within the frequencies of the multiverse that are considered fully energetic when separated out from the TES.

The second being the experiential knowledge base and skill set derived from working in the energies of the multiverse that require an incarnate vehicle, the physical universe, with the physical universe providing the specialisms relating to certain types of environment-, community-, and relationship based interactions. These specialisms become individualized in their own right over the indeterminable number of times that the Aspect experiences separation from the TES, both in the fully energetic state and the low-frequency energetic of the incarnate state. Because they become specialized they start to be used in a specialized way by the TES, the TES selecting a specific Aspect to work in a particular energetic or incarnate state where that Aspect will make the most of the challenges presented to it in the most efficient way possible.

ME: Making the incarnation efficient? Doesn't that negate the whole point of the challenge of being incarnate, that a certain experience is supposed to be experienced without prior experience? Negating a karmic need!

A: Who said that an incarnation should be experienced without the benefit of experience? I certainly didn't and The Source didn't either. But I will say this, though. Each and every Aspect that is maintained in the state of partial communion will have experienced everything as if it was the first time, when it experiences it for the first time. It's just that over the number of states of individualization the Aspect gains experience in certain things, and so the difficulty of experience can be recalibrated to take account of the level of Aspect experience, to maximize that experience as a function of prior knowledge—in essence, making it harder, thereby increasing the efficiency of the incarnation. A TES therefore chooses to either have a full set of Aspects in partial communion, or a number of Aspects in partial communion with the rest of its sentient energy in full communion as the basis for its experiential plan. As I have previously described, the TES can create a temporary "thirteenth" Aspect that is a hybrid of the experiential and evolutionary components of the other twelve Aspects that are either in partial communion or are individualized (incarnate) in some part of the multiversal environment that would allow it to work with a certain environment that none of its current Aspects have experience of in the individualized state. Upon reintegration of this temporary Aspect the experiential and evolutionary content is shared between the Aspects whose components have been used, which ultimately adds on to the total TES evolution.

ME: How does the TES function when all of its Aspects are integrated in a state of partial communion?

A: Again, as I previously described, they function a little bit like the programs in a computer. Thinking of the TES in terms of a computer, it has access to all of the functionality of the programs (Aspects) and the data (experiential and evolutionary content) surrounding them and so uses them as a repository, an experiential and evolutionary memory database that is part of its Over-All self. In the last dialogue on this subject I described the Aspects in terms of souls and the TES as the Over-All soul, (the Over-Soul). Also note that the energetic volume of the sentient energies that are the Aspects in totality are only a small percentage (circa 30 percent) of that which is the TES.

ME: So if the TES is comprised of individualized sentient energies and that which remain as its "self," what is the process that the individualized Aspects of the TES go through upon reintegration to the point of partial communion?

A: To a certain extent at the start of reintegration there is similar process followed by the Aspect that is undergoing partial communion with that of the Aspect that undergoes full communion. As you are aware, the Aspect experiences significant memory-, knowledge-, and ability-based expansion when it separates from the incarnate vehicle upon its demise. It becomes that which it is when individualized from the TES but not incarnate, a fully functional and, to a certain level, independent Aspect of the TES sentience and energy set. However, although it can communicate without hindrance with the TES, and knows that it is an Aspect of the TES, it is uniquely individualized from the TES. This level of uniqueness is a product of the individualized work that it has done on behalf of the TES. The uniqueness is the total cumulative experiential and evolutionary content which can be expressed, in no specific order, in terms of its application of power, wisdom, and love—in essence, its specialized properties or personality.

It is this specialization, and the benefits of being specialized, that causes the TES to keep the sentience assigned to the individualized energies of the TES, which are the Aspect, in an individualized state, even in communion. This is why it is called partial communion. And so, the Aspect that undergoes reintegration to create a condition of what partial communion is undergoes the experience of expansion while being individualized twice, once at the point of the demise of the incarnate vehicle and once at the point of reintegration with the TES. Whereas, the Aspect that is due for full communion undergoes expansion only once while individualized because the momentary feeling of expansion experienced by the Aspect upon reintegration is dissolved when the sentient energies assigned to the Aspect become diluted into the overall sentient energy set of the TES. The Aspect, in experiencing partial communion, therefore experiences a second and more profound level of expansion, one that includes access to three sets of experiential memory, the Aspects' memories, the memories of other integrated and individualized Aspects, and those of the overall TES itself. Although these experiential memory sets are available to the Aspect reintegrating into partial communion they are not as instantaneously accessible to it as they are to the TES itself, it's more of a feeling of expansion than actual expansion. Think of it as being a localized version of the Akashic, one that is specific to the TES and its overall experiences. It's not the Akashic per se, though; I just use this description for illustrative purposes as the Akashic is a function of The

Source that is specific to experience that is based upon the incarnate human vehicle condition within the physical universe and no other incarnate vehicles.

ME: How does this localized memory work then?

A: The Aspect has instantaneous access to its own experiential memory set while individualized, but when integrated in partial communion it has access to other Aspect memory sets and the memory set of the TES only via its communion with the TES.

ME: From the perspective of the Aspect in partial communion I find that rather limiting. I think I prefer to be in full communion as an Aspect becomes truly one with its TES.

A: It's as good as it gets for the Aspect in partial communion. Actually, it's very good because the Aspect has to formally request access to the memory sets of the other Aspects that are in the states of individualization or partial communion. If the Aspect had full instantaneous access to all memory sets, it could create psychosis within the TES. You see, the TES has its own overall personality that is the sum of its own personal experiential memory and evolutionary content, and the memories of all its Aspects that are either individualized, in partial communion, or have been absorbed into full communion. If one or all of the Aspects gained full instantaneous access to all of these memory sets it/they would start to behave like it/they was/were the TES and not an Aspect/s of the TES. This of course is not a real problem because the total percentage of the sentient energies that the TES projects in an individualized form external to itself, and/or is in partial communion with, is no more than 30 percent. Based upon this, there is a significant difference in the mass, so to speak, of sentient energies between the TES and any or all of its individualized Aspects. Although not a real problem, it would and could cause a certain level of distraction for the TES in its need to remedy the matter.

149

The evolutionary content, by the way, is solely accrued by the TES and not the individual Aspects or Shards employed to perform this role. The evolutionary content is therefore only owned by the TES, The Source Entity, and ultimately The Origin, although in reality it can only ever be wholly owned by The Origin.

ME: So the Aspect in partial communion feels expanded and has permission-based access to the total experience of the TES and its Aspects?

A: Correct. But it also feels something else. From the perspective of the Aspect in partial communion it feels like they are connected again, part of a bigger organism so to speak, like being an essential piece of code in a computer program, one that has its own role and reason to be within a community of interconnected and integrated pieces of code within the program rather than being an isolated piece of code with no sight of its role or reason for being in existence. It feels rather cuddly.

ME: Cuddly?

A: Yes, cuddly. Like being whole but without experiencing personal un-wholeness, because you are part of the wholeness and not part of the separateness—the un-wholeness being the feeling that something is separate from you, that something is missing. You are reconnected to a much bigger part of yourself, rather than integrated.

ME: As a descriptor then, there is a difference between being reconnected rather than being reintegrated?

A: Think of it in these terms. Reintegration leads to a level of communion. Full communion is equal to full integration and partial communion is equal to reconnection—integration being assimilation by the whole, whereas connection is being connected to the whole.

ME: All of this is looking at it from the perspective of the Aspect, isn't it? How does the TES experience reintegration of the Aspect?

A: Simply put, it doesn't make that much difference to it.

ME: Why? I would assume that with up to twelve Aspects projected into the various frequencies of the multiverse it would make some sort of difference to it.

A: You forget that the TES remains connected to the Aspect at all times, and at all times is cognizant of everything that the Aspect experiences. That includes all of the experiences in all of the parallel conditions created by Event Space. Based upon this, there is no real feeling of separation experienced by the TES at any time, irrespective of how low down the frequencies an Aspect is projected.

ME: So it's only the Aspect that experiences expansion due to reintegration then?

A: In general, yes. You see, when the Aspect is projected into the lowest frequencies of the multiverse, the physical universe, it remains in the frequencies associated with its level of evolution and not that which its Aspects are projected into. As a result, it experiences everything as if it was in this frequential level and not that which the Aspect is projected into.

ME: But doesn't this go against what the Aspect experiences in the lowest frequencies, pure lack of communicative bandwidth?

A: This is only relevant to the Aspect because it is ultimately the Aspect that is experiencing the low frequencies and the loss of communicative bandwidth as a result. This is the whole reason for the TES to project an Aspect of itself into the low frequencies of the multiverse, to experience almost total separation while not actually being separate. But, it is only a small part of the TES that experiences this, and as a result the experience is limited to the Aspect itself, in respect that is to the loss of communicative bandwidth.

ME: How does the TES continue to experience that which the Aspect experiences then if the Aspect is experiencing a lack of communicative bandwidth?

A: Remember, the Aspect is located in a low frequency and so it has very limited functionality and communicative ability. From its perspective nothing exists above its frequential position. The TES on the other hand has access to all the functionality it has at the frequency attributed to its evolutionary level and so can see and experience everything it needs to in all levels below it.

ME: Yes, but how is this achieved? I mean, there must be some loss in the ability of the TES when it projects some part of its sentience into these low frequencies.

A: Correct, but that is only the sentience that is attributed to the energies that are the Aspect. The sentience that remains within the main body of the TES does not experience such loss of communicative bandwidth primarily because it is in a body of energy that is at a higher frequential state and can access all experience from this level.

ME: And again, how does it do this?

A: By accessing The Source Entity's energetic state.

ME: Sorry?

A: In accessing The Source the TES places itself in a temporary condition of Omnipresent sentience, that being, "it is" The Source. You know we are all one with The Source?

ME: Yes, of course.

A: Well, being one with The Source has its advantages, and in this instance the TES can enter into temporary communion with The Source to affect an uninterrupted level of connectivity with any or all of its Aspects and/or Shards that are projected from it and are personally experiencing the temporary levels of separation experienced in low-frequency environments. In this way the TES, when integrated with The Source in this temporary form of communion, experiences all that its Aspects and Shards are experiencing, as they are experiencing them.

ME: I have just been told that this is achieved only while in this temporary state of communion and that it uses Event Space in some way—that it experiences all Event Spaces created by its Aspects and/or Shards concurrently, and so in some respects experiences that which the Aspect and/or Shard is linearly experiencing before they actually experience it.

A: Yes. And an Aspect that is well connected, one that has a higher level of frequential state even when projected into the lowest frequencies, can access this information from the TES. This is how mediums can see the future, how they see another Event Space.

ME: So that is achieved by accessing the TES only?

A: Yes, and because a well-connected Aspect can access this information from its TES, it can also access all other events as well. Simply put, when an Aspect is connected to the TES in this way, it has access to all the information that the TES itself has while in communion with The Source.

Getting back to the question about what the TES feels upon the reintegration of an Aspect or Aspect and its Shards or Aspects and their Shards, it is not about the integration of the experiences and the memories, as I have just stated. It is more about the reintegration of the sentience and energies that they are assigned to in a holistic sense rather than operational sense. It's a bit like having full lungs and then breathing in to a higher percentage of fullness. The lungs don't notice anything different other than having more air. This is the same for the TES energetically and sentiently.

ME: Is there a real need for the Aspect to reintegrate with the TES then?

A: If you think of it in terms of the experiential memories, no, but if you think of it in terms of the TES and what it is holistically, sentient energy, then the answer is yes because the Aspect is just that, an Aspect of the TES itself and not separate from the TES. The only reason the TES projects an Aspect of itself into the lower frequencies of the multiverse is to experience near separation from Source, while not actually being separate. It can only do this via a smaller Aspect of itself, just as The Source can only experience itself fully by the use of the billions of TES it created to occupy the structure of the multiverse.

ME: Why is something like the life review performed if the TES knows what the Aspect has achieved in its state of near separation and existence in an incarnate state? It also seems pointless.

A: The life review in this instance is very important because it allows the TES to understand how well that Aspect of itself performed in this state of near separation. In essence, the TES lives, or should I say exists, in the incarnate through the Aspect, and so in this way it establishes how it may have performed if it itself had incarnated, and not just as a small or a series of small Aspects.

My illustration of using the lungs in a state of inflation and how the additional air affects them is quite relevant to how the additional sentience and energy affects the TES. In this instance, both the sentience and its assigned energy is part of the TES, even in projection, and so integration is not an increase in its overall condition, just as the air is either inside or outside the lungs. It is the same air, it's just that it's in a different location. The air exists within and without the lungs and is therefore "air" and so the TES sentience and the energy assigned to the Aspect exists within and without the TES boundary and is therefore the TES.

10

The Period in between Being Integrated with the TES and the Need to Incarnate

The information I was gaining through Anne was starting to shape up nicely. I was delighted with the combination of new information with links into the existing knowledge base. It not only validated the historical information but illustrated where we deviated from the true knowledge path due to our "Humanity"— the level of humanization resulting from the level of individualized total immersion in the physical we are experiencing through being incarnate. For me the humanized aspect of the existing knowledge was not only a distraction, it was a blockage, an inhibitor to knowing the real truth of what we are. It makes us forget what we are and makes us think that we are the human body and not sentience given a body of energy.

With this thought in mind I considered where we were going next with this dialogue. The logical step would be to move on to the space experienced before the next incarnation the Aspect embarks upon, but I had a feeling that this was not going to be an easy subject, simply because there is no real known information. What I mean is, everything we have to date is based upon our sentience being individualized as the Aspect or soul, which can be identified as being those periods when the Aspect is projected out from the TES in either the pre-incarnate, incarnate, or post-incarnate states that don't include the states of communion we may find ourselves in. Based upon this, I decided to find out what we do while in the state of communion.

10.1

What We Do while in Communion

A: First of all, you have to remember that there are two types of communion: full communion and partial communion.

ME: I expected that we would need to differentiate based upon the types of communion, but isn't it really only one state of communion that we will be discussing? Partial communion?

A: From the human perspective I would agree, but that only works because, when incarnate in the human form, we rely on the perspective of seeing things from the individualized sense and not the collective sense.

ME: Full communion is a collective condition then?

A: Sort of.

ME: What do you mean, sort of?

A: Well, as you are aware from the descriptions in your previous dialogues in *Beyond The Source—Book 2* and *The Origin Speaks*, a collective is not just a group of entities that work together in unison toward a single goal or outcome. There are different types of collective. In the instance of full communion, the collective state is transcended to the state of "Oneness." Partial communion is a collective state.

You're frowning again.

ME: Sorry, it's something I do these days.

A: You've always frowned; it's just that you can't see yourself.

ME: Mmmm. OK, back to the dialogue if you please. Let's start with what we do in the state of full communion.

A: Nothing in the singular sense.

ME: What do you mean nothing in the singular sense?

A: Like I said, nothing. As an Aspect that has either elected to be in full communion with its TES, or has been reintegrated by the TES into the state of full communion, there can be no relation to anyone or anything that is in the singular. In this instance, the sentience and the energy that was the Aspect is dissolved into the energies that are the overall TES energies. It becomes the overall sentient energies that are the TES mind, memory, experience, and evolution if you like. There is no individuality of any kind that is produced when an Aspect is reintegrated into the TES in this way. The Aspect becomes the TES.

ME: Can the TES reestablish those energies that were used as that Aspect for future incarnate use?

A: In essence, yes, but it is not easy because the TES would need to track down and recreate all of the specific energy/ies that were used and the sentience that was assigned to it/them. It would be a mammoth task but not one that is unachievable. It's just that the TES would need to look for those smaller Aspects of sentience that were exposed to the experiences incurred while individualized, and put them all together. In reality it's not something that the TES would do on a regular basis.

ME: Why not? I would have thought that the TES would only have to use its intention to reassemble all that represented the Aspect that was dissolved into full communion and it would happen.

A: Agreed, but a TES has a better way of achieving this.

ME: And that is?

A: Do you remember we talked about a hybrid Aspect, one where the total sentience and its body of energy is taken from some or all of the individualized sentient energy/ies of those Aspects that are currently in partial communion to create an Aspect that has an ideal set of specialisms for the environment it is being projected into?

157

ME: Yes, I do. Such an Aspect, although temporary in its individualized state, would be able to experience the incarnation it was planned for and only need to experience that incarnation once, not having to reincarnate due to the accrual of karma or missing some part of, or not fully experiencing, the desired set of experiences it was projected into.

A: Correctly remembered. Well, in this instance, those parts of the sentient energies that were taken from the Aspects that were in partial communion will have two signatures. The first is of the total experiential and evolutionary content associated with a specific Aspect. The second is the signature associated with the experiential and evolutionary content associated with an existence that was not experienced with the Aspect as a whole, but were associated with the sentient energies of other Aspects that it was integrated with to become the/a temporary thirteenth Aspect, so to speak. So, based upon this, when the thirteenth Aspect finishes its experiential and evolutionary commitments, and the sentient energies are separated out into the other integrated Aspects that are in partial communion, they are easy to separate out and be recreated as the thirteenth Aspect. Or, depending upon the configuration of such Aspects of Aspects, not to be confused with Shards by the way, this may be the temporary fourteenth, fifteenth, or nineteenth, etc., Aspect.

ME: So there can be multiple numbers of temporary Aspects created to suit the type of environment a TES wants to experience, the configuration of which are endless?

A: That's right.

ME: OK, based upon this, a TES would be able to project specialized Aspects into the lower frequencies of the physical universe pretty much all of the time, and in doing so it would be able to evolve fast because each incarnation would be optimized to suit the environment it was assembled for.

A: In general, this is correct, but a TES does not do this.

ME: Why not? As far as I can see it would be the best plan of all, wouldn't it? I mean, why would a TES project any Aspect of itself into the low frequencies of the multiverse knowing that doing so accelerates its evolutionary content, and then not create a specialist Aspect for every incarnation?

A: To experience growth.

ME: To experience growth?

A: Yes, experience growth. You see, it's not all about being incarnate in the most effective way. It's about growing from the experience, and growth can only really be achieved by learning from the experience. It's the ability to learn from an experience when in the experience that ensures that a TES doesn't always project into the experience the optimal Aspect for that experience. It's a bit like saying, I want to experience putting my hand in boiling water, and the hand is temperature resistant. In this instance, the true experience of placing the hand in the boiling water, feeling the discomfort or pain caused by the boiling water, then rapidly removing the hand, and later maybe feeling the sensation of the skin being burned, is not experienced.

ME: It looks like I have taken a wrong turn in my understanding then, as I thought that the best route was based upon experiencing the attributes of the low frequencies associated with the physical in the most efficient way possible, negating the need to perpetuate incarnation.

A: It is but it cannot be to the detriment to the prime direction of experiencing that which is planned to be experienced. I will explain further. The most important aspect of being incarnate is to experience, learn, and evolve. If the incarnation is made too easy by the use of an Aspect, or hybrid Aspect, that is too good, that is too specialized, then the opportunity to experience, learn, and evolve is negated.

ME: What is the point of a TES projecting an Aspect that is specialized into the incarnate condition then?

A: To create a dichotomy.

ME: Now you are playing with me!

A: No, I am not, my beloved. Listen. The whole point of being incarnate is to accelerate the evolutionary progression of the TES. That being, the whole reason behind a TES projecting part of itself into the frequencies associated with the physical is to establish ways that accelerate the learning opportunities to it that are only available through incarnation.

Sometimes this requires the TES to project part of itself into the physical that has a specialism relative to the environment and experiences planned, which may include the dissolution of some form of karma, hence the specialism. Remember, karma is an attraction or addiction to low-frequency thoughts, behaviors, actions, and sensations, and so when part of a TES, an Aspect, is attracted to the low frequencies of the physical universe through one or many of these functions, it needs to remove that attraction before it itself can ascend the frequencies. Through attraction to the low frequencies of the physical, the Aspect becomes a frequential anchor. In this case, it needs to send the Aspect that has this attraction back into a similar or same environment or circumstances to enable it to dissolve the attraction. So in this instance, the Aspect that is projected has a specialism relative to the environment, circumstances, and method/s of attraction/addiction by default. The specialism is created by the accumulation of experiences, ways/methods of dealing/responding with/to those experiences, and the number of times the experiences were experienced before the optimal response was achieved.

Sometimes this requires the TES to project part of itself into the physical that does not have a specialism relative to the environment and experiences planned, which may include the creation of some form of karma, and later the need to dissolve that karma. The creation and dissolution of the karma being part of the incarnate life plan—this being the dichotomy because this in itself specializes the Aspect in some way.

If we look at a hybrid Aspect that is created on a temporary basis from the specialisms found in a number of Aspects that are in partial communion, we see an Aspect that is designed to enter into an environment and its circumstances with a view to work with the experiences the environment presents to the Aspect in the most efficient way possible. The Aspect responds to the experiences with the correct method/s or responses on a right first-time basis without creating karma. Such Aspects are designed to perform a specific incarnate role and then leave without becoming attracted to the low-frequency thoughts, behaviors, actions, and sensations that are available when incarnate in the physical universe.

ME: And I would guess that this type of Aspect would be someone like Babaji, Jesus, Mohammed, or Buddha.

A: Correct. They incarnated, mastered themselves and their environment, taught other incarnates how to do the same, and left. But we have digressed somewhat, this is not answering the question of what we do while in communion with the TES.

ME: No, but it has put another part of the jigsaw puzzle in place. Thank you for digressing. I would like to ask a final question on this subject, though, before we realign ourselves.

A: Fire away.

ME: If we consider that the hybrid Aspect would be similar in status to Babaji, Jesus, Mohammed, or Buddha, then there have not been many hybrid Aspects created. Or have I got this totally wrong?

A: There are vast numbers of incarnations that are undertaken by hybrid Aspects. Most of them are not as publicly prominent as those you have just mentioned and so go about their incarnate duties in a most invisible way. Just look around you. You can easily spot one if you look for them. They are usually being in some form of unselfish service.

Also, note that Earth is not the only place where a TES can project an Aspect of itself into. The physical universe and the frequencies associated with it is a VERY big place, and there are myriad opportunities within it to incarnate via the hybrid Aspect route.

ME: Yes, of course. OK, thank you. This explains it.

A: Now, let's look at what we do while in communion. Actually you will find this rather unremarkable.

ME: Why? I would have thought that it would be rather interesting.

A: Let me explain what we do, and you can then decide if you find it interesting or remarkable, or not, as the case may be.

ME: I am sure it will be, but I am intrigued as to why you think it would be unremarkable.

A: Wait and see. As I have recently described, when an Aspect is reintegrated with the TES at the full communion level, it becomes the TES in totality and so there is no individuality to talk about or any function that is achieved on an individual or separate basis. The Aspect in this case is simply part of the overall TES sentient energy.

ME: Even though it can actually be traced by the TES if it wanted to use those specific sentient energies for a role if it decided.

A: Correct. In this instance, the individuality is created by the TES and not the Aspect because it is dissolved and its component energy is evenly distributed throughout the TES. When the Aspect is reintegrated with the TES at the partial communion level it maintains its individuality in one of three main ways.

The sentient energies associated with the Aspect are maintained in a fully individualized state while connected within the main body of sentient energy of the TES. Think of this as being a "bolt on" part to the TES within the TES which operates both as the individualized Aspect and as a component part of the TES. You may also think of it as a computer that is now connected to a network; it is separate from an individual perspective but is part of the overall structure of the network.

The sentient energies associated with the Aspect are maintained in a disseminated state. That being, they are dissected and positioned within the main body of sentient energy of the TES in areas where they are best placed based upon their level of functionality, experience, and evolutionary content and how it best serves the overall TES sentience on a macro level. In this state, the disseminated component parts of the Aspect act as if they are still connected together as one individual Aspect while being located in different areas within the TES. They are separately together.

The sentient energies associated with the Aspect are maintained in a dissolved state. That being, they are dissolved and positioned within the main body of sentient energy of the TES in areas where they are best placed based upon their level of functionality, experience, and evolutionary content and how it best serves the overall TES sentience on a micro level. In this state, the dissolved sentient energies of the Aspect act as if they are still connected together as one individual Aspect while being dissolved throughout the TES. They are together in separation, rather than being separately together, and as such experience the level of omnipresence that the overall TES itself experiences while still maintaining their overall individuality. This level of connectivity with the TES is the most beneficial to the Aspect and TES. It is like having computer programs within computer programs within computer programs.

ME: This third state is what I would have expected to see within the state of full communion.

A: No, it's a completely different state of communion. In full communion the Aspect totally loses its individuality to become the TES. In essence, the Aspect returns to its original state of nonindividualized beingness. In the third state the Aspect is still in a state of individualized beingness, it's just that its sentient energies are spread throughout the main body of TES sentient energy. This is a function of partial communion. In partial communion an Aspect maintains its individuality, irrespective of how its sentient energy is reintegrated back within the main body of TES sentient energy.

ME: How does the Aspect relate to the TES while in partial communion?

A: Ah! Now we can properly get on to what we do while in communion.

ME: Sorry?

A: The answer to this question directly answers the previous comment on what we do while in partial communion with our TES, and that it is unremarkable for my/our energetic perspective, that being, not incarnate.

ME: OK, let's go for it.

A: Well, once an Aspect is reintegrated within the main body of TES sentient energy, it becomes the TES, it is the TES, but it is also capable of individualized thought and contribution to the TES.

ME: And ... ?

A: And so it works as a fully functional and individually aware Aspect of the TES, doing what the TES wants that part of itself to do.

ME: Mmmm!

A: Don't "Mmmm" me! It's simple! Look, the Aspect in the state of partial communion is independent and individual and so acts as a subroutine in a computer program. However, in this case, although it works for the overall program, it can advise the overall program of other ways to manipulate or handle the data it is working with.

ME: So the Aspect is not as free as it was when projected from the TES?

A: No, it can't be. When an Aspect is projected out from the main body of the TES sentient energy it is allowed to work within the rules of the environment it is projected into. In the Earth environment of the physical universe this is fully individualized free will. This is the only time an Aspect can operate on a totally independent basis. As you are aware there are various other forms of free will that include various forms of collectivity as part of its functionality. The Aspect therefore works within the level of free will associated with the environment it is projected into. When the Aspect is in partial communion with its TES it has no free will, but it does maintain its individuality and ability to think in an individual way—all of it on behalf of its TES. It's just that this form of individuality is relative to it being a part of, an Aspect of, a larger, much larger, entity operating for and on behalf of the TES from an "internal" perspective in terms of functionality. Try to think of it in this way, that which we do when in partial communion with the TES is to perform as an integral component of the TES but with individual sentient intelligence that can allow us to optimize what we do as an integral Aspect of the TES.

ME: So we support whatever the TES desires, whatever it creates, whatever its intention is?

A: Yes, we become intelligent cells within a much larger cell, doing what is required to support the larger cell, the TES being a cell within a much larger cell—The Source Entity, which in turn is a cell within The Origin.

ME: You're right, it was unremarkable.

A: Told you so!

ME: Just one final thought. The thought that we maintain individuality but lose free will as a result of our communion with our TES may well be a cause for some concern with some readers.

A: I agree and understand. This is one of the reasons why the ego struggles to maintain its dominance over us while we are incarnate. The ego, created by the Aspect undergoing incarnation, in experiencing individualized free will, wants to maintain this condition, which of course is ultimately not a condition that we exist within normally.

I want to tell you something else, though, something that will help with your readers' understanding.

ME: Fire away.

A: The TES itself can enter into any of the forms of full or partial communion with The Source Entity, and in turn The Source Entity can enter into any of the forms of full or partial communion with The Origin. You see, ultimately we are all smaller Aspects of Sentient Origin energy. As a TES we have the free will to enter into any of these levels of communion with our Source Entity, just as our Source has the free will to enter into any of these levels of communion with The Origin. The result is the same but at different levels of expansion.

The reason why mankind is in fear of communion is because it is not experiencing it while incarnate. If it, the Aspect, was able to experience communion with the TES or The Source Entity while incarnate then there would be no fear of any form of communion.

ME: But we can experience communion while being incarnate. We can achieve this via deep meditation, what the Hindus call "Samadhi," what westerners call "Transcendental" meditation?

A: Yes, this is true but it takes dedication and many years of committed meditation to achieve such levels of connectivity. Many give up due to lack of success, which is only a product of continuous dedication.

ME: One more quick question before we move on to the next subject.

A: Just one?

ME: Yes, just one, I promise. It's just for clarification. Those Aspects that are projected into the low frequencies of the physical universe don't always enter back into communion, do they?

A: Not all do. Some TES elect to keep their Aspect/s outside of communion, specifically if they are following a certain type of incarnate speciality, or if they are involved in "back-to-back" incarnations.

ME: Ah! So, in this instance, does the Aspect retain its level of individualized free will?

A: No. Once an Aspect is withdrawn from its incarnate state it assumes its normal state of connectivity with its TES and the role it plays as an Aspect of TES sentient energy, even if its condition remains in the projected state.

ME: And the projected state doesn't affect connectivity?

A: Not while the Aspect is in the frequencies associated with the evolutionary state of the TES itself.

No, there is no degradation in the Aspect's communicative functionality with the TES while in the projected state. This only happens when incarnate, or in frequencies that are close to those used to create the physical universe.

ME: And all of these states are only available to the Aspect while the TES is in the evolutionary cycle associated with progression through the frequencies of the multiverse?

A: Correct. Once the evolutionary cycle has ended the TES has to decide whether to stay in the individualized condition separate to the main body of The Source's un-individualized sentient energies, or enter into one of the states of communion just described itself. In any of these states the TES will have reintegrated all Aspects and positioned them in the type of communion best suited to their experience and specialism. This of course is repeated at the Aspect level with reference to any Shards projected, which are always reintegrated back into full communion before an Aspect itself would be accepted back for communion.

ME: Thank you.

10.2

The Choice of Aspect to Incarnate

Having established that the Aspect can enter full communion, any form of partial communion, or remain in the projected state, either by its own choice or at the choice of the TES in the case of hybrid Aspects, it was hard to see how any report of existence in between incarnations can be considered the norm. Everything appeared to be in a state of flux from my limited understanding. Everything appeared to be individual, nothing was truly common or consistent to the point where it could be used as a good example for people to read and understand what they would do after the demise of the incarnate vehicle and the use of a new one. However, looking throughout the previous dialogues I have had with Anne, I did start to see a number of commonalities, the commonalities being that everything was based upon how the individual TES was evolving and how its Aspects were being used to support it. I also noted that certain processes used by each TES to establish the effectiveness of its Aspect/s ability to experience, learn, and evolve as a result of being incarnate were common, as was the need to improve this efficiency. I was just about to think that I had gone full circle in my current thought process by suggesting that there was no commonality and then finding it when Anne decided to advise me that things were not as common or commonly un-common as they would seem.

A: I can see that you are in a right muddle.

ME: You see that I almost deleted that paragraph. It's not as common or commonly un-common as they would seem. It's an example of what each and every Aspect does.

A: Nonsense. The whole process or set of processes we have discussed over the last eight months are repeatable. Everything can be achieved in a different way. This is the most important thing to come out of this dialogue. If everything was the same, or achieved in the same way, there would be no diversification of experience and no need for any of us to experience the myriad ways of progressing through the multiversal structure. Every TES and Aspect has a choice as to how to reconnect with itself and its experience. Some of the processes are multiversal, others are individual, but there is always commonality in the methods of reintegration, of communion. One of those commonalities is the process used to choose an Aspect to project into the physical universe via the incarnate route.

ME: Thank you for clarifying that for me. Yes, let's dive into the detail behind how a TES decides what Aspect it uses for a specific incarnation. Hold on! What am I thinking? We as human beings think/believe that the Aspect, the soul, is the entity that makes the decision to incarnate. That it is an individualized Aspect- or soul-based decision. This dialogue is about to change the direction of this thought to one where the TES is in total control and that the Aspect does exactly what the TES wants it to do—the fundamental decision process starting at the choice of Aspect to use in a certain incarnate opportunity.

A: Ultimately the TES does have the final say in which Aspect it uses for a certain incarnation, but this is not always the case.

ME: Can you elaborate?

A: It is the TES that is the primary individualized unit of Source Entity sentience, but as you are aware it can choose to delegate that responsibility to a smaller individualized

Aspect of its self. Based upon this, we have three options to discuss.

1. The TES making the decision as to which Aspect to project into incarnation, or other conditions of existence and its location within the TES body of sentient energy. The decision being based upon the experience required and the experiential and evolutionary status of the Aspect in terms of its contribution to the overall TES knowledge and evolutionary base. This can be split into two further groups based upon The Origin of the Aspect and evolution, if it is in full communion or one of the three substates of partial communion.

2. The TES making the decision as to which Aspect to use that is still projected and external to the main body of TES sentient energy. The decision being based upon the Aspect itself. The decision, for instance, being if it is still incarnate and/or if it conforms to any experiential or evolutionary requirements.

3. The Aspect itself making the decision to incarnate. This can also be split into two further groups based upon The Origin of the Aspect in terms of being in partial communion or if the Aspect is still projected and is external to the main body of TES sentient energy, either incarnate or disincarnate.

ME: This seems like a lot of nested conditions to me.

A: It is nested but there is some level of commonality which will help with understanding the process. The thing to note here, though, is the level of autonomy that the Aspect has— whether it is in communion or is in the projected state.

ME: And what is the difference in the level of autonomy?

A: Wait and see. Let's work with the first condition, with the TES making the decision as to which Aspect to project into incarnation, or other conditions of existence if its location is within the TES body of sentient energies.

It may well interest you to know that the TES also has to consider what role the Aspect is currently performing within its body of sentient energies as well as the level of communion it is experiencing to achieve this role.

ME: You mean an Aspect, although ideal for a certain incarnation, may be ideal for an essential role within the state of communion?

A: Correct. The TES decides upon which Aspect to use first by its experiential and evolutionary status, secondly by its current level of communion-based integration, and then by the importance of the role it is currently playing as an autonomous but fully integrated Aspect of the TES. If the Aspect conforms to the first two criteria but not the last, because the Aspect is performing a role that it cannot be removed from, then another Aspect is chosen.

ME: I would have thought that the TES would be able to swap out any Aspect for any Aspect?

A: Ultimately it can, but if the Aspect is performing a role within the body of sentient energies that it feels is important enough to leave it in, it will do so.

ME: Even if the opportunity for an efficient incarnation is placed at risk?

A: There is no risk.

ME: Why?

A: Because the TES will review the outcomes of the incarnation with all the possible Aspects that are a close fit and create an order of experience via Event Space. What I mean by this is that The Original Aspect chosen will ultimately be projected from the TES into the preferred incarnate state it was selected for; it's just that it will achieve this when it has finished its role within the TES body of sentient energies.

ME: OK, now it makes sense.

A: I want to focus for a moment on the Aspect that is in full communion, because this is a unique condition in comparison with those that are in partial communion or in the projected state.

ME: Please carry on.

A: Assuming that the TES has no issue with the use of the sentient energies that are now fully integrated with it and are part of its wider TES sentience, it may choose to use an Aspect that is now in full communion if The Original experiential and evolutionary content accrued by that Aspect is ideal for being placed in an autonomous and individualized projected state for a certain desired experience. This is because an Aspect can be used to experience any level of frequential environment or set of conditions in parallel with the TES experiencing other things—that being in, or the need to be in, the incarnate state. Also notice that as stated above the TES may decide to employ other Aspects within partial communion or even in the projected state that is not quite the same fit "first" by the use of Event Space. It can then later use the energies of the Aspect that did fit the bill when the role or roles or functionality/ies that it or its distributed sentient energies were employed for has either come to a natural end or can be safely extracted from the main body of TES sentient energies without detriment to the overall TES functions they were working within.

With the decision process made as to which Aspect to use, and that it is currently in the state of full communion, it searches within itself for all of the energies and sentience attributed to that Aspect and reconstructs it. The sentience being attached, or not as the case may be, to the energies they were initially assigned to—the TES achieves this by looking for the unique experiential and evolutionary signature that the sentient energies or stand-alone sentience or stand-alone energies gained as a result of being within an individualized Aspect that has experienced all that it has experienced and evolved on behalf of the TES to a level correlating to that experiential set.

When the Aspect is reconstructed, it is then educated as to its reason for being removed from full communion, separated (projected) out from the TES, and introduced to its guide and helpers. It then creates a life plan (the details of how this is created will be discussed in a subsequent dialogue) along with the selection of the human form or other incarnate form that the Aspect can take that will allow it to work within the environment that the opportunity for evolution is present. All of this will be discussed in further detail as we move through the process.

ME: How is this different to the Aspect that is in partial communion?

A: The extraction, so to speak, from being in communion has varying degrees of difficulty to perform, with extraction and reconstruction from full communion being the hardest to achieve, relatively speaking, due to the level of dissolution of the sentient energies associated with the Aspect. In essence, the Aspect is not an Aspect as such but more of a collection of energies that becomes an Aspect. With partial communion the TES is no longer dealing with a fully dissolved Aspect, but an Aspect that is either compartmentalized as one whole group of sentient energies that are located in a known area of the main body of TES sentient energies, or is separated out into a number of smaller groups of sentient energies that are located throughout the main body of TES sentient energies, the locations and roles of which are known. In both of these instances, the Aspect remains in an individualized state while in communion. This is why it is called partial communion—partial communion being only a state of energetic connectivity, with the sentience remaining individualized while still performing a task or series of tasks for the TES. The Aspect's sentience has the ability to link all the separated energies together while they are in different locations, and so they still operate as one. Based upon this, the Aspect that is in partial communion, either whole or separated, is much easier to extract because it remains as a fully functioning individualized Aspect of the TES and not TES sentient energy. Suffice to say, the separation and projection of both of these Aspects is the same. The only difference is the need to collect the component parts of the Aspect that is separated out within the main body of TES sentient energies. The separated Aspect works with the TES, once it is aware of its new role, by actively collecting itself together as one, it then awaits the TES's decision as to when it will be projected. The functions of the separate components of the Aspect that were being performed on behalf of the TES need to be completed by these components, though, so if the TES decides that it wants to use an Aspect that is separated, it employs the use of Event Space to ensure that all separated components of the chosen Aspect become free of their tasks concurrently. Once this is achieved, it is projected out from the main body of TES sentient energies and introduced to its guide and helpers. It then creates a life plan along with selecting the human or other form that the Aspect can take that will allow it to work within the environment that the opportunity for evolution is present—just the same as the Aspect that was reconstructed from full communion.

The easiest extraction by far is the Aspect that remains in the "whole" state within the main body of TES sentient energies. In this instance, the Aspect will be performing either a whole function for the TES or will be being used as "additional processing power."

ME: What do you mean, "additional processing power?"

A: An Aspect that is retained in its whole state while being in partial communion has two main functions: one to remain functionally separate while enjoying the connectivity that being in communion offers; or two, participating in any function that the TES requires it to do that can in fact be performed on its own. This is the whole point of remaining individual and whole while in partial communion, to be able to experience communion or perform tasks for the TES in isolation to the rest of the TES while still being within the main body of TES sentient energies. From the perspective of the TES it is just like having the Aspect projected outside of its main body of sentient energies while also being able to use it for individual tasks. From the perspective of the Aspect it is just like being projected outside the main body of TES sentient energies while also being able to be in communion with its TES and be of service. If in rare occasions the Aspect is not functioning on behalf of the TES, it can be projected outside of the main body of TES sentient energies straight away and advised of its new role. If the Aspect is functioning as additional processing power for the TES, the TES either waits for the Aspect to finish the task and then projects it external to its main body of sentient energies and then advises it of its new role, etc., or places the Aspect in an Event Space where the function can be completed in a parallel environment, allowing it to work on its life plan and human or other form selection in the right chronological order, so to speak, chronology being a function of the lowest frequencies of the physical universe.

ME: What happens if the circumstances of the opportunity are lost due to a delay in projecting the Aspect external to the main body of TES sentient energies?

A: Simply put, the TES changes the location of the Aspect from the Event Space it is occupying to one where the circumstances are still in play. Don't forget, linearity is only a function of the lowest frequencies of the physical universe in one specific Event Space. Other Event Spaces can be accessed and the start point can be reestablished at will by the TES.

ME: So the opportunity is never lost.

A: No—never.

ME: And the process thereafter and before incarnation is similar or the same for all Aspects?

A: By and large, yes. All Aspects that are projected into the low frequencies of the physical universe and that enter into the incarnate state, and are following the experiential desires of their TES, follow similar processes of preparation—the preparation being relative to the TES and the desired experiential work. This process only changes when the Aspect is in control of its own experiences. Not all Aspects that are projected away from the main body of TES energies have free will. Those that don't have free will are undergoing the process of post- or pre-incarnate work and will be reintegrated into one of the states of communion or have been recently removed from communion and projected external to the main body of TES energies. Once projected or while still in projection the TES can use the Aspect in any experiential way it sees fit.

ME: When does the process change to when the Aspect is in control of its own experiences?

A: When an Aspect is given individualized free will and is left in the projected state external to the main body of TES sentient energies.

ME: What mankind experiences?

A: What some of mankind experiences.

ME: I don't understand.

A: I will explain further.

I stated that not all of mankind experiences this, shall I say, "continued" state of projection. Some enter into one of the various states of communion as previously described and so an Aspect that incarnates in the human body cannot have its energetic experience described in the words of "what mankind experiences," because Aspects that incarnate don't always stay in the projected state or experience incarnation in the human body. Some choose never to incarnate in the human body. Also note that "mankind" is not what we really are. We are Aspects of our TES who use the human body, along with others in the physical universe, as a means to experience existence in the lowest frequencies of the multiverse in the way they are supposed to be experienced, as if one is of that frequency.

This is a problem with incarnate mankind because most, if not all, of the channeled information that has been published, broadcast, or lectured on is based upon contact with Aspects that are in the projected state. Moreover, most are still close to the Earth from an experiential perspective. This means that they give a very human viewpoint on their post- or pre-incarnate experience. In this projected state they work close to the frequencies that are used in the incarnate condition because it makes reincarnation easier.

ME: Why does it make reincarnation easier?

A: It makes it easier for the projected Aspect because it is exposed to the lower frequencies of the multiverse while not actually being in those of the physical universe. Think of it in terms of being like a saturation diver, an oil rig diver, where they are kept at certain depths so that they can work on the sea bed without having to decompress every time they finish the task that required them to work in the water.

ME: The Aspect doesn't "decompress" that frequently in this case then?

A: No, of course not, but the level of sentient freedom is increased the closer to the TES the Aspect gets frequentially.

ME: And the level of connectivity doesn't get affected too much?

A: Not drastically. When I mentioned that the level of sentient freedom is increased this means the sentience driving the energies. Then, I mentioned that the level of sentient freedom is increased, this means that the use of reincarnation is made easier. It can do this without entering into the state of communion.

ME: So if the Aspect remains in the projected state and that state is in the lower frequencies of the multiverse doesn't this maintain the ego—the temporary personality created as a function of incarnation?

A: No, the ego is always dissolved when an Aspect is released from the incarnate state. I will say it again; the Aspect has full connectivity with the TES once disincarnate, even when in the projected state at lower frequencies. It is the level of freedom the sentience experiences that changes.

ME: Thank you. This explains things for me. Now, getting back to those Aspects that have free will and stay in the projected state, you said that they can choose their own incarnations.

A: I want to make one thing clear, though, before I start. In general, when an Aspect is in any of the states of partial communion, it maintains its individuality but loses its free will. It loses its free will simply because it is in communion and is functioning solely for the benefit of the TES functionality from a holistic perspective. When the Aspect is maintained in the projected state this is because the TES wants the Aspect to stay in that state. It wants the Aspect to experiment with its own level of willfulness—with free will. Part of this level of will is the ability to pick and choose certain experiences, the content associated with the experiences, and the planning and analysis behind the experiences. An Aspect, in this instance, is totally in control of everything it has, will, or could experience.

Based upon this, the Aspect has to make judgments as to what it can experience without accruing attachment to the sensations, thought processes, and behavioral patterns associated with low-frequency immersion (incarnation), if low-frequency immersion is what a projected Aspect with free will wishes to experience, that is.

ME: Not all projected Aspects incarnate then?

A: No. The vast majority, and in comparison with the total number of TES created by The Source Entity, and the number of Aspects that are in the projected state, the number is small.

ME:OK. So the projected Aspect gets to do all of the work associated with understanding its own evolutionary content. That being, the evolutionary content of the TES that is associated to its contribution, planning the experiences that will augment that evolutionary content, choosing the environment to have those experiences in, choosing the best incarnate vehicle to have those experiences in, establishing ways to avoid low-frequency attractivity to karma, establishing ways to remove low-frequency attractivity, creating the life plan, and choosing suitable Aspects that can act as a guide or helpers. That was a long sentence.

A: Yes, it was, but that is about the size of it. Of course, the Aspect can utilize the memory functionality of The Source Entity that is associated with incarnating in the human body, the Akashic, as a point of reference and for scenarios associated with the mainstream life plan and the associated Event Spaces that could be created within the life plan. The guide and helpers will be available from a group of Aspects that are either projected or are in one of the states of communion within other TES. The Aspect will choose one that it either has prior experience of, and this can be long-term experience in terms of the work they have done together, its ability to assist in the overall evolutionary opportunity available in the chosen incarnation, or its skill in guiding other Aspects in the environment and experiential set that the Aspect has chosen. Please note that this is only an overview. We will go into some more detail on this subject later.

ME:You also mentioned that the Aspect may be able to choose its level of personal experience when it is in one of the states of partial communion. I thought you said that all Aspects lose their free will when in communion?

A: I did and I haven't forgotten. In some instances, an Aspect is allowed to retain its free will while in one of the states of communion, usually one where the level of dissolution within the main body of TES energies is minor. This means that the decision process is initiated while in communion but the rest of the process must be orchestrated when projected external to the main body of TES energies. To elaborate further, in these cases the Aspect decides on what it wants to achieve while it is in communion and then initiates separation. It decides on what it wants to action to put its plans into action. It is only in the projected state that the Aspect can access the Akashic, guide, helpers, and environment it needs to complete its plan, its life or experience plan. These Aspects tend to be very highly experienced/evolved Aspects. You might call them ascended masters if you want to because they will have progressed beyond the need to incarnate to assist in the evolution of their TES. This is why they remain in the state of being individualized—with individualized free will—while in communion; they are important Aspects of the overall TES sentience.

ME: OK, let's go backward a moment and assume we are talking about an Aspect that is in partial communion and has been chosen for projection.

A: OK. Let me first of all finalize the last dialogue. There are many Aspects that are highly evolved. Many, if not most of these, no longer need to incarnate and so therefore stay within the state of communion with their TES. A large number of them go into service and become guides or high-level helpers for other incarnate Aspects or even guides and helpers for whole incarnate civilizations. This is irrespective of size or distribution within or without a galactic locale. In the event that they decide to act as a guide/helper they invariably need to enter into some form of what I will call semi-separation from their TES. This means they commune with their TES and request projected status based upon the presentation of their own desires and how these desires will help to increase the evolutionary content of the TES. Once these desires are agreed with the TES, the Aspect is allowed to separate the energies that their particular individualized TES sentience is assigned to, into a state that is external to the main body of TES sentient energies. They become a smaller body of TES sentient energies, an Aspect, with a small link of sentient energies that are perfectly capable of allowing full communicative function between the Aspect and the TES. In this state, these Aspects are in constant communion with their TES even though they are, for all intents and purposes, individualized and separated. Notice that I used desire in the first instance and not intention.

ME: Why? I thought that intention preceded thought, which preceded action? No mention of desire in that train of thought!

A: Correct, but desire precedes intention for it is the area of the sentience where prototype intentions are made. I will explain the process in summary. When an entity has a desire it can be like wishful thinking with no intention to go out and make that desire come to fruition. However, when an entity has a desire for a certain creative outcome, it can work around that desire by changing the desired outcome to suit certain conditions. It may still have no intention to make that desire come into fruition. When the desire is acceptable to the entity, in all of its outcomes, it can then use its intention to make it happen. Once intention is invoked, thought about how to make the intention surrounding the desire manifest is created, which results in the actions required to create that manifestation.

ME: For the record then, and to simplify this even further, I see the following process surrounding the manifestation of creative desire.

Initial Desire—Modified Desire—Final Desire— Intention (to create the desire)—**Thought** (on how to create the intended desire)—**Action** (the creation or manifestation of the intended desire).

181

A: Very well done.

ME: Thank you; this clarifies things further for me. Moving on, at this point the Aspect is largely autonomous then?

A: Totally, and that is the whole point. I will describe the commonality between an Aspect in partial communion with free will with one that is in partial communion without free will in a moment because the actual separation process, and actions supporting the incarnation process, are identical once the Aspect is identified by its TES for separation/projection, or has decided to become separated/projected from the TES by its own free will.

In variance to the Aspect in partial communion with free will having to discuss its desire for experience, and that it is best achieved via separation/projection outside of the main body of TES sentient energies before initiating separation, the Aspect that does not have free will is selected by the TES to perform a certain desire of the TES itself. I have alluded to this before but I won't illustrate it again.

In this instance, the overall TES sentience is active in making the decisions on what it wishes to experience to augment its current evolutionary content and subsequent progression.

ME: You just said the TES is to experience, to augment the decisions. Is the TES not making the decisions on its evolutionary progression normally?

A: Not always. Many TES allow their Aspects to make the decisions, just to see what happens when they don't make the decisions for them. This is normal and is what The Source Entity does with all TES; it lets them make the decisions.

ME: Isn't it devolved responsibility?

A: It's not devolved responsibility because in the case of the TES it is a smaller individualized unit of The Source, and in the case of the Aspect, at least when in separation from the TES, it is a smaller individualized unit of the TES, and so on with the Shard and the Aspect. In fact, no matter how small the level of devolution is, it is ultimately The Source that is making the decisions anyway. Looking at it from another perspective, it is ultimately The Origin that is making the decisions because The Origin is the ultimate creative force and everything is ultimately made from the energies and sentience that is The Origin.

ME: Got it!

A: Getting back to the TES then. The TES is, of course, cognizant of all it has experienced, will experience, or could experience, and so its decision to project an Aspect of itself into a lower frequency is simply an experiment. It is an experiment in understanding how a part of itself would perform if it didn't have this ability to see all that is past, present, or future and all the Event Space–based permutations created by duality, triality, and quadruality, etc., etc. It is also an experiment in how much it will experience, learn, and evolve as a result of the experiment and the environment the experiment is set in. So, it has a number of choices when it decides on which Aspect to use.

1. Use an Aspect that has NO prior experiential knowledge of the experience it may be selected for. This would gain the maximum experiential and evolutionary content for the experience because everything would be new. An issue here, though, is the accrual of karma.

2. Use an Aspect that HAS prior experiential knowledge of the experience it may be selected for. This would gain the minimal experiential and evolutionary content for the experience because everything should be known, and the way to act and react in the situations that present themselves would be readily available. This should allow minimal accrual of karma.

3. Use an Aspect that has LIMITED prior experiential knowledge of the experience it may be selected for. This would gain nominal experiential and evolutionary content for the experience because not all ways to act and react, or the best karma-free responses in the

183

situations that present themselves, would be readily available. This should allow nominal accrual of karma.

4. Use an Aspect that is a hybrid of all Aspects that HAVE full experiential knowledge of any of the sub-experiences within the main experience it may be selected for. This would gain almost no experiential content for the experience because every action and reaction is known in the perfect sense with no mistakes being made. This should allow no accrual of karma. This Aspect would be used to make big changes for other incarnate Aspects, such as being a guru, avatar, president, or other leader on the world/universal stage.

Once the decision has been made as to which Aspect is to be used, or which components of other Aspects are to be used to create a hybrid Aspect, the Aspect is briefed, for want of a better word, on what it is to achieve and the environment that it is to achieve it in. Once this process is finished, the Aspect is exposed to the separation process, and when this is complete, it is given free will in order to make plans on how it will achieve its task.

11

Separation from the TES

A: Separation from the TES employs the same process whether the Aspect is chosen for separation/projection, or due to having free will, has chosen it itself. Therefore, the process for separating the Aspect from the main body of sentient TES energy is the same whether it is actioned by the TES or a highly evolved Aspect *[see "major sentient component" later in this dialogue because a highly evolved Aspect is really a function of the TES itself —GSN].*

ME: It's nice to know some things are common.

A: Yes, it is, and this is one of them.

As you are aware the Aspect is in one of three states of partial communion. Dissolved energy, component compartmentalized energy, and wholly compartmentalized energy. The dissolved and component compartmentalized energy-based Aspects first need to be placed into the same state as the wholly compartmentalized energy-based Aspect. I will describe the first two as separate items and then continue with the description with the wholly compartmentalized state.

When the Aspect is in the dissolved state, the TES or the highly evolved Aspect itself has to seek out the locations of all those small dissolved parts of sentient energy that has the same signature as the Aspect that is to be reconstructed/ reassembled. When all of the locations of these dissolved sentient energies are identified, the TES or a major component of the sentience of the Aspect projects the desire, intention, and thought required to create a form of sentient attractivity as its action. When this is in place, the sentient energies that are the Aspect start to gravitate together under a form of natural attractivity. In this way they are naturally drawn together.

The TES or major area of Aspect sentience, having projected the initial desire for reconstruction, then waits for the sentient energies to gravitate together. Before this happens, though, the desired intention needs to populate the total area of the main body of TES sentient energies in order to find those smaller sentient energies of the right signature and program them with the desired intention of reconstruction/reassembly.

ME: How does that work?

A: Desired intention is a very powerful communicator. It makes no assumption relating to the location of where a component of sentient energy of the Aspect under reconstruction resides within the TES. It elects instead to tell every minute component of the TES, no matter how small, of the desired intention to reconstruct an Aspect and what the signature of that Aspect is. In this way, all sentient energies pass the desired intention on to all surrounding sentient energies, who in turn pass on the desired intention to all sentient energies that surround it. Think of it in terms of a multifrequential version of the 2, 4, 8, 16, 32, 64, 128, 256, 512, etc., etc., mathematical progression. In this way, the desired intention passes through each sentient energy in an exponential cascade that is always recreated the moment it is received by another component of sentient energy that has not yet received it. As each component of the "correct" sentient energy is contacted, it instantaneously changes its state from wanting to be in its state of separation relative to its state of partial communion within the base area of TES sentient energies, to needing to be in communion-based connectivity with sentient energies of the same signature in a collective "Aspect-" and not "TES"-based function. Additionally, these sentient energies of the same Aspect signature send out forces of "attraction" that seek out the sentient energies of the same signature.

ME:I have just received an image that this actually accelerates the process of reconstruction, because they literally meet in the middle and pull each other together.

A: Yes, it is a fast process. You could call it a "viral" process, except that it would be viral to the power of twelve!

ME:It's that fast?

A: What I have described appears to be slow, whereas in actuality it is instantaneous.

ME:What time frame would instantaneous be, let's say from the point of initial desire to the wholly completed reconstruction of the Aspect?

A: It is the speed of desire, which is faster than the speed of intention, which is faster than the speed of thought, which in turn is faster than the speed of action.

ME:What is the speed of desire? I have heard of the speed of thought!

A: It would be difficult to explain in human language but suffice to say it is as fast as, in human terms, having the initial desire for a certain product of desire flash across your mind to seeing the end product manifest in front of you at the same moment as the desire starts to leave the mind.

ME:I have just experienced that. It's like the desire was always manifest. Like there was never a time when the desire wasn't in existence!

A: That's correct. That's what instantaneous means.

ME:Now I understand, yes, now I understand. The speed of desire is quick, quick beyond belief.

A: Yes, it is, and it is just as quick in manifestation in the lowest frequencies of the physical universe as well. Soooo, be careful what you desire or wish for.

ME: A wish is a desire?

A: Yes, it's a desire in disguise.

ME: Interesting.

A: Isn't it.

ME: Getting back to the dissolved Aspect that is in partial communion, what happens once the Aspect is reconstructed?

A: You are jumping ahead of yourself; we need to discuss the Aspect that is in a larger compartmentalized state first.

ME: OK, let's go for it, it can't be much different to what you have just shared with me.

A: It's not, that is, except for what I am about to tell you.

ME: What's the difference?

A: I will explain. When an Aspect is in the dissolved version of partial communion, the desire to become whole again either comes from the TES or that area of dissolved sentient energies that are close enough together to create an area of major sentient activity; that being, enough activity to make the decision, or more importantly to have the desire to reconstruct itself to being "wholly" represented sentient energies. When it is compartmentalized into, say, four or five, or more, areas of sentient energy/ies, it is usually the largest area of sentient energies that creates the desire to become whole and then projected into separation and then incarnation or location into one of the energetic simultaneous universes of an Aspect.

ME: Doesn't this require a need to be reconstructed before the desire can come into play?

A: Yes, of course. The desire to become whole is a function of the need to experience a certain experience and gain the subsequent learning and evolutionary content associated with it. This is also a function of the major area of sentient activity, for it is that area that creates the desire to incarnate again, among other opportunities.

ME: Among other opportunities?

A: Not all Aspects that are projected from the main body of TES sentient energies are reconstructed with a view to being incarnate, they are also used to experience any part of the different simultaneous universes that the Aspect or TES has either not experienced or has a desire to experience in a differing or similar way. Of course all of this is before the plan of exactly what to experience has been ratified with the TES—ratification being required if the Aspect is the driving force behind the desire to incarnate, or experience an Aspect of a simultaneous universal environment. We can discuss this in the next chapter, so to speak.

ME: So the largest area of compartmentalization, that with the largest area of sentient energies, is the one that initiates the desire for a certain experience and then broadcasts the desire to become reconstructed to the other compartmentalized components?

A: Correct, and, as with the speed of reconstruction, it is an instantaneous function of desire. The only difference is that the exponential cascade effect is not necessary because the sentient energies are grouped together in compartments. It is therefore the compartments that use the forces of desire-based attraction to become wholly represented as one Aspect of TES sentient energy.

ME: What about the work that these sentient energies are doing for the TES? What is the process for decoupling those energies that have a role within the wider area of base TES sentient energies that are now being requested for reconstruction?

A: They finish their work.

ME: OK, they finish their work! How can they finish their work and become instantaneously reconstructed?

A: The desire to be reconstructed with the whole "Aspect" opens a gate, so to speak, with a certain tract of Event Space that is used specifically for the termination of any current workload that any area of sentient energy is working on, no matter how big or how small that workload is.

ME: What happens to any downstream workload? Is it dropped, left behind, or forgotten?

A: No, it is assigned to another area or other areas of sentience within the TES; that being TES or Aspect in full or partial communion. This is done complete with the previous experience or knowledge of that or those sentient energies that were originally performing the role but were identified for reconstruction.

ME: So it looks like there are no "processing" holes left as a result of the desire for a certain Aspect in communion being reconstructed.

A: No. None!

ME: And, once we have the Aspect in a state of being fully reconstructed it can undergo the process of separation from the main body of TES sentient energies?

A: Yes, we can.

ME: And this includes the Aspect that was already in the wholly compartmentalized state of partial communion?

A: Yes, it does.

ME: I imagine this is a simple process.

A: It has its simple parts and it has its not so simple parts.

ME: OK, explain away.

A: In actuality, this is a process that is almost always created by the TES and not the Aspect.

ME: Why almost always? I would have thought that the TES would be the one who supervised the separation except for those times when an Aspect of high evolution is selected or selects itself.

A: It is, but as you alluded to there are rare occasions when it is the Aspect itself that creates the separation. We should really discuss this in isolation, maybe toward the end of this dialogue, but I can see that it is appropriate to discuss it in a summarized way now.

ME: Why is it rare?

A: Because this is when the Aspect is simply a vehicle for the main body of TES sentience to experience the lowest frequencies of the multiverse, the physical universe, itself, rather than an individualized Aspect of its sentience being selected to do the job for it.

ME: What you are saying then is an Aspect never actually drives the separation/projection process from the main body of TES sentient energies, even though the Aspect is individualized within them? And, that this also suggests that any highly evolved Aspects are really only the main body of TES sentience projected into a smaller body of its energies.

A: Correct. It is only when the TES is using an Aspect of its sentient energies as a house for a major component of its sentient energies that that Aspect is able to initiate and drive the separation process.

ME: When would a TES decide to project a major component of its sentience into a smaller vehicle, an Aspect of itself?

A: When it has a significant role to play within a specific universal environment, one that needs a certain level of functionality to make the changes necessary or desired and that these changes are on a global scale, for want of a better word. Maybe even galactic or bigger.

ME: Now I get it. In these circumstances it needs a high level of TES sentience to make these "changes" possible.

A: Yes, it does. As you can imagine, these types of change are not insignificant, and some of these levels of change are written in mankind's history. For example, a flood, major falls and rises in civilizations, the movement of planets, etc., etc.

Getting back to the process of separation, once the sentience that is the Aspect is whole, the TES relocates it close to the periphery of its main body of sentient energies, creates a teardrop, so to speak, and populates it with the sentient energies that are the Aspect. It then moves this teardrop fully external to its main body of sentient energies and projects it into an area of frequency that is lower than that occupied by the TES where it can plan on how to successfully integrate with the desired experience in the environment it is desired to be experienced within, in its newly separated state. From this point onward it is the responsibility of the projected Aspect to create and identify the conditions that will allow it to be successful in this task, with no level of experience being deemed as a failure as all experience creates learning and the accrual of evolutionary content.

11.1

Deciding on What to Plan the Incarnation On, Having Had the Desire Affirmed by the TES

So far this particular section was settling into a theme that was holistically similar to that already broadcast by other spiritual authors, albeit, from the perspective of the subject headings. What was new news was the deeper information surrounding the subjects. I was acutely aware that I may well have mentioned this before, more than once, but I felt the need to display my thoughts just one more time. Again, I thought, these common headings will be the bridge for those people who are familiar with the subjects associated with the incarnation process, but who want to know more information about what lies behind it.

This next subject heading was missing something, though. It was making the assumption that the decision on what to plan the incarnation on was the responsibility of the Aspect, but affirmed by the TES as being bona fide. I knew from previous dialogues that the TES itself also had reasons for projecting an Aspect external to its main body of sentient energy and wanted to make sure that I captured all areas of interest. I was just about to consider this further when Anne came in to make things clear. It would seem that things are not so clear, though!

A: I gave you these headings to work with, and I would suggest that you need to read them and the space in between them.

ME: Are you suggesting that I need to read in between the lines?

A: Yes, of course. We will deal with the function of the TES in this instance first and then continue with the function of the Aspect directly afterward.

In the event of the TES making the decision to project an Aspect of itself into whatever environment it chooses to experience a certain experience, it also has an idea of how it wants to experience it and so directs the Aspect as such. In terms of an incarnate experiential desire, the life plan is described in overview to the Aspect and the Aspect is allowed to fill in the rest of the detail, the subject of the incarnation being already decided by the TES. All the Aspect has to do in this instance is illustrate how it can be achieved and in what way it will achieve it. This process, being similar if not the same as an Aspect that has chosen to incarnate by its own volition, will be described as such. Suffice to say, once the TES has decided on what it wants to experience and has identified an Aspect to experience it on its behalf, it allows the Aspect to do the rest of the work.

ME: The TES gives the Aspect its free will at this point then?

A: Yes and no. Initially, yes, the Aspect has to have free will to be able to create the life plan and to involve all of the Aspects that will also be incarnate to interact with the Aspect in their correct order of interactive appearance, and that the order is optimal to the learning and evolutionary content accrued by the Aspect while incarnate. Not forgetting, of course, the way in which the Aspect interacts with the environment itself. If the incarnation is on the Earth and is in the same frequential state as you are in now, the Aspect retains its individualized free will. If, however, the Aspect incarnates in one of myriad other incarnate vehicles available to it in the low frequencies of the physical universe it will relinquish its individualized free will to the version of "will" that is associated with the incarnate vehicle it is going to work with and its version of civilization it has to interact with.

ME: Are you suggesting that there may be different variations on the theme of an experience that a specific incarnate vehicle or form may be used for?

A: I am not suggesting it; it is a fact. For information, the human vehicle is not only used on the Earth. As you can see from the diversity of the human race, it is not possible for so many variants to come from the same planet. Each of them has been used to seed the planet with a variant of the human form that was in harmony with the changes in the frequencies and environmental conditions as they (the incarnate vehicles) descended the frequencies. All of them being the third variant in terms of density and referring to their description in your first book, *The History of God*.

ME: And the version is adopted at the point of incarnation?

A: Yes, it's adopted at the point of incarnation but the functionality of the incarnation is taken into account from the start of the creation of the life plan.

ME: Thank you. We should continue on the subject of the heading.

A: Yes, we should. In the case of the Aspect making the decision on what to base the incarnation on, it needs to conform to a number of prerequisites before it can be agreed with the TES and therefore before continuing with the plan.

In essence, the TES, in recognizing how rare a resource the incarnate vehicles are that are used within the physical universe, needs to ensure the experience, learning, and evolutionary content that will be accrued as a result of the incarnation is enough to justify the use of the incarnate vehicle.

ME: The use of a body needs to be justified? That seems extreme.

A: No, it's not. You see, the TES and the Aspect know all too well that experiencing the environment offered by the lowest frequencies of the multiverse experiencing the environment, via incarnation, provides the most efficient route to gaining evolutionary content, and so the TES wants the overall plan of what the incarnation is based upon to illustrate that it will provide the maximum evolutionary opportunity, the biggest bang for your buck, so to speak. Based upon this, the plan should include the following:

1. The ability to address existing karma and break the links to other entities and/or low-frequency addictions or attractions that the Aspect has accrued.

2. Experiencing existence from a different direction than that previously experienced. Seeing both or multiple sides of the coin, so to speak.

3. Experiencing something completely new.

4. The illustration of ways to improve communications with the Aspects who become the guide and helpers.

5. Understanding how many helpers are required and how the guide and the helpers can benefit from an evolutionary perspective through this incarnation.

6. Showing new or existing pathways to self-realization negating the need for further incarnation.

7. Ways in which the Aspect can affect a wider population (global) from an evolutionary perspective.

8. Ways in which the Aspect can be of service.

9. The number of Event Spaces that can be created and therefore the number of ways in which parallel evolution can be accrued.

10. Knowing how many other Aspects will need to be working with the Aspect.

11. Understand how many direct interactions are required by other Aspects and identifying who they are and what roles they will play.

12. Knowing the level of profundity expected in the personalized experiences.

ME: This does explain personalized experiences. I imagine that it covers all corners rather well.

A: It does. When the Aspect can give in-depth examples of how these requirements can be met, recognizing that the Aspect is unable to know these requirements when incarnate, the TES then allows the Aspect to commit to the process of planning the functional detail behind the incarnation. It decides on where to incarnate, what body to use, and its longevity.

11.2

Where to Incarnate, How Long to Stay

ME: I am somewhat confused. I expected the detail behind the twelve points above, that being the examples that are given to the TES, to include such detail as where the incarnation will be located, the duration of the incarnation, and of course the body to be used.

A: No. The points above are an overview that is presented to the TES on the functional detail that can be integrated within the plan.

ME: It all seems a bit backward to me. I would have expected the body and the family the body will be born into to be part of the initial twelve-point justification.

A: Well, it isn't. The work I have just described is the way in which the desired outcomes of the incarnation are established. The incarnate vehicle and the family the vehicle is born into is one of the last things that are decided upon.

ME: OK, so what's decided?

A: The Aspect now has a plan of what it wants to experience and the desired outcomes attributed with those experiences. This is the minimum requirement necessary for it to use the interactive Event Space and memory of The Source Entity that is attributed to the genre of incarnate vehicle expected to be used for the incarnation. In the instance that the incarnate vehicle is based on the human form it is the Akashic.

ME: I had an interesting thought just go through my mind that the Akashic is not just used for the human body on Earth, but the human vehicle that is available in the rest of the physical universe.

A: Correct. However, although there are many variations on the human vehicle, it is only the variants that are seen on Earth that are aligned to the Akashic. This includes the other locations in the physical universe where these exact variants are used.

ME: Right, got it.

A: Good. At this point in the plan, the Aspect enters into the Akashic and enters the desired outcomes into the space it occupies. The Akashic then illustrates a number of locations on Earth that will offer the best chance of success. It's rather like using a medical diagnostic computer where the operator inputs the symptoms and the computer offers the issues that creates these symptoms as its output.

There are always a number of options available to the Aspect; this is the beauty of using the Akashic. What's more, the Aspect also has the opportunity to analyze each of these options and the Event Spaces that are created, and potentially created, to see which offers the best opportunities.

ME: Is a body chosen at this point?

A: No. This analysis is all about choosing the environment to work within and not the incarnate vehicle itself.

ME: But I would have thought that the incarnate vehicle, the body, was the key player in the analysis?

A: It is, but we have to use a top-down approach.

ME: How do you mean?

A: I will explain it again in a different way. Once the TES has agreed the overall plan the Aspect presented to it, the Aspect then has to look at the locations that can offer the best opportunities to fulfill the plan, the environment itself. It is not an easy task, for the Aspect has to look at how its plan would integrate with all the other plans that other Aspects are either planning, have planned and are currently not incarnate, have planned and are currently incarnate, or will plan. This also includes all of the possible parallel variations offered by Event Space intervention resulting from dualistic, trilistic, and quadrulistic decisions that it may decide upon are presented within the environments that it could incarnate into. All of this is taken into account, and as a result the Aspect is able to choose a location that is befitting its desired plan. Note, though, that the Aspect may not choose the most efficient location to incarnate into.

ME: Why not? I would have thought that the Aspect may choose the most efficient location as a means to gain as much evolutionary content as it can from the location and the incarnation itself!

A: Logically I would agree with you. However, incarnation is not always about efficiency in the experience. It is also about the inefficiency as well.

ME: Wait a moment. Are you suggesting that an Aspect may actually choose an inefficient incarnation location?

A: Yes, and many Aspects choose to do so.

ME: Why?

A: Simply because they are looking at the total experience of the TES and not just the experience of itself as an Aspect. You see, it is most important that the TES, as the overall sentient entity, gains experience, learning, and evolution in all possible ways. And that means every way possible.

ME: And although an optimal location may be identified, it is up to the Aspect to decide whether to use it or not.

A: Correct.

ME: Phew! OK, why, in what circumstances may the Aspect decide not to choose the optimal location? That is, taking into account that the TES may have already experienced the optimal location for a previous plan that was similar to one that the Aspect (we are discussing) may be planning?

A: Precisely that. That another Aspect of the same, or another TES, may have already experienced a similar incarnate existence.

ME: Another Aspect of another TES?

A: Yes, why not? All TES communicate with each other and as a result all Aspects know what the Aspects of all other TES have experienced. Based upon this, the Aspect, together with the information gained from running an "experience" scenario, now has the ability to choose the best location for its incarnation. The next thing for it to do is to narrow down the focus to the incarnate vehicle that would offer it the best operational fit, so to speak, within the location.

199

ME: You mean that as there are many potential locations that an Aspect can incarnate into, that there are also many incarnate vehicles within the chosen location that the Aspect may choose to incarnate into?

A: That's about the size of it. Yes.

ME: And how does it decide that?

A: By going over the plan within the location and the various incarnate possibilities.

ME: The Aspect goes over the plan all over again, with all of the possible incarnate vehicles and all of the possible Event Spaces that could be created?

A: Yes.

ME: I am just considering all of this prework; it's an amazing amount of work.

A: Who said incarnation was easy!

ME: I didn't. What about the incarnate vehicle to use?

A: What about the incarnate vehicle to use?

11.3

Which Body

As far as I was concerned this next section was going to be the one that most people would relate to. As incarnate human beings we all relate to the human body as the one in which we incarnate into, time after time until we no longer need to incarnate as a result of mastering the addictions and attractions that the physical universe presents to us. We stop incarnating when we no longer have any karma to work out. When we can incarnate and be in the physical but not of the physical. Suffice to say this also counts for those Aspects that incarnate in the rest of the physical universe. No one Aspect that incarnates in the physical universe is immune to the possibility of accruing karma, irrespective of the form of the incarnate vehicle used, and irrespective of the frequency within the physical universe that it is incarnated within. Clearly, the higher the frequency the incarnation is within, the lower the chance of accruing karma. Also, the more of a collective-based system the Aspect incarnates into, the lower the chance of accruing karma. With this in mind and the knowledge that incarnating in the lowest frequencies of the physical universe, in reality the multiverse, presents the greatest risk of accruing karma, and that the Earth is the only planet with incarnate vehicles that are both low frequency and have individualized free will, it makes total sense to focus on the human vehicle as the body to choose in this dialogue. I therefore requested of Anne that we only work with humankind in this section.

A: You took your time to get to the end of that train of thought.

ME: Sorry. I just wanted to make sure that the readers recognized that the human vehicle, the human body, is but one of a vast number of incarnate vehicles that an Aspect may choose to incarnate into within the frequencies associated with the physical universe.

A: I think they are aware of that by now, but I understand the need to reiterate, so I will also reiterate. All the information to date is relevant to all Aspects that incarnate within the frequencies of the multiverse we call the physical universe. Everything carries over. There is no advantage other than the frequential advantage of being more "in tune," in a more accomplished level of communication with the TES and The Source. The human vehicle is the most difficult to work with, the most complicated, the most addictive, and the most accomplished method in accruing both karma and evolutionary content. In this respect, incarnating within the human vehicle is a dichotomy, a form of quadruality, and as a result it is unique. Additionally, because most of your

201

readers can only relate to the human vehicle, and as it is the one most Aspects that incarnate on the Earth use, it makes perfect logical sense to only consider it within these continued dialogues.

ME: This feels like we have both just rambled on a bit.

A: That may be so but it was a necessary ramble, and informative too. Now, though, is the time to continue with the information. We have discussed the top-down approach of the overall plan resulting in the focus on the location for the incarnation, and now I will look at the selection of the incarnate vehicle.

As I have just stated there are many incarnate vehicles that could be used within each of the possible locations and deciding the incarnate vehicle to be used, in this case the human body, is the hardest decision an Aspect can make. The Aspect has to look at the parents of the "potential" vehicle, what advantage, in terms of education, health, longevity, peer group, career, pastime, being of service (local, group, and world), and therefore evolutionary opportunity the potential incarnate vehicle has to offer. Not only that, the level of difficulty and percentage chance of success also has to be taken account of, as well, of course, as the number of parallel existences that can be utilized in order to maximize the evolutionary opportunity.

ME: And I would guess that all of this is checked out within the environment and the Event Space/s to be incarnated into, and the Akashic from the human perspective?

A: Of course. And it takes time, so to speak, to understand every possible opportunity, experience, and learning outcome. All things considered, the choice of the vehicle is the most important decision an Aspect will make.

11.3.1

Termination Junctures

ME: Earlier you talked about termination junctures, areas within the longevity of the incarnation where the Aspect may elect to end the incarnation early without affecting the overall expectations of the life plan.

A: Yes, these are an essential part of the life plan. They are a normal method of ending the incarnation if the overall requirements of the incarnation have been fulfilled, or where the Aspect may feel that it has experienced enough in a particular incarnation and has a desire to return to the energetic.

There are normally up to five termination junctures. Each of them has a relevance to the level of actualization of the life plan versus the ultimate desired outcomes. Each of them allows the Aspect to move away from the incarnate state without detriment to the overall requirements of the life plan.

ME: I would have thought that the life plan was cast in stone, so to speak, and that the Aspect needed to finish the incarnation in totality in order to make a reasonable stab at completing the intended experiences?

A: There are no rules about taking an incarnation to its natural demise, apart from the need for the Aspect to achieve certain basic requirements.

ME: But I would have thought, based upon previous dialogues, that the whole point of the TES, or the Aspect justifying to the TES the experiential opportunities of a life plan, was to experience as much as possible in the incarnation it is authorized to have or is assigned to?

A: Again, that's a myth. It is all about the quality of that which is experienced in the incarnation and not the quantity of experiences. Once an incarnation has achieved a minimum requirement, that being the experiences that were used to justify the incarnation, it can be terminated if the Aspect wishes it.

ME: What about if the Aspect gets a few things wrong in the incarnation? Can it can be terminated if the Aspect wishes it? The Aspect may feel that it is required in certain interactions?

A: It's not necessary in the bigger picture to correct things in the same incarnation. You can take as long as you like. It is more important to gain the overall direction than to get it absolutely correct, to get it right first time.

ME: Why?

A: Because once the overall direction is secured the errors can be ironed out over a period of time that can be expressed either in the same life, one life, or many lives. You experienced and commented on this as a result of the corrections in understanding that you have had over the seven years since finishing your first book, *The History of God*, that you were allowed to go forward in error because the overall direction was correct. I will remind you that there are no real rules, only desires, intentions, thoughts, and actions—those commitments we make to evolutionary growth. As long as we remain committed, and every TES, Aspect, and Shard are also committed, then the duration experienced in an experience or the number of times an experience is experienced is immaterial. It's what you, your TES, and ultimately The Source Entity, not forgetting The Origin gain from them that counts.

ME: But how does that work from the perspective of karma—the objective being that the Aspect endeavors to navigate the lowest frequencies in the multiverse without becoming attracted, attached, or addicted to them in the duration it is incarnate, relieving its self from karma at the earliest opportunity?

A: I see where you are coming from. You feel that this information flies in the face of the need to progress as fast as possible to evolve away from the need to incarnate.

ME: Yes, that would be a correct assessment of my current thought process.

A: Well, both are true. You see, and you will find that this is a common theme throughout these dialogues, as I have just said, it's all about the quality of experience and the evolutionary opportunity attached to it.

ME: So I see. Just when I think I have got a grip on understanding what the process is, of anything, I seem to find out that I still haven't got it!

A: You seem to find out that you still need to dive deep into the questions surrounding what reality is and improve your understanding.

ME: Yes.

A: And, think about how hard that work is going to be for those who succeed you and your work. Not to mention all those other truth seekers that are broadcasting what they are experiencing and finding out.

ME: Understood. It's OK; I am not complaining, just looking for some commonality that I can work with, something that I can use as a datum.

A: You have your datums, big ones!

ME: I know.

A: Now about the five termination junctures. As I stated each of them has a relevance to the level of actualization of the life plan versus the ultimate desired outcomes of the life plan. If I identify them as individual stages, this might help you and your readers understand. Note that all termination junctures are positioned in the life plan at points where the termination of the incarnation has little or no downstream effect on those other incarnates that would be part of the life plan, in any Event Space. This means that the Termination juncture is a natural departure point.

The First Termination Juncture is where the Aspect has achieved the incarnate state and has some experience of it from the perspective of being associated with the incarnate vehicle. This does not necessarily mean full integration with the vehicle because this juncture can be activated while the fetus is still in the womb. The first junction can be initiated at any time up to, and including, the incarnate duration necessary for full integration of the Aspect with the incarnate vehicle, which is seven years of clock time. This may not be a popular comment but it does have to be noted here though that the Aspect may incarnate purely to allow it to experience the gestation period and/or the experience of stillbirths, cot death, premature birth, major organ disorder, disability, disease, etc., that can occur in the infantile stages of incarnation.

The Second Termination Juncture can be applied at any point in a period within the next seven to fourteen years—that being seven to twenty-one years of age. At this time the Aspect will have achieved full integration and will have mastered the control of the incarnate vehicle. The Aspect will have experienced education; integration within the community, in most cases has an overall sense of purpose or direction, how to form and dissolve relationships, and what responsibility means. Methods of termination in all junctures from here onward can be via illness, accident, poisoning, or sudden organ failure.

The termination of an incarnation at this point in the life plan is only generally actioned if a short incarnation was planned and the desired experiences and subsequent evolutionary content has been accrued within a pre-agreed tolerance. If, or when, all experiences and evolutionary content have been met, the guide and helpers start to work with all those other guides and helpers that the incarnate Aspect would have worked or interfaced with had it continued the incarnation and actively work on dissolving those Event Spaces that are affected. At this time the incarnate Aspect is guided toward one specific Event Space, that which results in the termination of the incarnation.

The Third Termination Juncture is when the incarnate is in the next seven to twenty-one years and takes the incarnation up to forty-two. At this point in the incarnation the Aspect is starting to make headway in its life plan and, in most cases, is becoming a useful citizen. The incarnate will have found its career path, its partnerships, and its recreational preferences. It may be actively pursuing them, perfecting them or honing them, working to achieve its maximum potential. Clearly, this "potential" is relative to the evolutionary level of the Aspect and the environment it incarnates into. Many Aspects never actually meet their full potential as this is a goal and not a requirement. Remember, it's the journey that is important and not the end product. It is the way in which the journey is experienced that gives the Aspect its depth of knowledge and evolutionary content, so long that is, that the Aspect illustrates growth in all that it experiences, irrespective of whether one would call it good or bad from the human perspective. The duration of the incarnation at this point in the plan is now fully under review and the desired experiences versus the minimum expected experiences are compared on a regular basis with the possibility of introducing new additional preplanned experiences into the life plan. The decisions are made by the guide, helpers, and the Aspect as to whether the incarnation should continue or can be terminated within the framework of the third termination juncture. There is an unadvertised thought process within incarnating Aspects when in the energetic that suggests that most Aspects prefer to return to the energetic early from an incarnation than stay on in what is a difficult environment to exist within. As a result the third termination juncture is a popular one to use.

The Fourth Termination Juncture is anytime within the next twenty-eight years, taking the incarnate up to the potential age of seventy. It is at this time in the duration of the incarnation that the Aspect will have met most, if not all, or at least have sight of, its expected experiences in some level of depth and is able to consider additional opportunities and/or spiritual progression. The spiritual work being available at all times throughout an incarnation but is predominantly available when the Aspect has met most of its commitments, the continuation of which provide little additional worth in the incarnation other than the need to complete the cycle they are part of. Based upon this, the period between the ages of forty-two to seventy is when those who are due to experience spiritual awakening will become awake in some way, shape, or form, and those who are already awake at some level may become more profoundly awake and will have a yearning to perform some spiritual service for the benefit of others. This termination juncture is therefore only utilized if the continuation of the incarnation is no longer advantageous, or a spiritual opportunity is not available or has been completed.

Many Aspects do elect to continue the incarnation irrespective of the comments previously stated and take the opportunity to experience existence in a decaying incarnate vehicle to illicit additional growth, noting that the method of decay would have already been known by the Aspect and that the particular process of decay would provide a unique experiential point above those already experienced. Suffice to say, those Aspects that are on the spiritual path at this point in the life plan are not specifically destined to live a long life for they may only be required to be of service in a certain way for a certain time or experience a certain level of spiritual functionality for a certain time. At this point in the incarnation the downstream interactions are starting to diminish and so the amount of work required by the guide and helpers to initiate the process of termination starts to become less complicated.

The Fifth Termination Juncture is essentially the last opportunity to end the incarnation in a way that is outside of the planned duration of the incarnation, the planned duration being the natural demise of the incarnate vehicle through disease, decrepitude, or organ failure. It is available between the age of seventy and the anticipated natural age of demise of the incarnate vehicle selected. As with the fourth juncture the depth of work required by the guide and helpers to apply termination process and sever the downstream interactions is further reduced in complexity. This juncture is used when the Aspect has completed all desired experiences and has completed any spiritual education, progression, or wider spiritual service it has committed to. In essence, this juncture is used when the Aspect, guide, and helpers are satisfied with the experiential performance of the Aspect, and they collectively decide that there is no advantage to continuing the incarnation and that it can therefore be terminated early and safely without affecting any downstream interactions detrimentally.

ME: As you previously stated then, these are just points in the life plan where the Aspect can, with prior agreement and work with the guide and helpers, bail out from the incarnation early.

A: Correct, the important thing being that all downstream interactions are tidied up, so to speak.

ME: During this description you suggested that quite a number of Aspects choose to terminate their incarnation early.

A: A lot do. Many change their minds about the incarnation they are having as a result of experiencing it for real, so to speak. Incarnation is quite a shock to the energetic system and many who try to do too much recalibrate their expectations and desires while incarnate and as a result reduce the amount of experiential content or decide to end the incarnation early after a certain level of experience is experienced. I will say, though, that the vast majority of Aspects follow through with their commitment to the incarnate state and take the association with the incarnate vehicle right through to its natural demise.

ME: Based upon all of this, it looks to me like it is really very important to have a good team behind you.

A: It is. A good guide and a group of experienced helpers can make a big difference in the quality of experience in an incarnation. They allow the incarnate to respond to the demands of the environment and the interaction with other incarnates while working with the requirements of the life plan. They also work with the desires of the Aspect to either extend the duration of the incarnation in order to maximize the evolutionary opportunity or reduce it if the basic criteria are met and the Aspect wishes to terminate the incarnation early by using one of the termination junctures. They are the entities that make it all happen. They make the termination junctures work.

ME: The Aspect cannot action termination junctures on its own?

A: No, it has to be completed by the guide and helpers because of the downstream interactions.

12

The Guide and Helpers:
Levels of Guides, Master Guides, Etc.

ME:How do we choose our guides and helpers then?

A: Very carefully. No, I am joking.

I could see that this was a joke and that Anne was trying to get me to be less serious about all of this, to be more relaxed, to enjoy the journey and not make it a chore. She was right, though. Over the last couple of years, in fact since she had ascended, I had kept myself very, very busy. Busy to the point of not letting my emotions come out, specifically those emotions associated with enjoying life in the incarnate.

A: No one said that you couldn't let your emotions come out.

ME:I know. I realize it's just a defense mechanism. Such is my integration with the physical that I sometimes have to remind myself that incarnation is just a blink of the eye in real terms and that I will be integrated with you and our TES soon enough.

A: Sooner than you think.

ME:What! Why, when, how long have I got? I need to plan.

A: I am only teasing you. You have plenty of time to do the work we planned, and more. That includes writing the next six books as well as having well-earned rests. *[I wasn't getting any rests to date!! So this was a pleasant announcement, or was it another joke? —GSN]* It's not important to get all of the books done in one go.

ME: Good, I almost went into overdrive then, in planning what to do and when to do it.

Let's plan on going into the selection of the guide and helpers. I know we would have to be careful about which ones we select, but I would have thought that all guides and helpers would be competent; otherwise, they would not be allowed to hold such roles and/or positions.

A: Correct. Although this plays a part, I will allude to it shortly. It's more about the environments, interactions, and circumstances that are planned within the life and the best guide for the job based upon their experience with the environments, interactions, and circumstances, as well as our relationships with them.

ME: Go on.

A: There are a number of things to consider when choosing a guide and helpers, each of them is as important as the other and forms part of the justification for incarnation. This list will not be exhaustive but will give the reader an idea of the criteria surrounding the selection of a guide, bearing in mind that an Aspect may elect to use the same guide for a number of incarnations, that number being in single figures to the tens of thousands of incarnations. These criteria are:

• The overall experience of the guide.

• The number of incarnations the guide has orchestrated.

• How many wards (incarnates) the guide can work with at once.

• How many Event Spaces the guide can work in concurrently—for all wards together.

- The guides' specialities in terms of environments, circumstances, interactions, and locations/frequency.

- Whether it has incarnated itself, either together with one of the wards, in a reverse role with one of the wards, or to test the evolutionary quality of the environment before, during, or after a change has been made in favor of the life plan of the ward/s under its care.

- Whether it has been associated with the evolutionary cycle itself, that being it has been through the process of experiencing incarnation on a regular basis to accelerate its own evolution. (Note here that guides generally do not enter into the evolutionary cycle themselves because they gain evolution through receiving evolutionary donations from those Aspects who are on the evolutionary cycle that they have guided. All a guide wants in existence is to be of service.)

- The number of helpers the guide has used and which ones they can offer in the proposed incarnation.

- The experience of the helpers.

- The specialisms of the helpers.

- How many helpers are required.

- Previous incarnations under the guidance of the proposed guide.

- How well the Aspect works with the guide.

- How many Aspects the guide is currently guiding and therefore its capacity to provide accurate guidance taking into account the workload of the other wards under its guidance.

- The status of the guide, that being if it is under guidance itself, is a fully fledged guide, or is a master guide.

- Whether or not the guide has worked on the overall maintenance of the multiverse or not. This gives the Aspect an understanding of how well a guide can manipulate the environment it will be projected into in its favor.

I could go on but this list will suffice.

ME: Thank you. You mentioned the status of the guide. Can you elaborate on that a little?

A: With ease. All guides obtain a status as a result of the work they undertook, undertake, and could undertake. As I have stated before, the guides and helpers themselves are not generally part of the evolutionary cycle but do gain evolution through the gracious giving of evolutionary content by grateful TES in recognition of the work they do for them when they take on an Aspect or Shard as one of their wards. It is their level of evolutionary content that depicts the status of a guide. Guides and their helpers work solely for the benefit of being of service. They enjoy the opportunity to work behind the scenes, to guide, control, and put into place all of the processes, procedures, and actions necessary to support an incarnation and all of the interactions with other incarnate Aspects or Shards and those Event Spaces that are created through such interactions and decisions surrounding the interactions themselves. The level of success, that being, the amount of evolutionary content accrued by a guide's ward or wards during an incarnation and the repeatability of this level of accrual in subsequent incarnations being a mark of its ability. It is the level of ability and sustained (high) levels of evolutionary content that a guide is able to allow an Aspect, etc., to accrue that give it its status.

ME: I have just had a thought. Does this mean that a master guide would be able to make a, shall I say, a silk purse out of a sow's ear, that being, assist the Aspect in such a way that allows it to accrue a maximum of evolutionary content irrespective of the performance of the Aspect while incarnate?

A: A master guide has the ability to make the changes necessary to allow, shall I say, even a poor performing Aspect shine from the perspective of the accrual of evolution. This is not their purpose, though, because they tend to work with Aspects that embark upon a series of difficult incarnations and therefore need a guide of significant experience. Shards also incarnate and therefore need a guide, by the way, due to them being a subincarnation from an Aspect. Having said that, a master guide does provide advice and guidance to fully fledged guides, and those entities/Aspects that are just starting out on the road to being a guide. They can also help a guide who is experiencing difficulties with its ward. Suffice to say, though, a master guide is not in employment as a master purely to sort out the problems associated with poorly performing Aspects, guides, or helpers. Its main role is to work with those Aspects that are either of evolutionary interest, have a long-term relationship with them, that being they worked with an Aspect before being granted master status, can work on their own mostly when incarnate, allowing the guide to work with other Aspects concurrently or the Aspect has a major role to play, one that could affect the evolutionary content of others. In fact, this last comment, where an incarnation is one that that could affect the evolutionary content of others, that is the main reason for an Aspect having the benefit of being associated with a master guide.

ME: OK, so it looks like the status of a guide is based upon its level of evolutionary content, even though it is not part of the evolutionary cycle, so to speak.

A: Correct.

ME: But how is it that a guide that is based outside of the evolutionary cycle can still accrue evolutionary content?

A: Through the grace of the Aspects that they work with. You see, even though a guide, or a helper, does not actively seek evolutionary content as a result of being of service, that service being in the most pure way, it can still accrue evolutionary content. Every TES or Aspect, if outside the evolutionary cycle, can accrue evolution. Again note that a

Shard does not operate outside of the evolutionary cycle because it is an Aspect's subincarnation.

ME:How?

A: By simply being of help.

ME:I don't understand.

A: OK, I will describe it another way. Ultimately everything evolves to the point where it can be accepted back into communion with the creator, The Source. So how does this happen if not all TES's or Aspects of a TES enter into the evolutionary cycle.

ME:By the evolution being absorbed by those who assist, as a function of their interaction, with those who enter into the evolutionary cycle?

A: Good answer, it looks like you have it. It even looks like you read my mind. OK, elaborate a little for me to prove you do have it.

ME:Wow, you are a taskmaster, aren't you!

A: Even you have to be kept on your evolutionary toes, so to speak.

ME:Mmmm, I think I am receiving the information to help me explain this. Here we go. Absorption is a natural function of association with entities that are evolving. It's the triangulation effect that I was told to call inflational triangulation in *The Origin Speaks*. It happens automatically. When an Aspect shows appreciation of the work a guide has undertaken for them, that has resulted in the accrual of certain levels of evolution, that appreciation is expressed in the giving of some of that evolutionary content to the guide. This is not a tithe, a tax, it's a gift to show appreciation. Because it is directly given to the guide it creates a function of direct line triangulation, and so the guide's evolutionary level is elevated to a level equal to that of its previous evolutionary content plus that evolutionary content which it is given. This is in variation to the function of balancing the frequential content of two entities, where the one pulls the other up to its level. It is purely a function of accrual, and so a guide, although not actively part of the evolutionary cycle, can in fact accrue more evolutionary content than any of its wards simply because it is associated with those Aspects that are in the evolutionary cycle and that they, the guide, may be working with many more than just one or two Aspects. The association with more than one Aspect accelerating the accrual of the guide's evolutionary level in the process.

The guides actually evolve faster than those TES, Aspects, or Shards that enter into the evolutionary cycle!

A: Yes, that is correct. It is the reason why a guide can become a master guide in a shorter length of time, so to speak, than an Aspect that is doing back-to-back incarnations. It is also the reason why a guide can gain a certain level of evolutionary status. In effect, the better the guide, the faster it evolves, the faster its wards evolve, the higher the status, and the higher the demand on its ability to guide others. It is also the reason why some incarnates choose to become guides.

ME:Because they can evolve faster by being outside of the evolutionary cycle.

A: And deeply respect those TES and Aspects that choose to evolve through the evolutionary cycle, specifically by the use of incarnation.

ME:Got it.

A: I think you do. You see, a team comprising of a good guide and competent helpers makes a big difference to the way an Aspect experiences its incarnation, and the synergetic aspect of this is the evolutionary progression of the guide and of course the helpers, so even though the guides primary reason to be is to be of service to those Aspects who enter into the evolutionary cycle, it is in the best interest of the guide to be of service because it ultimately benefits from an evolutionary perspective.

12.1

Changing Places

As well as writing about spiritual physics, conducting workshops, giving lectures, writing articles and posts for my website, etc., etc., I also take weekly healing and reading appointments. As a result of the vast number of readings I have with my clients I am constantly exposed to new information about the greater reality that is specifically related to incarnation. In a number of readings, I have come across incarnate Aspects that were previously in the role of a guide or a maintenance entity and that are now working with the evolutionary cycle as an incarnate. This leads me to understand that it is not cast in stone that once a TES or an Aspect has decided to choose a path of either being in service or being in the evolutionary cycle it has to stay in that role for the duration of the existence of the multiverse in its current version—the current version of the multiverse ending when all TES have evolved to the point where they can once more enter into communion with The Source. I will digress a little here to state that this current evolutionary cycle is the third—the information behind this statement being in my fifth book The Origin Speaks. Suffice to say, though, that once the evolutionary cycle has been completed, The Source reassigns its sentience to another location within the area of The Origin's omnipresent area of energetic sentient self-awareness, and starts all over again. Based upon this, I will state again that it appears that a TES or an Aspect may wish to either stay in the same roles for the duration of the evolutionary cycle or change roles if they feel the desire to. Having said that, to date, I had only been exposed to clients who had changed from the role of being in service to being in the incarnate cycle. This was logical I suppose because I am not likely to meet incarnate Aspects that have moved out of the evolutionary cycle and back into being of service. However logical this seemed, I was about to be given a deeper level of understanding by Anne.

A: TES or Aspects of a TES that have chosen to be in service can and do elect to participate in the evolutionary cycle, and incarnate within the frequencies and environments associated with the physical universe. They can also elect to return whenever they feel that they have experienced enough.

ME: OK, you have just given me a nugget of gold here that I think we should work with.

A: And which particular nugget is that?

ME: That a guide or a helper can also elect to return whenever they feel that they have experienced enough.

A: Mmmm, I think you may have the wrong end of the stick here, so to speak. I will elaborate further.

A TES or Aspect of a TES can elect to be in either the evolutionary cycle or be of service at the start of a particular evolutionary cycle or at any point in the existence of the cycle; most, however, choose to stay on the path that they have chosen. Others, specifically those in service as guides, helpers, maintenance entities, or overseers ...

ME: What are overseers?

A: Overseers are the entities that guide the guides.

ME: Are they master guides?

A: No, they are part of another function. They are part of a hierarchy of entities that work with the, shall I say, work with their function.

ME: Are you talking about the so-called council of twelve?

A: One of them.

ME: There is more than one council of twelve?

A: Yes, there is a group of twelve entities for each of the frequency levels used to create the physical universe. Each of them has a role to play in orchestrating the evolutionary efficiency of the frequency they work with. I was going to say "assigned to," so I will say why they are assigned. The Source assigns certain TES to maintain the structure of the multiverse. There is a hierarchy of entities that help with this maintenance below them; some of these you would call angels or elementals. You will write a book on this subject later. The TES that are assigned to the physical universe assign other TES to orchestrate the evolutionary efficiency of their assigned frequency. These are the entities that guide the guides and can also be classified as overseers.

ME: Interesting.

A: Yes, it is, and I expect I may help you with the compilation of the book that will describe them and their roles. We still have a lot of work to do together with this book, though.

ME: Thank you for that reassurance.

A: Good, I will continue with delivering the information I was supposed to before you asked your question.

ME: Please do.

A: Others, specifically those in service as guides, helpers, maintenance entities, or overseers, can elect to enter into the evolutionary cycle for any period they wish. Some choose to complete the remaining period of a cycle of the multiversal existence; others choose to experience only a certain period of events. Many more only experience a few incarnations before returning back to their role as guide, helper, maintenance entity, etc. More frequently, though, incarnation is used as a method of checking the performance of a ward on an almost side-by-side basis, the period being minutes to days to weeks to months to a few years. Even whole lifetimes are used in this sense. What should be of interest to you is that those TES and/or their Aspects that are already in the evolutionary cycle can, and do, choose to become guides or helpers and therefore choose to be of service rather than be in the evolutionary cycle.

ME: Would these Aspects or TES need to be free of karma, to actually be in the position where they no longer need to incarnate in the first place?

A: Ordinarily, yes. But an Aspect or a TES whose Aspects are carrying minimal karma can elect to leave the evolutionary cycle and work out the karma in another way.

ME: How would they do that?

A: Where the karma is a link between Aspects there can be a trade of evolutionary content to negate the link. If the karma is based upon attractivity then the TES can work the addictions out by working directly with the Aspects, their guides, and helpers to dissolve it.

ME: And that allows the overall sentient energy that is the TES and/or its Aspects to move out of the evolutionary cycle and into service.

A: Yes.

ME: Just exactly how many Aspects or TES, or Aspects and TES together, move out of the evolutionary cycle in preference to being in service to those that remain in the evolutionary cycle?

A: I cannot give you a figure per se.

ME: Why not?

A: Because it is not a number that you would recognize as being reasonable.

ME: Try me.

A: OK, it is in the billions, that being, if we include all of the frequencies of the physical universe. However, this number is only a transient figure.

ME: How do you mean "transient?"

221

A: I say transient because ultimately any entity that chooses to move outside of its initially chosen path needs to move back into it again prior to communion with The Source, hence the figure being transient.

ME: Does this not affect their evolutionary content?

A: No. Nothing is lost from an evolutionary perspective by moving back into your initially chosen path of being either in the evolutionary cycle or being of service.

ME: Why does it need to move back to its original evolutionary cycle? I wouldn't have thought that this mattered.

A: We have a path, an evolutionary path, to follow and that path is one that we choose at the start of the evolutionary cycle of the multiverse. That being, when The Source has accepted all TES back into sentient communion, moved its sentience from one group of energies within The Origins area of polyomniscient sentient self-awareness to commandeer another, and then populates it with TES again, our TES choose a main path to work with. As I have alluded to, there are only two main paths: the personalized evolutionary cycle and being of service. The reason for the need to return to this "originating path" is because it invokes a primary Event Space associated with it.

Although Event Space is a parallel condition, it has functionality associated with it that is aligned to the accrual of evolutionary content. This demands that, no matter how many Event Spaces are created by an Aspect or TES, it must return to The Originating Event Space.

ME: Surely this means that there is only one ultimate path that an Aspect or TES can follow, that all others are supplementary.

A: No, it means that although all parallel conditions are created from one ultimate start point, and finish at one end point, they are just as valid as individual, but parallel, spatial environments. It's the evolution that is linear, and it is the evolutionary condition that determines whether an Event

Space should continue to expand fractally or collapse back into the main evolutionary line of progression.

ME: Got it. This means then that if the evolutionary path chosen is to be of service, taking into account that being of service is not the personalized evolutionary cycle, it is an evolutionary path, at the start of the evolutionary cycle of the/a multiversal environment, then the Aspect or TES has no choice but to return to this evolutionary path at the end of the end of the evolutionary cycle of the/a multiversal environment. This is irrespective of how many times it swaps from the personal evolutionary cycle to being of service and vice versa, including the number of Event Spaces it creates.

A: Correct.

ME: And this is simply because The Originating Event Space is either in the evolutionary path of being of service or the evolutionary path of the personalized evolutionary cycle.

A: Correct again.

ME: So Event Space controls us even though we create it?

A: Only in so much as it is a function of our own choices and that we must return to The Originating Event Space, an Event Space which we initially chose to work with.

ME: Is there any difference in the, shall I say, "flavor" or "function" of Event Space that is chosen by an entity, the TES or Aspect, if it desires to be of service or be in the evolutionary cycle?

A: Only in so much as there is a specific direction that the TES or Aspect that invoked the Event Space needs to go in, in terms of the roles and responsibilities that they would operate within in a particular evolutionary path.

ME: And these are the creation of Aspects and or Shards to animate the incarnate vehicles within their chosen environment for those that chose the evolutionary cycle. For those that choose to be of service it is remaining as a whole

TES with no Aspects, or be a TES with Aspects created to be multiversal maintenance entities, guides, or helpers.

A: Correct again, but with one caveat.

ME: What's the caveat?

A: I will describe it in a moment.

ME: Oh, OK. What about the TES at the originating Event Space? I would have thought that a TES would not create/project Aspects of itself so early on in the evolutionary cycle of a new multiversal environment to be in a position of choosing which path to take.

A: Two main things happen at the point of population of a multiverse during a new multiversal evolutionary cycle.

One: the individualized Source Entity sentience that are TES are allowed to consider their direction before they are assigned a body of energy, that being they are individualized while still in communion with the overall Source Entity sentience. In this instance, individuality can be carried over from a previous multiversal evolutionary cycle, it can be a new individualization, or it can be an individualization that is re-individualized after entering into full communion with The Source at the end of its personal evolutionary cycle in a previous multiversal evolutionary cycle. During this time, the TES decides on which evolutionary path to take and whether or not to create Aspects of itself to help it in its chosen method of experience.

Two: once they have made this decision and are assigned a body of energy, if they have already chosen to create Aspects of themselves they assign smaller portions of their own individualized sentience to certain areas of their energy (creating smaller Aspects of themselves) and assign certain desired experiences to certain Aspects. These experiences are either within the evolutionary cycle or being of service. In this instance, the TES remains outside of both the evolutionary cycle and/or being of service remaining only in the evolutionary cycle of the multiversal environment while their Aspects work either in the personal evolutionary cycle or are of service. This is the normal state of a TES if it has some Aspects that are of service and some that are in the evolutionary cycle. Those TES who create Aspects that are all of service enter into service in totality. Those TES whose Aspects are all within the personal evolutionary cycle enter into the personal evolutionary cycle in totality.

Alternatively, if a TES wishes to remain whole and not create Aspects of its self, it can choose to be of service by working with the maintenance of the greater multiversal environment. In rare instances, and this is the caveat, a TES can elect to remain whole and enter into the evolutionary cycle as well. But, this is only chosen by a TES if they wish to make a change to a certain universal environment and that that change requires all of the sentient energies of a TES and not just an Aspect of a TES.

ME:Doesn't this last option run the risk of a TES creating TES-sized karma?

A: If the TES is incarnating into the lowest frequencies of this particular multiverse, yes. But in this instance a whole TES would be the sentience behind a number of, shall I say larger bodies, such as galaxies rather than an incarnate vehicle like the human body.

ME:Well, that would ensure that the TES avoided TES-sized karma, wouldn't it?

A: Yes, it would.

ME:Hold on a moment. Aren't we supposed to be of a whole Om TES?

A: We are each a single projection of a whole Om TES. We are the only two projections, the only two Aspects. There are no Shards projected from us. As you already know, Om, pure Om, don't generally incarnate.

I would like to touch upon how a guide works now, for we are getting close to the end of this dialogue.

ME:How close to finishing are we?

A: We are within the last 15 percent or so of the work necessary to complete this dialogue.

ME:There is quite a bit more to come then?

A: Yes, but we are coming to the end of the subjects I wanted to discuss with you and your readers.

ME:OK, let's go for it. We are on the home straight!

I have to say that at this point in the proceedings I did actually feel that the "end was nigh," so to speak. I felt this even though I noted that we had another four main chapters to work with and another subheading within the current chapter to finish. My logical mind had a dichotomy to deal with, though. Anne had stated that there were only two main ways to progress, the evolutionary cycle and being in service. She also stated that an entity must return to the path of origin if that path was deviated from. For example, if The Originating path was the evolutionary cycle and the entity changed over to being of service it must return to the evolutionary cycle in order to commune with The Source. In The Origin Speaks, *The Origin identified six ways to progress and that once a path was taken, any migration to another path was a one-way street. Something didn't feel right here. Based upon this, I felt a strong urge to clear this up before moving on to the next subject. As I paused for thought for a moment, I noticed that my connectivity with Anne was being activated. Anne was quick to clarify the situation.*

A: There is no dichotomy, just a limitation in the information being portrayed.

ME:How do you mean, a limitation in the information being portrayed?

A: The Origin gave a holistic rendition of the information surrounding the way an entity, as an individualized unit of sentience, can progress. It was considering everything relating to a TES in general and not just those TES that are created by The Source Entity you refer to as SE1, which is what we were discussing. What's more, although there are many form factors throughout the physical universe that an entity can project an Aspect (soul) of its self into, it is still the "evolutionary cycle" and as such is still relevant to incarnation as the evolutionary method of progression. It is incarnation and the use of the human form that are being used as a datum. Based on this, we are only really interested in the two main ways a TES can relate to as methods of progression while in the evolutionary cycle, the evolutionary cycle itself and being of service. The other methods of progression are nice to know, but are of a higher context when considering this human-centric dialogue on the processes surrounding incarnation.

In terms of the comment about migration from one path to another being a one-way street The Origin itself later stated that this was not strictly true because some entities do swap paths on a secondment basis. Note here, though, that they must still return to their original path before communion with The Source can be achieved, so migration is by definition a two-way street. Even if the entity stays in its second path for the rest of its individualization and that the second path ends up being 99 percent of its total existence it needs to return to The Original path for it to ascend into communion with The Source.

ME: So there is no dichotomy, just a limitation in the depth of information being broadcast because of its applicability to incarnation within the physical universe, which in this instance is human-centric.

A: Correct.

ME: And the one-way street comment really referred to the need to return to the original progressive path taken?

A: Again correct.

ME: OK, thank you.

227

With this cleared up, I relaxed a little. It made perfect sense to me that the information in this book would be human-centric and the information in The Origin Speaks *would be more holistic. I also noted that in some respects I had placed the cart in front of the horse by being presented with deeper information from a higher authority and then working on a new project that by definition would present less information in the holistic sense but would go deeper in the specialized subject of human incarnation and with a lower authority.*

A: It is nevertheless important for human kind's understanding of that which is invisible to them in the incarnate state. It will make them more cognizant of how the decisions they make and the actions resulting from them ultimately affect them in their true state. A lower authority, eh! From where I exist, you are the lower authority.

ME: That I can fully accept, and I accept full responsibility for maintaining the level of accuracy necessary to ensure the information is clear and concise. Especially as it is up to me to get the information in the right order and ensure that there is continuity in the information that is being presented. I know we are allowed to be in error as long as we are heading in the right general direction, but it is important to get it as accurate as possible.

Right now I again recognized that it is the way questions are asked, and the need to interpret the answers correctly, that ensures that the information is clear, concise, and has continuity, giving it ultimate validity. I have always known this but for some reason, when dealing with different levels of information to capture the attention of truth seekers that are at different levels of interest and understanding, it has become even more important.

12.2

The Guide Hierarchy and More on
How a Guide and Its Helpers Function

I was going to enjoy this part of the dialogue with Anne. I had met many guides over the past couple of years and to be given the chance to explain, through Anne, something about how they work was going to be both a personal delight and a further chance to correlate what I have experienced in the myriad readings I have performed for my clients, which result in communication with their guide and helpers. Anne was quick to connect with me and start the ball rolling.

A: We have only discussed in brief that there is a structure to those who are in service as a guide.

ME: You're right! Is there more to this that we can pass on to the readers?

A: Just a little. We will have to explain this in human terms because there is a hierarchy, and this is expressed by the abilities of the guide and the helpers employed by the guide to assist in steering the incarnate along the life plan.

ME: So we are not in control of our life plan?

A: Ultimately it is up to the incarnate Aspect to work with the life plan. It is the role of the guide and helpers to ensure that the incarnate Aspect has minor levels of assistance when it is required. This includes repeating experiences that are required to clear any karma.

I think it is best to split out the hierarchy of the types of guides and helpers, identifying their roles and responsibilities and how they function. You may recall from our previous dialogues about the life review that the guide and its helpers have to go through this post-incarnate analysis as well as the Aspect, so it is important that they maximize their efficiency of assistance and how they interface with the incarnate Aspect.

I am aware that we may be going over some old ground here so I will be as brief as possible while maintaining the depth of knowledge surrounding the information to be broadcast.

Master Guides

A: A master guide is not only an accomplished guide in its own right but one that is capable of working with, advising, or managing twelve main (fully fledged) guides and their wards (a "ward" is the descriptor used for the incarnate Aspect that the guide is working with). They not only operate as a tutor to the guides they work with, but they also use other guides to allow them to work with multiple wards. Each master guide, as are all guides, is capable of representing twelve wards. This includes all of the parallel versions of the ward/s that are created by Event Space.

ME: The means that a master guide has the potential to be responsible for up to one hundred and forty-four wards and their parallel versions!

A: Correct. If you realize that this means that they have the responsibility for one hundred and forty-four times the myriad Event Space created versions of their wards it is an awful lot. For example, this could easily be around three thousand per ward at times. Multiplying three thousand by one hundred and forty-four equals 432,000 incarnations to represent.

ME: That's a lot of incarnations to look after.

A: Isn't it just.

ME: How do they do it?

A: They create a version of themselves for each of the Event Spaces that are in play. This means that they are not only able to divide their sentient attention efficiently among all of the wards that are under their control, but they are able to offer one-to-one tutoring for each of the fully fledged guides they are responsible for at the point of the diversification of the guides sentience required for each of the guide's wards.

Additionally, the master guide can also work individually with each of the helpers under the control of the guides it is responsible for, adding another multiple to the number of versions of itself that it is capable of creating. The number of helpers that a particular Aspect has looking after it is variable and is dependent upon the level of help the Aspect needs at a particular point in its incarnation. Based upon this, the number of versions of its self and its sentience a master guide has to divide itself into is in a state of constant flux.

A master guide is also referred to when an Aspect chooses to use one of its termination junctures in order to end its incarnation early because it is capable of communing with all versions of the guides that are responsible for those Aspects that are affected downstream of the chosen termination juncture.

A guide can only achieve master status when it has accrued the equivalent evolutionary content of a TES that has completed its evolutionary cycle within the current overall evolutionary cycle created by The Source Entity. Note that guides, although not within the evolutionary cycle themselves, can accrue evolutionary content faster than their wards due to their ability to work with up to twelve wards and their Event Space–created parallel incarnations.

ME: So you're saying by inference here that a master guide is only achievable at TES level and not at Aspect level?

A: Yes, and the TES must be capable of having all of its Aspects operate at main guide level.

Main (Fully Fledged) Guides

A: As just discussed in our dialogue on master guides, each guide can be responsible for up to twelve wards. This includes the myriad Event Space–created parallel incarnations. Whereas the master guide is capable of dividing its sentience up between all the guides, helpers, wards, and the Event Space–created parallel incarnations, the main guide is not. In this instance, the guide has a different function available to it—which the master guide has, but has no need to use as a master guide. The guide can create new helpers that are specifically designed to act as a monitor, a remote viewing function for want of a better word, for the guide—allowing it to devolve responsibility for the incarnate Aspect to the helpers assigned to each Event Space–created parallel incarnation. Note that the number of helpers is variable for each of the Event Space–created parallel incarnations. Also note that they are not the same helpers per se for they themselves are created by the creation of a new Event Space.

ME: Why doesn't a master guide use the ability of creating new helpers to act as a remote viewing function?

A: Simply because they don't need to because they have the ability to divide up their sentience. This achieves a better and more omniscient version of the same thing. In essence, they are present with each of the Event Space–created parallel incarnations, whereas the main guide is only able to observe via the helper created as a remote viewing function. If its attention is needed to solve an issue with a certain Event Space–created parallel incarnation, it needs to move its whole sentience to that incarnation and commune with the helpers associated with that incarnation.

ME: I imagine that takes quite a bit of time and effort.

A: Time doesn't exist, of course, but the effort required to move around the Event Spaces associated with the different Event Space–created parallel incarnations, touching base with all the helpers involved, can be challenging.

ME: I would have thought that a guide would be more than capable of such actions.

A: They are but when the guide is being asked to participate in multiple incarnations concurrently it can be quite a task to be able to negotiate the finer details of all of the life plans and associated interactions with those incarnate Aspects that the life plan/s are involved with.

ME: You said life plan/s. Does an incarnate Aspect have more than one life plan?

A: No, there is only one life plan that a guide needs to work with. But there are variations on the life plan that are a result of the way the Aspect is multiplied by the Event Space–created parallel versions of itself.

ME: So there is only one life plan, but there are multiple ways that the life plan is being addressed, and the guide has to deal with all of the different ways in which the Event Space–created parallel versions are working with the plan.

A: Or not, as the case may be.

ME: What do you mean?

A: An incarnate Aspect can, as a result of their decision process, have an Event Space–created parallel version that is completely off course, or one where it chooses not to have the mentorship of a guide.

ME: How does an incarnate Aspect operate without a guide or helpers?

A: Some do well, others have a difficult time. Some start to work with the environment that they are in, in the way that it is supposed to be worked with, going with the flow of the particular version of the physical universe they have created through their decisions. There are some, though, who never have a guide.

ME: And they would be advanced Aspects from highly evolved TES that are incarnate only to assist in the growth of the general incarnate population, I would guess.

A: Correct. They are a rare breed. An Aspect is capable of becoming a main guide in its own right but this is as far as it can go from the position of being an individualized projection from its TES. Master guide status is a communal level of achievement that the projecting TES attains when all of its Aspects have achieved main or fully fledged status.

ME: Would this mean that the master guide uses its own Aspects as main guides in your description? How many guides they are in control of?

A: No, a master guide generally remains in, or returns to, the un-individualized TES state once all its Aspects have reached the level of main guide. It reintegrates its main guide Aspects within its main body of sentient TES energies. The main guides that it is in control of are usually those Aspects of other TES that are operating as main guides. It has moved beyond the need for the parallel experience available to it via the use of its Aspects as main guides and can now achieve the same and more by diversifying its sentience in the way I previously described.

New Guide

New guides are those Aspects of a TES that have finished the process of being an aspiring guide *[see later —GSN]* and have been assessed as being capable of taking independent control of a ward. New guides were once a rarity but with the ever-increasing queue of entities that are lining up to enter into the evolutionary cycle, and specifically the use of incarnation to accelerate their evolutionary progression, they are becoming more common.

ME: Why is that? I thought that, in general, guides decided to be guides at the start of the multiversal evolutionary cycle. In fact, I thought it was the choice of the TES itself to go down this route.

A: It is, but those TES that enter into the evolutionary cycle at the start of the multiversal evolutionary cycle can and do elect to use Aspects of themselves as smaller individualized guides as a way of achieving their own progression in an accelerated way while being outside of the evolutionary cycle itself.

ME: OK, so they don't stay as TES per se?

A: No. I thought this would have been clear from the previous dialogues we have had.

ME: You're right, it is. I must be getting tired!

A: I will come to your rescue. It is worth repeating this information a couple of times in different ways in the same series of dialogues because with the depth and breadth of the information being portrayed, a lot of information can be forgotten.

ME: Thank you.

A: Also remember that there are those TES or Aspects of a TES that change their direction midstream of being in the evolutionary cycle, and they will either project Aspects of themselves to be of service as aspiring guides or their already projected Aspects will enter into service by electing to become an aspiring guide. Note that a TES must have achieved a certain level of evolution in the evolutionary cycle before it or any of its Aspects can elect to go into service and become an aspiring guide.

ME: What level of evolution do they need to have achieved?

A: They need to have moved into the fifth full dimension of the multiversal structure. They need to have reached the point where they can elect to stop using incarnation as a means of evolutionary progression, to be at the point where they could continue to evolve through the evolutionary cycle within the energetic only.

ME: So they need to have experienced enough incarnate existence to make them able to work with the convoluted ways in which an incarnate Aspect can operate when it is not aware of its downstream opportunities, when it's not aware of its life plan.

A: Correct.

ME: So how does this work at the start of the multiversal evolutionary cycle? Just how does a guide gain experience at the start, when it has no hands-on experience of either incarnation or attending to an incarnate Aspect?

A: Through the use of Event Space.

ME: It has to select an Event Space where it can experience that which it has experienced in a future Event Space to allow it to operate at the start of an Event Space that is the start of the multiversal evolutionary cycle?

A: Correct.

ME: Oh boy! I thought I had finished with the chicken and egg stuff with The Origin in *The Origin Speaks*!

A: You had to some extent.

ME: But doesn't the use of Event Space this early on in the evolutionary cycle negate the whole point of being incarnate to accelerate one's evolution?

A: No.

ME: Why not?

A: Because it is only TES that have elected to be of service as their primary route of progression at the start of the multiversal evolutionary cycle that can access Event Space to gain the experience required to assist in the guidance of TES who elect to enter into the evolutionary cycle and use incarnation as a means of accelerating their evolutionary progression.

ME: So the guides are only TES at this stage of the multiversal evolutionary cycle—there are no Aspects of TES?

A: Not at this stage, no.

ME: And at what point in the cycle do they access their experiential data?

A: You were thinking at the end, weren't you?

ME: Yes, I was.

A: Wrong, they can only access the data from the Event Space that provides them with enough experience to be an efficient guide. At this point in the proceedings, it has to be noted, there is a limited number of individuals using the function of incarnation.

Food for thought here. It is highly likely that this, the third multiversal evolutionary cycle, is looking like it is the last cycle where the lowest frequencies of the structure of any Source Entity will be used in the creation of an environment, multiversal or otherwise, for evolutionary progression.

ME: Why is that?

A: Because every "created" entity is progressing in an accelerated rate and as a result the need to incarnate to experience a lower frequency will be negated because lower frequencies will no longer need to be experienced to evolve.

ME: Again, why is that?

A: There are bigger challenges waiting!

ME: Can you allude to some of those challenges now?

A: No. That will be part of the next series of dialogues you have with The Origin. They will be part of the dialogues that will be called *Beyond The Origin!*

ME:I can't wait!

A: You will need to; it will be hard work—the hardest work you will ever do in this incarnation. We have strayed completely off our path and need to continue with the discussion on the new guides.

New guides are just like an aircraft pilot who has just passed the stage where it can take its first solo flight and as such they are only allowed to work with one Aspect at a time. They of course have a group of helpers to assist in the management of their ward, but they are usually experienced and specialist helpers with a known track record, so to speak. Helpers that already have experience and/or a specialism make the workload of the new guide more manageable, especially during the periods when it is responsible for its first few wards.

A new guide will have all of the abilities of a main guide bestowed upon it once it has proven its ability to work with its wards in an efficient and productive way. It starts to get experienced once it has guided one hundred and forty-four and above wards. Until this time, it has a very much hands-on and one-on-one relationship with its wards and no special functionality.

ME:It needs to learn the basics first.

A: Yes, it needs to learn the basics first.

Aspiring Guides

Aspiring guides are TES or Aspects of a TES whose TES has either elected to change from the evolutionary cycle but has not completed the minimum evolutionary requirements necessary to work as a main guide or are helpers who wish to expand their level of commitment in terms of being of service or are TES that are allowing their Aspects to remain in the projected state to enter into service as individualized Aspects. They are also a temporary state for those Aspects who, in the projected state from their TES, were selected to go into service as guides from the start of their existence.

ME:If you consider that in the previous dialogue that a TES can use Event Space to experience future learning and evolutionary content related to being a guide, why is there a need to be an aspiring guide if this is the start of the evolutionary cycle? Or even any part of the evolutionary cycle?

A: I can see that you think that this doesn't make sense.

ME:You would be correct in that assumption, although I very much feel that there will be an explanation.

A: There is. The position described is an experiential concept. This means that it is only there as an opportunity to experience another method of progression.

ME:Aren't all things experiential? Isn't this the whole point of any level of existence?

A: Yes, of course. It's just that this experience is not what you would call being in the mainstream, and this is simply because it is not a logical part of the progression for a TES or Aspect of a TES that wants to be of service or is chosen to be of service.

ME:I felt like it was in the description you gave.

A: I apologize if that was the impression you gained but the descriptor is just that, and not a justification for the position that creates the experience.

ME:OK, got it, it is simply a variation on the experiential theme of being in service.

A: That's right. Can I continue with the description?

ME:Yes, of course.

A: Thank you. The aspiring guide cannot be totally responsible for a ward (incarnate Aspect) in its own right until it can illustrate that it can work with the helpers associated with it, the helpers and guide/s of those Aspects that have chosen to work with the evolutionary cycle, and is able to consider the parallel Aspects of the incarnate Aspect in terms of how Event Space affects the accrual of its experiential content and the opportunity to gain additional evolutionary content through its use. It does this by being an assistant to a main guide, or if the aspiring guide requests it, a master guide.

ME: Why would the aspiring guide request being an assistant to a master guide?

A: When it has the overall aspiration of becoming a master guide itself or it feels that it would benefit from being given direction from an Aspect or TES that has had significant experience looking after and orchestrating the direction of the incarnate Aspect in terms of its life plan. Master guides, as you are now aware, have functions above that of a main guide so the aspiring guide, or even a main guide who aspires to be a master guide, will elect to be under further guidance, even though it could be working autonomously and therefore gaining experience from a different angle.

However, getting back to the thread of the dialogue associated with when the aspiring guide can demonstrate its required minimum expected requirements, it is allowed to be the guide of a single incarnate Aspect and select the specialized and generalized helpers necessary to guide the Aspect through its state of incarnate beingness. In the instance of the first time the aspiring guide is responsible for an incarnate Aspect in its own right, it is overseen by a master guide as stated just a moment ago.

Specialist Helpers

A: First of all, I would like to identify a line of demarcation for you.

ME: OK, go ahead.

A: At this point in the game, so to speak, the position of guide in its three versions of master, main, or aspiring guide can be either a TES or the projected Aspect of a TES. When considering the role of a helper of any of the two roles to be described, the helper can only be the projected Aspect of a TES.

ME: Why is this?

A: Simply because this level of being of service is only relative to the projected Aspect of a TES and not a TES in its own right.

ME: Can you explain some more?

A: Of course. It's quite simple in actuality. The helpers are at the same level as those projected and therefore individualized Aspects of a TES that allow the TES to evolve through the use of incarnation to accelerate the progression of the TES through the evolutionary cycle.

ME: They are the same?

A: In so much as they are individualized from the TES, yes. When in the energetic, the disincarnate state, there is nothing energetically to tell them apart from each other. Apart from, that is, that they are progressing on behalf of their TES by the use of different paths. One using the evolutionary cycle and the other being of service and progressing by the donation of evolutionary content by the guide it is associated to.

ME: As you stated before, guides get their evolutionary content from the donations from the wards they are responsible for. Is this not the case with helpers then?

A: No. The evolutionary content initially goes to the guide, who if it feels the helper/s were significant service with a particular ward will offer them evolutionary content in return.

ME: This all feels like a bartering system.

A: It isn't. It is simply one of the myriad ways of progressing. It is also part of the hierarchical structure and its functionality.

ME: That being, I guess, the more advanced an entity is, the more evolutionary content it can accrue and therefore the more it can donate to those that help it accrue evolutionary content.

A: Very well done. I will carry on with the description of the specialized helper. As you can imagine, this type of helper is specifically capable of assisting the incarnate Aspect with successfully navigating that/those experience/s that it has worked with itself and has mastered. In a similar way to how incarnate Aspects choose their career path for their life on Earth, the specialist helper gains its specialism by choice, by actively seeking a specialism that they feel is right for them, or one where there are a limited number of other specialists available. It can also find its self as a specialist by divine decree or by chance.

ME: What do you mean divine decree or chance?

A: The specialist helper may, in effect, be subjected to a number of similar experiences to deal with by their wards over a number of incarnations which create a specialism in their own right. Although, usually, the specialism doesn't necessarily mean that the helper is permanently biased toward the universal location of its wards' incarnations, where the helper gained its specialist knowledge and ability, it can and does use this knowledge when working with wards that are in different universal locations but with similar experiential expectations within the life plan. As a result of this, if a ward has most of its incarnations in locations within the physical universe other than Earth, and wishes to either bring in knowledge to Earth, or work with knowledge that is new to Earth, but that is common in other locations within the physical universe, it can elect to request the help of a helper that is specialized in the desired experience or role.

Note that it is not uncommon for an incarnate Aspect to have or request the assistance of more than one specialist helper, and it is also not uncommon for all of the helpers enlisted for an incarnation to be specialized. This can especially be seen when an incarnate Aspect chooses to be either a world leader, or of significant influence, such as the inventor of a certain technology or medical process.

In terms of a specialism being assigned as "divine decree," this is when a TES that is on the path of being of service uses Event Space to identify what specialism/s will be best suited to its level of service, absorbs that specialism from the knowledge offered in that Event Space and then projects an Aspect of its self into individuality with the absorbed specialism preloaded, so to speak, into the sentience assigned to the projected energies.

As with both classes of helper, the specialist helper can only work with one ward and the Event Spaces associated with that ward. They are chosen by the incarnating Aspect and the guide during the compilation of the life plan and the key experiences associated with it. Additionally, the incarnating Aspect has the opportunity to work with the guide before the specialist helper/s is/are chosen. This ensures that the guide is fully briefed on the life plan and what is expected in terms of its specialized support. When this is established, the guide can then suggest the use of either its own projected Aspects as helpers (if the guide is a TES) or enlist the use of those helpers that are the projected Aspects of another guide (TES) that have the appropriate specialist experience.

The specialist helper operates autonomously to the guide when working with the ward in areas relative to its specialism, but is and can be directed by the guide to make changes relative to the ward's life plan requirements that infringe upon its specialism should the guide feel these are necessary.

The General Helper

As with the specialist helper, the general helper can only work with one ward and the Event Spaces associated with the ward that it is assigned to. The general helper, although autonomous to the guide, operates exclusively under the direction of the guide, if required, under the direction of the specialist helper should it need additional assistance.

The general helper can remain generalized or, in time, can also become specialized. However, general helpers can actually specialize as a general helper and gain a wide breadth of experience with some level of depth of knowledge of their experiences, making them an extremely important commodity in their own right.

ME:So, taking all of this into consideration the specialist helper has a deep understanding of its specializations, whereas the general helper can apply itself to any experience with enough depth of understanding to make it effective.

A: Correct. The general helper is actually a very important role and although it has a different level of interface with the ward, it is just as important as the specialist helper.

13

How We Incarnate (Soul Mates, Twin Flames, etc.) and How It Affects Us Psychologically

Although the information on how we incarnate and how it affects us psychologically was described to some extent during my dialogues with The Origin in The Origin Speaks, *I feel that Anne will offer a different perspective on this subject. I specifically feel this because Anne is working with me on the human level, so to speak, and not on the higher level that The Origin would offer. Also, Anne has been giving me more in-depth information about the process in and around how we as sentient energetic beings incarnate in the Earth realm and not in the physical universe per se, although much of what has been discussed would carry over. We enjoy individualized free will here on Earth and that is not available in the same way in the rest of the physical universe, even though we may incarnate in the higher frequencies associated with it. Incarnation on Earth is a unique experience, and we subject ourselves to certain extremes of this unique experience. Understanding how we can and do incarnate is one way in which we will be able to rationalize our experience here, specifically those Aspects of incarnate existence that are not quite as understandable as we would like them to be, that being the psychology surrounding them. I do have to say here that I am no psychologist, but if the information that was discussed with The Origin on this subject is anything to go by then the information we are about to discuss will provide the answer to many of the questions surrounding psychological or mental illnesses.*

I do have to say here that I don't expect to go into the fine details of the psychological aspect because I am aware that this is the subject of another book in its own right, one that I am destined to write. What we will see here, though, is the executive summary of how the way we incarnate affects us.

The Hierarchical Structure Associated with the TES

A: This could be of psychological benefit.

ME: How do you mean?

A: Offering the general public the solution to their psychological problems in one breath and then in the next, telling them that the detail surrounding the solutions will come later.

ME: I understand what you are saying, but I do feel that we will have more than enough information to digest in this dialogue without going in to the real depth. Anyway, the book I am told to work on that will focus on this subject will also go into the therapy associated with it.

A: Touché.

ME: Great, that's settled then. What do you want to start with?

A: Let's go over the hierarchy of the TES and its projections first.

ME: OK. Lead on.

A: The True Energetic Self (TES) can project up to twelve smaller Aspects of itself into any universal environment within the structure of the multiverse. These are what are sometimes described as souls. I will, however, no longer use the word soul, because it naturally associates the Aspect as being the "Self," the dominant sentience and not the TES as the True Self, the real dominate sentience. It is this error in thought that stops us as incarnate Aspects from moving outside of our understanding of self, that being our association with the human vehicle being predominant in our thought processes.

ME: That makes sense.

A: There is a structure below the Aspect level, and this structure is where the Aspect itself can project up to twelve smaller Aspects of itself into other universal environments within the multiversal structure. These smaller Aspects are called Shards.

ME: A quick calculation tells me that the TES can, in the most extreme case, have twelve Aspects projected with each Aspect projecting twelve Shards, making one hundred and forty-four individualizations of the TES.

A: Aspects and Shards experience individualization when projected from their TES or Aspect and so as with the Aspect in relationship to the TES, the Shard can and does experience true individuality while in the projected state. That being, it is capable of individual incarnations and the parallel conditions created by Event Space associated with it.

[I know I will be going over old ground here, ground that The Origin went over in The Origin Speaks, *so I will make my apologies right here and now. —GSN]*

The TES cannot commune with The Source until it has evolved through the structure of the multiverse and all of its projected Aspects are back in a state of communion with it. This is similar with the projected Aspect in relation to its Shards. The projected Aspect cannot commune with its TES until all of its Shards are reintegrated with it. Note the use of the word reintegration relative to the Shard rather than communion. This is because the Shard, being of significantly reduced sentience in comparison to the Aspect, cannot enter into any of the states of communion in the individualized state I previously described.

ME: So a Shard is only individualized while in the projected state, and that it is always reintegrated with the Aspect when its role, incarnate or other, is finished.

A: Yes.

ME: How does that affect the way that an incarnating Shard thinks or feels about itself?

A: An incarnating Shard is not usually capable of thinking of itself as being anything other than the vehicle it incarnates into, such is the level of sentience associated with it.

ME: You said "not usually." This means that there is a potential for those that can.

A: There is but that is a different description. You see, a Shard can be an individual projection or a partial (single) migration of sentience. I will deal with these when I am at the correct point in this dialogue. Suffice to say, though, that the rule surrounding the percentage of overall sentience that can be projected from an Aspect to create its Shards is the same as for a TES projecting its sentience to create its Aspects. This is that there is always 70 percent of the sentience that remains in the main body of the TES, and therefore there is always 70 percent of the sentience that remains in the main body of the Aspect.

ME: And this explains why the sentience associated with a Shard, which is circa 2 1/2 percent of the total sentience of the Aspect, and the sentient functionality associated with it, would create a limitation in the ability to think outside of the incarnate self.

A: Now you have it. The variation to this, though, is that the Shard that is a single migration of sentience into another incarnate vehicle can, if the Aspect has no other Shards projected, assign the full 30 percent of its available sentience for projection to that Shard.

ME: And I would guess that this would be the same for an Aspect if the TES was only using a single migration of sentience into another incarnate vehicle?

A: Correct. This means that in the case of the TES, it would experience its own experiences at the same time as the Aspect its sentience was migrated into.

ME: So the TES experiences the ability to drive its own energies and the incarnate vehicle its migrated sentience is in at the same time?

A: Yes, but this is normal for the TES because that is how it experiences things via its projections normally. With the exception, that is, that the projected Aspects drive the incarnate vehicle they are projected into, whereas in this instance, the TES is driving the incarnate vehicle on behalf of its migrated sentience. Think of it in terms of driving two motor cars at the same time.

ME: And this would be the same for the Aspect that migrates its sentience into a Shard?

A: Yes. There is a slight difference, though, because the TES that migrates its sentience is not incarnate but the Aspect that projects its sentience is. In this instance, the Aspect being already incarnate is usually incarnate at a frequency within the physical universe where it retains a large proportion of its connectivity with its TES. It also enjoys the functionality associated with that frequency which includes the command and control of the energies associated with its environment, which includes the incarnate vehicle it occupies.

ME: What frequencies within the physical universe would this be relative to, that being the ability to know who and what you are while incarnate, and be in the level of control where an Aspect could manipulate its incarnate vehicle?

A: That would be all frequencies above the eighth, with some minor ability in the sixth and seventh.

ME: So the Aspect's sentience and its associated energies are in both the primary incarnation and the secondary incarnation, which are both controlled directly by the Aspect.

A: Correct.

ME: And does the Shard think of itself as an independent entity in this case?

A: No. If the Shard was projected and was given autonomy, the answer would be yes, and the Aspect would receive the experiences in the normal parallel way a TES with a projected Aspect and an Aspect with a projected Shard are recorded. But in this instance, because the sentience and its associated energies are in the state of migration, the Aspect drives both the incarnate vehicle it resides within and the incarnate vehicle its Shard is incarnate into. In this instance, the sentience in its state of migration is split between the two vehicles and drives both of them, it drives both motor cars if you like, at the same time and experiences everything in both vehicles concurrently as a single function of sentience. In summary, the Shard does not think of itself as a single autonomic entity; it is simply an extension of the Aspect's sentience, and thinks of itself as being both the Shard and Aspect, just as the Aspect thinks of itself as the Shard as well. It's just that the sentience is in two vehicles. Another way to think of this is to be looking at two TV's!

ME: That last comment makes it easier to understand.

A: Good. I hope it is also understood by the readers as well.

ME: I expect it will. Well, we seem to have moved on very quickly into the detail behind the demarcation of subincarnations and secondary incarnations!

A: We do, and it was at the right time. I will use this part of our dialogue as a means of referral for the time when we formally discuss the subject of Shards, secondary incarnations, and subincarnations as an itemized function of how we incarnate. Now, though, we have to start from the beginning of this itemization. To describe this, I will use some common and some new nomenclature.

Twin Flames

Twin Flames are thought of as being souls who are Soul Mates, but this is not true. The correct definition is given away by the name itself. Twin Flames are therefore incarnate vehicles that share the same Aspect. They share the same Aspect by the sentience and associated energies being split equally between the incarnate vehicles being used. From the human perspective the twinning of the Aspect into two separate incarnate vehicles is achieved by the use of embryos in the same womb, with the twins illustrating many similar or same features both physically and in personality, but this is not a strict method. Twinning of the Aspect can and is achieved on a regular basis with embryos originating from different wombs, and the Aspect is not limited to a single twinning function. The Aspect can split itself into up to twelve smaller versions of itself that are in essence its self, but in twelve different incarnate vehicles, which do not need to be within the same womb or in the same location within the physical universe.

Some of the aspects of Twin Flames are that they display telepathy, empathy, the need to be together, do the same things, dress in the same way, and marry another twin. They feel the same pain, they feel the same joy, have the same thoughts, and have the same friends. Twins are, in most human cases, duplicates of each other, physically, mentally, sentiently, and energetically when from the same womb. This, of course, can include triplets and quadruplets, etc., although this is not as common as twins.

Sympathetic Souls

Sympathetic Souls are Aspects that have worked together before. Although Sympathetic Souls are not Soul Mates, because they will originate from different TES, when they meet they will feel like they are. This is simply because they are connecting at the energetic level automatically and will recognize each other's energetic signature as being one that they have worked with in previous incarnations. The incarnations are not specific to Earth-based incarnations of course because we incarnate in myriad forms throughout the physical universe and its associated frequencies. Based upon this, any previous interaction, whatever the form and wherever the location or frequency, will be enough for two or more Sympathetic Souls to recognize each other in some way.

Also be aware that the work the Aspects undertake in the pre-incarnation stage can also create a certain level of recognition, even if the Aspects have not incarnated together before. However, this will simply be a low level of recognition and not give the same level of deep "knowing," this will simply be a low level of recognition.

Sympathetic Souls will share same or similar ideas and ideals. They may also share the same likes and dislikes, such as pastimes or careers.

Soul Mates

Soul Mates are Aspects that originate from the same TES. Aspects that originate from the same TES can collectively be called a "Soul Group." A Soul Group, however, is only specific to those Aspects that are projected from the main body of TES sentient energy and not in any of the forms of communion previously discussed. Suffice to say, meeting a Soul Mate is a rare and beautiful event and is one that is not often forgotten simply because of the feelings associated with being in the same space as one's Soul Group member are remarkable. Soul Mates can be both same sex or opposite sex, there are no rules in this respect, although, from the purely human perspective Soul Mates are thought of as being sexually opposite, which is inaccurate.

Soul Mates will experience a certain level of telepathic and empathic communication and will certainly be able to feel each other's energies. Along with enjoying an extremely deep level of love for each other, they will want to be with each other all of the time, will need to be married, and have similar or the same pastimes.

Entanglement with Other Aspects' Lines of Projection

Entanglement is when the energetic lines of projection between two or more Aspects occurs. It can occur between Aspects of the same TES or between Aspects of different TES. It may seem bizarre that this can happen at all in an environment where a TES can be a master of its energies and environment, but it does. Especially when the Aspects in question are being projected by TES that are close to each other frequentially and environmentally.

Although not an issue in the energetic because we experience a much higher level of individual and shared/collective connectivity and expansiveness from the perspective of being incarnate, entanglement can and does create issues between the Aspects whose lines are crossed or entangled, especially in the lowest frequencies of the physical universe and therefore the multiverse. When the lines of projection are crossed or entangled, the communication between the projected Aspect and its TES can be shared by those Aspects experiencing entanglement. However, if there is no understanding of the simultaneous experiences that can be achieved by the TES and its Aspects by the TES and that all Aspects experiencing entanglement also share these experiences, then when these simultaneous experiences are experienced, confusion reigns.

The incarnate Aspect, when in the lowest frequencies of the physical universe, generally has no knowledge of the ability of the functions associated with entanglement and so when they are experiencing the thoughts associated with the experience of imagery, knowledge, and audible data that is invariably divorced from the environment they are incarnate within, they lose their total association with the primary environment they are incarnate into. For example, if the Aspect experiencing the simultaneous environments and experiences of another incarnate is based on Earth and the Aspect that it is entangled with is based in another environment in another galaxy, then that audio visual data has no anchor point to the Earth-based environment the Earth-based incarnate Aspect has, and so it will have no place in the total vocabulary set of that incarnate Aspect. The total vocabulary set in this instance is not just the spoken language but is the sum of the total experiential content experienced; such as the five physical senses and thoughts, desires, lessons, etc., accrued by the incarnate Aspect. So the incarnate Aspect, experiencing the experiential content of another Aspect, either develops a fear of that which it experiences, specifically if it is not of the Earth-based environment or accepts it and openly tries to communicate with that which is experienced by it. The ultimate destination for the incarnate Aspect that develops either the fear of or desire to communicate with that which it experiences is psychosis and the development of mental health issues. The ultimate end-game is usually the administration of a regime of medication and/or sedation.

It is possible, with the correct teaching, to help the incarnate Aspect understand what it is experiencing and work with it in a positive and functional way that does not attract the attention of mental health professionals.

Maintained Connectivity with Other Aspects

In some respects, the experiential functionality associated with maintaining one's connectivity with other Aspects that are projected from the same TES are identical to those Aspects that find their lines of projection in a state of entanglement. Again, this can either be fully understood with the experiential audio visual, etc., information being enjoyed and absorbed/used in a positive way, or it can lead to psychosis if not understood, or indeed not wanted.

When in total control and full understanding, the Aspect experiencing maintained connectivity with other Aspects can use this function as a way to fully experience the environments those other connected Aspects are experiencing. This will be in the form of observation only and the Aspect will not be in the position of being able to manipulate or integrate any Aspect of the environment it is exposed to—while it is incarnate, that is.

Maintained Connectivity with Event Space

An incarnate Aspect that has maintained connectivity with Event Space is one that can either traverse all of the potential realities associated with its dualistic, trilistic, or quadrulistic decisions, etc., at will, or is forever confused as to where it is and what it has achieved.

In respect of the incarnate Aspect that is in control of this function, it can achieve two things. Firstly, it can position itself into the alternative events that may, could, or will present themselves to it and make an active decision as to which decision is optimal or desirable. Or secondly, it can communicate with those versions of itself that exist within these alternative realities and accelerate its own experiential and evolutionary content in the process.

ME: I feel a need to interject here because I have some questions.

A: Go ahead.

ME: Doesn't that assume that the primary Event Space is the one that is being experienced in the Earth-based Event Space?

A: No, this is relative to any of the versions of the incarnate Aspect that are created as a result of the creation of additional Event Spaces due to the decisions that the primary incarnate Aspect has made, and/or the decision of the other fracturalized versions. Each of them will consider that they are the primary incarnate Aspect existing in the primary Event Space. Normally none of them will recognize that they are the product of a previous decision and are therefore another version, a copy, so to speak. The only exception to this condition is the Aspect that incarnates with the ability to experience these different Event Spaces, these different realities, at will, knowing that it could be either the primary incarnation or one of the copies while not being affected by this thought process.

ME: Why would an incarnate Aspect not be affected by such knowledge? Surely it would be afraid that it could wink out of existence at a moment's notice if its experiential/ evolutionary dead end is reached and it converges into the nearest active Event Space.

A: It won't. It knows and fully understands that it could wink out of existence into the primary incarnation or one of the copies. This is because it knows what it ultimately is and therefore holds no fear of the reintegration of Event Space.

ME:So the Aspect that can steer its way around the Event Spaces that are fractualizations of its downstream decision processes not only optimizes its experience by the use of such navigation, but it also recognizes that in doing so it could accelerate its own reintegration with a more mainstream Event Space in the process, ending its own individual line of Events. In effect, it can choose its own future!

A: Correct.

ME:Heavy knowledge!

A: Only for the uneducated. Incarnates have been doing this for years, they are called psychics. Most of them, though, are not able to use this function to its true potential.

ME:Clearly. What about the incarnate Aspect that is able to communicate with those other versions or copies of its self in the other Event Spaces?

A: If it is aware and awake it will be in acceptance of the ultimate possibilities just discussed, and it will also be able to use the ability to project its consciousness into the Event Spaces occupied by those other versions of its self that it is experiencing.

ME:Would these other versions have the same level of connectivity?

A: Not necessarily. Some will and some won't, but mostly they won't, for it takes a certain number of circumstances and a certain type or set of decisions to place the fractal or incarnate version of the incarnate Aspect into the position of awareness and the functionality associated with it.

In essence, the Aspect that has the capability of experiencing the Event Spaces (while controlling its own Event Space) of other versions of itself will benefit (as will its primary Aspect and TES) from its ability to experience parallel existences by accruing the evolutionary content associated with these experiences and the evolutionary content associated with the ability to experience them concurrently rather than linearly.

Those incarnate Aspects that have either the ability to see or experience the myriad downstream Event Spaces associated with its own downstream potential Event Space/s in an uncontrollable way, that being, they don't have the awareness that is normally associated with such functionality, have a very hard time anchoring themselves to their current Event Space. They will experience things that their friends, relatives, and associates will not be able to relate to because some Event Spaces will be in the far future, or variations of a far future from a chronological perspective that could or may be diversified from its main line Event Space and the fracturalizations from it. They will be considered psychotic and unless they can be educated as to what is happening to them, including being trained to control this function, they run a great risk of being institutionalized.

Similarly, those incarnate Aspects that have ability to project their consciousness into the incarnate Aspects associated with the other versions of themselves in an uncontrollable way, including their downstream potential Event Spaces, will also have significant difficulty in working in their current Event Space. Their consciousness will move seamlessly from one Event Space to another, experiencing them as if they are one Event Space but without the continuity associated with being in the same line of Event Space. Any continuity errors experienced will create profound psychological issues because roles and tasks that they have undertaken may not be relevant in their Event Space or the roles and tasks that they should have done in their Event Space may not be actioned as a result of these errors. They will also have difficulty interfacing with people in their career, relationships, and recreational pastimes. They will not know what their reality is, how valid it is, and whether their memories/actions are real or fiction. Again, without the correct level of education and training they will be considered psychotic and run a great risk of being institutionalized.

Walk-Ins

ME:I have to admit that I am looking forward to this particular subject heading. It is one that most spiritualists are aware of and I expect that the content you will present will have a lot of common ground with the current level of knowledge.

A: Let's see, shall we? I expect that we will have some new knowledge to discuss as well.

ME:Thank you. It will be good to be back on the trail of new knowledge again.

A: That, my dear soul, is the whole reason for your role in this incarnation, to broadcast new knowledge. Enough of the pleasantries, though. I want to start.

ME:I know that we are now short of time. I know this event is drawing to a close, and I want to maximize the opportunities we have left.

A: I will continue then.

There are four main types of Walk-Ins and incarnate mankind experiences them as:

- One-to-one Walk-Ins

- Multiple Walk-Ins

- Multiple static Walk-Ins

- Single temporary active Walk-Ins

- Single temporary passive Walk-Ins

One-to-one Walk-Ins are what spiritualists generally recognize as a Walk-In. This is best described in two ways. Firstly, it can be the result of an Aspect deciding that it has learnt, experienced, and evolved enough from a particular incarnation, wants to return to the energetic, and subsequently desires the incarnate vehicle to be used by another Aspect because there is enough longevity in the vehicle to make a Walk-In viable. Or secondly, it made a decision prior to initiation, prior to integrating itself into the incarnate process, that as part of its life plan it would leave the physical state at a predetermined point and another known Aspect would take over the incarnate vehicle and continue the incarnation in accordance with its own life plan and that created by the first Aspect to incarnate into the incarnate vehicle. In this instance, the primary incarnating Aspect can choose to experience any length of incarnate experience from a few seconds to the whole incarnation with all but a few seconds. The secondary incarnating Aspect therefore can Walk-In to experience incarnate existence from the perspective of almost a whole incarnation, if the primary Aspect only desired to experience the conception, gestation period, and birth of the fetus, to the final few moments of the incarnation in the incarnate vehicle, which would include the demise process.

The psychological aspects of a Walk-In are loss of memory (of varying levels and durations), changes in personality, disorientation, and reduction in or increase in skill set/s.

Multiple Walk-Ins are a condition where the incarnate vehicle is used by either a known or an indeterminate number of Aspects throughout the longevity of the incarnate vehicle. In terms of the known number of Aspects using the incarnate vehicle, each of the Aspects that associated themselves with the vehicle as part of their life plan will have decided which or what part of the "life" they will be incarnate within the vehicle for, the total number of incarnations creating a whole coherent life from the perspective of the external incarnate Aspect that is in the "immersed" state of incarnation and is therefore not aware and awake to the point of recognizing the incarnate vehicle it sees as being anything other than one person one body.

From the psychological aspect the only issue here is that a long-term associate (friend) would see a gradual change in the personality of their friend over the years they know them, the changes being specific to when the Walk-Ins swap out.

In terms of the incarnate vehicle being used by an indeterminate number of Aspects, there is almost no plan to the "life" the incarnated vehicle will have. This is because those Aspects that use the vehicle will incarnate when and where the opportunity arises—that being when the currently incumbent Aspect decides that it has experienced enough, or its "life plan" has been satisfied. They will of course have their own life plan but it will not correlate or link in to the overall life experienced by the incarnate vehicle, their plan being able to experience what they can, when they can, and doing their best to work with the conditions of the life and its environment that it inherits from the previous Aspect.

From the psychological aspect the external observer would see a completely irrational change in behavior and personality of the incarnate vehicle over its longevity due to the lack of planning in integration with the experiences and environment the incarnate vehicle is exposed to with previously coherent or incoherent decision-making processes being negated and replaced with those associated with the newly incarnating Aspect. The external observer may also note additional specialisms being displayed by the incarnate vehicle that are specific to the Aspects that Walk-In.

Multiple nonanimate (passive) temporary Walk-Ins are totally unrelated to multiple Walk-Ins. These Walk-Ins are a function of the desire of a number of Aspects to experience the incarnate existence of the primary incarnate Aspect on a temporary basis while being in the passive role. That being, they are not in control of the animation of the incarnate vehicle. Provided the primary incarnate Aspect is in accordance with the addition or subtraction of multiple passive Walk-Ins, the number of different Aspects can change or swap out almost on a daily basis.

There is no obvious psychological function of this Walk-In that can be observed by the external observer because the incarnate vehicle is animated by the primary Aspect only, with no interference to the life plan from the passive Walk-Ins.

Multiple nonanimate (passive) permanent Walk-Ins are a function of the desire of a number of Aspects to experience the incarnate existence of the primary incarnate Aspect while being in the passive role throughout the total longevity of the incarnate vehicle. As with the Walk-In condition just mentioned they are not in control of the animation of the incarnate vehicle, they are simply back-seat passengers, so to speak.

As with the previous condition there is no obvious psychological function of this Walk-In that can be observed by the external observer because the incarnate vehicle is animated by the primary Aspect only. In both this instance and the previous instance of the multiple Walk-In, the only way the presence of the other Aspects would be noted would be in regressive or "in-depth" hypnosis.

Single temporary active Walk-Ins are Walk-Ins that occupy the incarnate vehicle at the same time as the primary incarnate Aspect and have the ability to animate (control) the incarnate vehicle. Animation is either achieved in isolation to, in parallel with, or in tandem with the primary incarnate Aspect.

From the psychological perspective, the outside observer would witness similar behavior patterns to those presented by the incarnate vehicle that experiences multiple Walk-Ins.

Single temporary passive Walk-Ins are Walk-Ins that occupy the incarnate vehicle at the same time as the primary incarnate Aspect on a temporary basis, but which don't have the ability to animate (control) the incarnate vehicle. In this instance, the temporary passive Walk-In is, as with the multiple passive Walk-In, a purely back-seat passenger, observing and experiencing the existence and life plan of the primary incarnate Aspect but not influencing it.

From the psychological perspective, the outside observer would not witness any unfamiliar behavior patterns to those presented by the primary incarnate vehicle. The only way to identify that the incarnate vehicle housed a temporary Aspect would be via regressive hypnosis.

Secondary Incarnations

Secondary incarnations are a function of the ability of the Aspect to move to a lower frequency incarnate vehicle when it incarnates into an incarnate vehicle at a frequency higher than, but including, the eighth frequency, associated with the physical universe and therefore the multiverse as a primary incarnation.

When an Aspect incarnates into an incarnate vehicle that is in the eighth frequency and above, it retains most of its connectivity and functionality associated with being in the energetic environment of its TES. This means that the Aspect can freely commune with its TES and can manipulate its self and its environment at will. Although the Aspect is incarnate, it will be, from the perspective of those Aspects who incarnate into the frequencies that are below the eighth frequency, in the energetic state. This perception of the next level above a frequency being energetic, from the perspective of the observer is a consistent perception that starts at the third frequency level and continues upward to the eleventh frequency. Please note here that at the Earth level the first three frequencies are needed to create the environment the Earth and those components of the physical universe that are represented at this level can exist within, so there is no similar function from the first in observance of the second, to second in observance of the third frequency levels that are observed at the third in observance to the fourth and the fourth to the fifth, etc. I will reiterate again that the functionality associated with being able to create a secondary incarnation, an incarnation within an incarnation, is ONLY available from the eighth frequency and above.

Getting back to the description of the functionality of the secondary incarnation then, an Aspect will actively move its sentience and associated energies from its primary incarnation into another lower frequency incarnate vehicle if it wishes to experience an existence at the desired lower level and that that experience will enhance those experiences within the primary incarnation that it would not have experienced otherwise. The experience in a lower frequency incarnate vehicle is expressed as a "secondary incarnation" and not a "subincarnation" as this is a different function, one that I will explain in the next subject heading. The Aspect that chooses to enter into the role of being in a secondary incarnation also has the ability to pass on its experiences to those other incarnates that are working with it at the frequency of domicile of the primary incarnate vehicle. This enhances the efficiency of experience by extending it to its counterpart incarnate Aspects or colleagues.

When an Aspect enters into the secondary incarnation it can either leave the primary incarnate vehicle in a form of stasis, leaving only 5 percent of its sentience and associated energies in the primary incarnate vehicle in a sort of "care-taker" role, allowing it to collect the experiences of the secondary incarnation and disseminate it to its counterparts or colleagues on an automatic basis. This has the effect of the Aspect only truly experiencing one incarnation, the secondary incarnation, until the demise of the incarnate vehicle that is being used for the secondary incarnation is experienced, wherein the primary incarnate vehicle is reanimated by the sentient energies used in the secondary incarnation returning to it. Alternatively, the primary incarnate vehicle can be left in a functional state by the Aspect leaving circa 20 to 30 percent of its sentience and associated energies within the primary incarnate vehicle and projecting the remaining energies into the secondary incarnate vehicle it has chosen. This is, although being classified as a secondary incarnation, the true state of the incarnation within the incarnation. It is classified as such because the sentience associated with the energies that animate the primary incarnation and the secondary incarnation can and does actively, effectively, and regularly migrate between the two incarnations, experiencing both and controlling both simultaneously. In this instance, the sentience associated with the secondary incarnation tends to migrate back to the primary incarnation during the times when the secondary incarnate vehicle needs to rest and remove the toxins accrued during its normal daytime animation—when it needs to sleep.

An interesting but basic fact of the use of the secondary incarnate vehicle is that it is regularly monitored by the Aspect's counterparts or colleagues and is accessed for information on the levels of integration and functionality expected/experienced by the Aspect in animating it. To do this the vehicle used as the secondary incarnation is removed from its environment (when necessary), it is monitored and information downloaded from it that is useful to the primary incarnation and/or its counterparts/colleagues. This action is one that is experienced on a regular basis and is the explanation for the experiences of many, but not all, UFO abductions reported.

Subincarnations

Subincarnations are the main descriptor for a Shard. The Shard is described as a subincarnation and not a secondary incarnation because it is a direct projection from the Aspect and follows the same distribution of sentient energy as that experienced when the TES projects an Aspect from it. That being, it will only project a maximum of 30 percent of its total sentient energy into a maximum of twelve Shards. This means that if all Aspects are projected external to itself by its TES then each Aspect only contains 2 1/2 percent of the TES total sentience. Similarly, if each Aspect only contains 2 1/2 percent of the TES total sentience then each Shard only contains 2 1/2 percent of the Aspect's total sentience. That suggests that the Shard can only ever have 2 1/2 percent of 2 1/2 percent of the total sentience projectable by the TES, which limits its incarnate capabilities. The Shard, when projected into an incarnate vehicle, is therefore able to enact a fully independent incarnation within an appropriate level of sentience from the Aspect it is projected from to make it feel like it is an Aspect or an Aspect of the Aspect. However, that level of sentience restricts its cognitive abilities in comparison with a true incarnate Aspect.

Whereas in the secondary incarnation the sentient energies of the Aspect are effectively moved or shared between the primary incarnate vehicle and the secondary incarnate vehicle throughout the use of the secondary incarnation, the sentient energies associated with the subincarnation are static in comparison.

ME: Does this mean that Shards are subject to low intelligence?

A: You could say that, but it would be as a generalized statement only.

ME: Go ahead.

A: There are Shards that appear, in all intents and purposes, to be intelligent, but in reality contain only the basic Shard sentience.

ME: Who or what would they be?

A: People who make it rich by accident *[of course there is no such thing as an accident!* —GSN] or through the application of intelligent people or friends around them who promote something that the Shard is good at or creates, and that has a new level of interest with the populous allowing the product, or the actions of, the Shard to be sold in some way.

ME: We have a saying for that type of person in the UK. I will refrain from repeating it. Nevertheless, this shows that just because an incarnate is a Shard, it doesn't mean it is destined to be financially challenged.

A: If being financially rich is a measure of intelligence then there are many Shards out there that are incorrectly identified as intelligent. The reality of the matter, though, is that each Shard, in general, has an average- to low-achievement life expectancy at best in terms of its experiential content and ability to work with those interactive experiences presented to it.

ME: Do Shards have life plans? What I mean is, do they have the same access to a life plan and the pre-incarnation planning that an Aspect has?

A: Not in the independent way that the Aspect does with its guide and helpers, no.

ME: What happens then?

A: Whereas the Aspect or the TES (together or separately) decides on what it wants to achieve in the incarnation as an upstream function of the life plan, electing who and what will be its guide and helpers and the specialisms they need to bring with them, and when to employ them in the guidance of the incarnate Aspect, the Shard has no such function or ability.

ME: But they do have guides and helpers, don't they?

A: Correct. In fact, the whole life plan of the Shard is developed by the Aspect and or TES and not the Shard itself in conjunction with the overall life plan of the Aspect.

ME: So, if the Aspect and/or TES have to work out the life plan of the Shard or Shards the Aspect projects as well, that means they also have to work with all of the parallel functions of the Shard/s incarnation/s that come into existence as a result of its dualistic, trilistic, or quadrulistic, etc., decisions that invoke different Event Spaces?

A: Of course.

ME: That's a massive task to undertake! Just a thought, what is the number of Shards projected by the average incarnate Aspect?

A: Four. Four is the average number of Shards projected by an Aspect, although there are many Aspects that project more, and some also project the full twelve, the vast majority project four plus or minus one or two Shards.

ME: I have a quick question for clarification before we end the dialogue of this subject.

A: Fire away.

ME: When are the Shards projected from the Aspect? Is this before Aspect incarnates or during its incarnation?

A: There are no real rules on this, although I can see from your thoughts that you think that there are.

ME: Yes, I would have thought that the Shards would be projected from the Aspect when it is in the energetic, before it is incarnate, and that they would be reintegrated when the Aspect returns to the energetic.

A: Well, I have already discussed this in a previous dialogue and although what you are thinking is in keeping with that dialogue, in reality, an Aspect may choose to project or reintegrate a Shard at any point in its incarnation. What I described previously is a logical presentation of what happens in the general sense.

ME:OK, thank you.

14

Projection into the Incarnate Vehicle

Again I had the feeling that I was running out of (clock) time. Things had moved on a pace in my incarnate life (I will explain later—or rather Anne tells me she will explain on my behalf, I have just been told), and my time was starting to become very precious indeed. In fact, it was now becoming almost nonexistent, but in a most wonderful way!

I knew that this book was due to be completed soon, and I also knew the remaining word count that was necessary to make that happen would soon be accomplished. That said, I looked at the chapter headings I had to deal with and wondered a little as to what depth we would be going into. I needn't have wondered too long because Anne came to my rescue.

A: She's lovely, a real sweetie, and is a perfect partner for you at this time of your incarnate life and the level of work you are doing.

Anne was obviously eager to advise you, dear reader, that I had been blessed with the presence of a most graceful lady in my life. She was guided to me and I had received guidance to her. "Celia" was a natural progression for me and appeared to be, no, "is," the perfect partner for me. The transition from Anne to Celia had been a surprise and was seamless from an emotional perspective. I was humbled at the mechanics of the process behind our joining together in such a loving partnership.

A: We worked hard to get you both in the same space to be able to make the connection. It needed to be the right time and place for both of you. Even though it was always in the plan, a plan that you were not allowed to see for yourself, the logistics were challenging, to say the least.

ME: Who is "we?"

A: Your peer group—those OM who are following your work, who are assisting in the background. You see, even though you don't have a guide and helpers per se, you do have a helping hand once in a while. Also, you are not allowed to be on your own, so to speak, and so Celia is a very special Soul/Aspect.

ME: She is also OM?

A: Yes, of course.

ME: But I thought that I/we were the only full OM's to incarnate?

A: You are not told everything, and we needed to keep you focused and on track in this period of your incarnation, hence the veil being drawn over this information. You would have been distracted and would have been looking for her, ultimately making a mess of the overall plan. Suffice to say, you "two" are still the only full OM to incarnate, for she is an Aspect of your TES, just as you are an Aspect of her TES, just as I was/am an Aspect of our TES. An OM can only enter into a relationship with an OM. All OM are one, even if the Aspect is individualized from the TES and/or the TES is individualized from the OM collective. This is important for there needs to be a certain level of "purity of function" that can only be achieved by OM with OM. Do you understand?

ME: Yes, I believe I do.

A: Good. Now let me continue with the rest of this dialogue, because as you said, we are running out of clock time.

ME: OK, please go ahead, please continue.

A: The process of projecting the individualized Aspect of TES into the incarnate vehicle is remarkably simple in real terms. In essence, it is like putting a suit of energetic clothes on, a low-frequency suit of energetic clothes, that is.

Once the Aspect is individualized and the previously identified incarnate vehicle is ready for integration with the Aspect, the Aspect commences the integration process. In order to achieve integration with the incarnate vehicle the Aspect needs to create a link between it and the energy system of the incarnate vehicle. This link creates an energetic "step-down" function that allows the high frequencies of the Aspect to integrate with the low frequencies of the incarnate vehicle, allowing it to animate it as if it was a naturally occurring appendage to the Aspect. To create this link, the Aspect weaves what can be described as an energetic pipe that is known by some as the "hara line." The hara line allows the sentient energies of the Aspect that are to be used in the integration with the incarnate vehicle to pass through the reduction of frequencies that are a natural function of the vehicle and its environment without being overly affected by them. In essence, it protects or separates the sentient energies of the Aspect from those of the environment and the incarnate vehicle so that they do not become affected by the low frequencies that the incarnation is proposed to be in. That being said, the sentient energies of the Aspect are not totally unaffected for there is a natural occurring reduction of communicative functionality experienced by the Aspect as it integrates with the incarnate vehicle that cannot be negated by the protection of the hara line. This is recognized as the "forgetting" function as is the main reason for the individualization of the Aspect that creates the "Ego" and the total association of the Aspect with the incarnate vehicle; the incarnate vehicle thereby being referred to as the "Self." For information the hara line can also be called the "Silver Cord," the energetic line observed by those incarnates that are able to perform the temporary separation of the Aspect from the incarnate vehicle called "Astral Traveling." This is also called "Samadhi" by Hindu yogis and "Transcendental Meditation" by western adepts.

Although the sentient energies of the Aspect move in and out of the incarnate vehicle from its very conception it can only fully integrate into incarnate vehicle when it is in the thirty-second week of gestation.

In order to integrate with the incarnate vehicle the sentient energies of the Aspect move through the hara line. This is connected to the energy bodies of the incarnate vehicle by the "tan tien" and "Soul Seat" via a function of the crown chakra. That being, it uses the same space as the crown chakra without affecting the functionality of the crown chakra and as a result it appears to go through it. The hara line therefore continues down to the tan tien, where it is connected to the energy bodies of the incarnate vehicle, thereby allowing the Aspect to animate the incarnate vehicle as if it was the incarnate vehicle. The hara line does not terminate at the tan tiem, however; it splits into two at this point and progresses down each leg, terminating at the soles of the feet, where it can and is used as a grounding function with the energies of the Earth, or area of local density within the physical universe, the planet, the environment, where the incarnation is planned to take place. Once the sentient energies are integrated with the incarnate vehicle at the tan tien, the "Essence" of the sentience, the "Beingness" of the Aspect moves into and occupies the area just behind the heart chakra. This area is called the Soul Seat *[see Barbara Brennan's books,* Hands of Light *and* Light Emerging, *for some excellent illustrations. —GSN]*. That which "is" the Aspect when incarnate is therefore resident within the Soul Seat and NOT the brain. As previously described much earlier in this dialogue, upon the demise of the incarnate vehicle the process of separation from integration with the incarnate vehicle is the reverse of the integration process.

At this point in the incarnation, the interactive opportunities with other incarnates are limited. Also, the integration with the incarnate vehicle is only at its most basic. It takes seven years for the Aspect to become fully integrated with its incarnate vehicle, and this is because the energetic templates and attributed energy systems become more complex as the gross physical aspects of the incarnate vehicle grow into maturity, allowing a more complete level of integration. In essence, this description is back to front, though, because it is only when the energetic templates are developed to the next stage of complexity that that gross physical can grow to the next stage. However, there is an interdependency between the gross physical and the spirituo-physical (the melting pot between the frequencies associated with the gross physical and those of the lower frequencies associated with the energetic), where the energetic templates need the gross physical to be at a certain stage of maturity before the next stage of template complexity can be added. As just stated, this interdependent growth occurs over the next seven years.

15

The First Seven Years Are the Most Important

I have just returned to this dialogue after a two-week break. Incarnate "life" had gotten on top of me, and like many incarnates right now, I was feeling that time was running away from me. As a result I had to place a few things into an order of priority. I had become very aware that I was close to the end of this work and needed to get it finished. I note that I have stated this many times in the last few thousand words; the difference here, though, is that I really feel it. I also know that it needs to be completed in the next few weeks as well, and needs to be proofed and presented to my publisher, Ozark Mountain Publishing, before the end of this year (2015) so that I had to finish the text ASAP. I took stock of the situation and observed that a few notes I had made to myself on some of the questions I was going to ask Anne were still relevant given the titles of the final two chapters. Knowing, of course, that not everything goes according to plan in this business I asked the first question relating to why the first seven years of incarnate existence are the most important.

ME: We have a saying here on Earth that goes something like this: "Give me the boy and I will give you the man."

A: Those years being the years that the boy in question is at his most "pliable" or those where he is most susceptible to the influence of others.

ME: Yes. I would expect that this equally relates to girls and women?

A: Of course it does. The correct statement should be "give me the child and I will give you the adult." This, however, is not relative to the Aspect and its incarnation from the perspective of the mechanics of incarnation because that deals with the function of free will and personal choice—that being, to actively choose to be affected by those surrounding us or to actively choose not to be affected by those surrounding us.

ME: OK, I will stop distracting you.

A: Thank you. In this instance, the first seven years are relative to the level of integration with the incarnate vehicle and therefore the depth of immersion into the incarnation itself. The depth of immersion is a direct function of the level of integration with the incarnate vehicle. I will say here, though, that what you may think of as being integrated and immersed is not the actuality of the function.

ME: You mean that the more integrated with the incarnate vehicle the Aspect is, the more immersed in the incarnation it becomes?

A: Correct. In the event that the Aspect is fully integrated with the incarnate vehicle it becomes fully immersed in the incarnate existence it planned. This means that the Aspect "is" the human body in the case of existence on Earth. If on the other hand, the Aspect is incompletely integrated, and there are various levels of this, then the Aspect either "knows" or "feels" that it is not the human body or incarnate vehicle and therefore has varying levels of access to its TES and the greater reality. This type of integration results in the person appearing to be of access to those who are fully integrated and therefore fully immersed.

I will therefore describe the mechanics of the first seven years of incarnate existence from the perspective of integration and functionality based upon the eras of integration the incarnate Aspect experiences as the flowing:

- Pre-birth

- Birth to first year

- Year one to year four

- Year four to year five

- Year five to year seven

- Year seven and beyond

In the **pre-birth** period the level of integration with the incarnate vehicle, the Aspect is simply learning how to work with the energies of the vehicle selected, getting the feel of its functionality/abilities, health, longevity, and strength. In effect, it is learning how to connect with the energies of the vehicle. Each and every Aspect that incarnates has to go through this process simply because the energies associated with the incarnate vehicle vary depending upon the vehicle itself. Those energies associated with its construction, that being those of the mother and father, make enough energetic difference to ensure that the Aspect needs to align itself to them in a way that is subtly different to the alignment used in its previous incarnation. Once it is happy with its level of integration, and happy with the level of harmony with the energies of the vehicle, it elects to fully integrate with it. It is at this point that the Aspect loses the energetic functionality associated with its normally high frequential state to a functionality associated with its temporary incarnate state. That being, it forgets who and what it is and loses its capabilities as a creator, the level of forgetting and functionality, of course, being a function of the level of integration with the incarnate vehicle and its associated immersion. Based upon this, an Aspect can incarnate in states of no awareness and memory of Self, with no communicative ability with its TES, to full awareness and total memory of Self and full communicative ability with its TES.

In the **pre-birth to year one** period the Aspect is busy establishing itself as the incarnate vehicle from a rudimentary sense, that being, relative to the level of awareness it has assigned to itself, or the level of immersion it desires to experience. Also included are the initiation of the relationships, from a human level, with the mother, father, and its siblings—if any at all at that juncture in its incarnate existence. During this time if the Aspect has a high level of awareness assigned to it, it can either choose to stay with the incarnate vehicle at all times or it can move away from it during rest periods (sleep). If on the other hand the Aspect has chosen total immersion, it will sink into a deeper and deeper level of integration and immersion with the incarnate vehicle and will fully associate itself in all ways with the incarnate vehicle, establishing the ego as a result. Note here that an ego is always created as a result of incarnation, irrespective of the depth of integration and immersion, but it is the depth of immersion that creates the size of the ego, so to speak—that being, the level of overall control it has over the incarnation during the incarnation from a purely human perspective. *[For additional information please see my article on the ego in the back of this book. —GSN]*

Energetically speaking the Aspect is learning how to control the incarnate vehicle through the experience of the five senses, anatomic/automatic bodily functions and movement of motor-based functions. Also, the chakras and auric field are not entirely developed at this point in the incarnation, which results in the Aspect having limited energetic functionality and personal protection from energetic attack of any kind. In aid of this, the Aspect, within the incarnate vehicle, needs to be close to, or better still within, the energies of its mother's (or father's) auric field for both protection and energetic nutrition. From the perspective of energetic operational and functional connectivity, that which allows the Aspect to animate the incarnate vehicle, connectivity is via the hara line, which is the energetic tube or micro vortex that protects the sentient energies that are projected out from the TES and into the incarnate vehicle, through a location close to the crown chakra to a point just above the pelvis where it splits into two and continues down each leg. The sentient energies of the Aspect coalesce at the tan tien, which is three inches (75mm) above the navel and three inches (75mm) inside of the physical body at this point. There they are connected with the energy matrix that is the energetic "Body" templates on all seven levels of the spirituo-physical components of the incarnate vehicle, the energy meridians, mini, minor, and major chakras. The essence of beingness of the Aspect, its sentience, coalesces at a point in line with the tan tien but behind the heart chakra known as the "Soul Seat." *[Again, see Barbara Brennan's work. —GSN]* The incarnate beingness or sentience of the Aspect is therefore located in the soul seat and NOT in the head.

From **year one to year four** the Aspect continues to develop the ego and as a result the start of a "Human Personality" can be seen by those who interact with the incarnate Aspect. Furthermore, accuracy of "Bodily" control is experienced and self-awareness as a human being is established. At this point the majority of the capacity for learning is established and the Aspect gains knowledge of itself (likes, dislikes, and abilities); its communicative abilities and functional abilities from a mental and physical perspective are becoming noticeable. Energetically the Aspect gradually reduces its dependence on the mother and father for energetic nutrition and protection. With that the incarnate Aspect becomes an independent incarnate entity around the age of four and is now capable of increasing its level of individuality in all perspectives and functions.

From **year four to year five** the Aspect is in a period of consolidation, and energetic autonomy from the parents is established. With the ability to be totally autonomous from the parents, it seeks to establish its own personal and energetic boundaries. This period can be either the start, or the end, of a phase of tantrums, which are created as the incarnate Aspect also establishes its boundaries of external control from others, internal power over the self, and external power over others.

In the instance of the fully immersed Aspect, evidence of selfishness can be observed along with varying levels of coercive ability becoming visible as the ego grows and takes hold of the sentient energies of the Aspect in this incarnate state. The memory of its real state being far in the energetic distance/past, the ego washes over the sentience and the relationship between the Aspect's sentience (its sentient energies); the incarnate vehicle and the ego are now merged as one.

In the instance of the semi-immersed Aspect, higher thoughts, function/abilities, and other incarnations percolate to the surface in random moments, making the incarnate Aspect feel that it is not quite what it is as an incarnate entity and start to question its self and its surroundings. This can lead to the Aspect asking strange questions of its parents, siblings, and friends that are totally out of context with its incarnate upbringing, age, and experience to date. Out-of-body excursions may be experienced.

From **year five to year seven** the Aspect completes its final stage of energetic development from the perspective of the growth of the three gross physical and four spirituo-physical energetic stages—seven in total—to that of the adult gross physicality of the incarnate vehicle. Note that this is a statement of functionality and not of size. All of the chakras, mini, minor, and major, are now fully developed and fully functional. From this point onward, the incarnate Aspect is capable of using its energies for purposes other than simply maintaining the incarnate state. They can be used for communication, coercion, healing, energetic attack, and defense as well as manipulating the Aspects local environment. Some or all of these functions are used on a subconscious basis in the main, irrespective of whether the Aspect is fully immersed in the incarnation or is in some level of spiritual awareness. For those Aspects that are in one of the various states of awareness, more exposure to the greater reality is experienced and/or at a greater depth. At this point the ego is almost fully developed.

From **year seven and beyond** the Aspect "is" the incarnate vehicle, the incarnate vehicle being in a state of seamless connectivity, functionality, and operation between the Aspect and its incarnate vehicle. Due to the ever-increasing need to work and interface with others in the physical environment, from the perspective of both the fully immersed and the aware Aspect (at whatever level), the thought processes revolve around the self being the incarnate vehicle and not its sentient energetic state. From here onward, the fully developed ego grows from strength to strength and is the dominant personality that drives the incarnate vehicle. Even at this age, the ego is what we are when incarnate, and it only gets bigger as we age and gain exposure to the experiences that incarnate existence gives us. External influences taint, mar, temper, encourage, satisfy, excite, and educate us on all levels giving us desires, prejudice, likes, dislikes, addictions, and overall experiential experience. From this juncture the personality is the ego and the ego is the personality, and the incarnate Aspect is ready to work in the physical as a function of its physical environment.

These seven years provide both the greatest and most complete integration and immersion into the incarnate state sentiently, energetically, physically, and mentally, providing a robust basis for the life plan to be introduced and worked with.

16

Control of the Incarnate Aspect's Direction versus the Life Plan during the Incarnation: An Overview

16.1

The Need for the Guide and Helpers

ME: You ended the last chapter by stating that on or after the seventh year of incarnation that *"These seven years provide both the greatest and most complete integration and immersion into the incarnate state sentiently, energetically, physically, and mentally, providing a robust basis for the life plan to be introduced and worked with."* What did you mean by that?

A: In essence, these seven years are the most important years of an Aspect's incarnation, for they form the basis of how the Aspect will address its life plan from an autonomous basis and how much work the guide and helpers will need to do to ensure the incarnate Aspect stays on track from an external influence basis, so to speak.

ME: I don't quite understand.

A: Well, think of it this way. If the integration with the incarnate vehicle is robust then the Aspect will be fully immersed in the incarnation at the depth it is supposed to be. Additionally, the Aspect's energetic functions will be identified to the guide and helpers so that they are aware of how to influence the Aspect and the Aspect will be aware of its higher functions as its incarnate vehicle matures. By this I mean that the cognition of the incarnate Aspect increases the longer it is integrated with the incarnate vehicle, that being, it recognizes its "self" and its energetic abilities and uses them accordingly. This means that the Aspect, while immersed in its incarnate state, will either use its intuition or gut feelings more than logic and will therefore know what it has to do in this incarnation with very little prompting.

You are aware of certain individuals who, at a very early age, want to be a pilot, a doctor, or a lawyer, etc.

ME: Yes, I have met many people who had "a mission," so to speak. I myself had a feeling from a very young age that I had/have something very important to do.

A: Yes, good, and this is the metric, albeit a simple one, that identifies how well the Aspect is integrated and immersed. Those Aspects that have the feeling of a "life mission" are in tune with their life plan. Those who do not have a feeling of a life mission are not tuned into their life plan so well. So, based upon this, at all points during the incarnation the incarnate Aspect is under the guidance and help of its main guide and helpers. I will say it again. The level of intervention by the guide and helpers is therefore a function of the level of integration and immersion in the incarnation.

ME: OK, I think I have it now.

A: Good. The life plan is, as previously described, a list of all the experiences the Aspect, or TES on behalf of one of its Aspects, chose / has chosen to allow the evolutionary content of the TES to increase within a single incarnation. It is designed to augment existing experience and its associated evolutionary content and provide new experiences that are either a progression from a previous experience or set of previous experiences or are a completely new genre. The Aspect may decide to be exposed to its desired experiences at either certain or known juncture points within the incarnation, or just "go with the flow," so to speak, allowing fully autonomous incarnate interaction from a known or chosen experiential point. This means it either chooses to be guided in a very interactive way, or it elects to have a primary experience as a springboard for all the other experiences to work from employing the guide and helpers only when it appears to be really off track. Either way, it needs to have an external resource that is able to see where the Aspect is in accordance with its life plan and knows how to influence the Aspect and those other incarnate Aspects that are part of its plan, ensuring that those things that it has elected to do that are part of their life plan are actioned. The life plan is therefore riddled with "interactive" contracts between Aspects that serve the function of ensuring that the chosen experiences are presented to the incarnate Aspect by those other incarnate Aspects that are working around it in the same environment as it is, that have agreed to present them. This of course is reciprocated.

ME: Does the Aspect know when it's off track? If so, how?

A: Only if it has a high level of energetic functionality will it be able to know this and act accordingly, negating the need for the guide and helpers to intervene. The general state of integration and immersion within the incarnate vehicle is such that the Aspect will not be aware of being off track, especially if the Aspect is enjoying the incarnate experience and maybe even getting addicted to its experience. It is therefore for this reason that the Aspect needs the guide and helpers to intervene on its behalf, steering it back on track, so to speak, back onto the main line of the life plan, or provide a way that allows the Aspect to get back on track itself.

16.2

How We Get Back on Track

ME: Now we are about to get to the meat and bones, the whole reason for this chapter, I would guess?

A: Correct, although it won't take much to explain.

ME: Why not?

A: Because from the human perspective it needs to be described in a fairly simple way. The detail behind what I am about to illustrate, however, is too complicated to describe because of the amount of preparatory work the guide and helpers go through. They undertake a significant amount of work, checking, double checking, treble checking, etc., to ensure that the method of intervention they are going to use will be successful enough. Furthermore, and as you would expect, they use the Akashic to validate the optimal junctures of insertion and the intensity of intervention required.

The optimal use of intervention is always to use the minimum possible interference allowing the Aspect to see the way forward itself and make the necessary corrections accordingly. Throughout the incarnation the guide and helpers monitor, or for want of a better word, "observe," the incarnate Aspect and its progression. The guide, as previously described, acts as a sort of "manager" of the helpers, overseeing the work they do, directing and assisting when necessary, intervening when there is a major diversion to the plan. In order to get back on track the guide, through the helpers, places events or experiences that can either make the incarnate Aspect change its direction or thought processes by minimal intervention, or introduce a major level of intervention if required.

Minimal intervention can be achieved by the guide and helpers "nudging" the incarnate Aspect by placing "niggling" thoughts of doubt about a certain experience or series of experiences creating a want to change direction. Feelings of actual "desire" to change direction or experience can also be inserted into the thoughts or feelings of the incarnate Aspect. This is usually manifest in a "need" to do something or experience a certain thing. The desire to "follow" a person or way is also a method of minor intervention.

Major intervention can be achieved by making a change in personal circumstances such as by the introduction of an illness or an external influence such as the loss of career or accident.

In essence, and for illustrative purposes, one can visualize this as the guide and helpers dropping "bombs" in the way of the incarnate Aspect making it change its direction in a way that allows it to go back on track, back on to the main line of the life plan in terms of experience, learning, and evolutionary content gained versus the junctures within the life plan where the expected experience, learning, and evolutionary content is supposed to be gained.

16.3

The Parallel Experiences

A: I have only talked about one specific incarnation here and have not touched upon the parallel conditions that are created by Event Space when the incarnate Aspect is presented with a choice, of any sort.

ME: I thought we had as part of the description of the structure of the guide and helpers?

A: In that context we have, yes, but I just wanted to make a point here about parallel experiences and what the guide and helpers do in these instances—just for clarity.

ME:OK.

I was sensing a level of detachment coming as I typed, like Anne was about to sever the link and move on.

A: Every time the incarnate Aspect has a choice to make, a parallel version is created by Event Space. This includes the possibility of making a choice or choices, the possible possibility of making a choice or choices or the possibility of the possible possibility of making a choice or choices. When this happens the work of the guide and helpers is magnified by the number of parallel versions of the incarnate Aspect and its environment that are created. These are created in a fractal sense, and dissolved in a fractal sense when an evolutionary or choice-based "dead end" is experienced. In doing this, the guide orchestrates the helpers into Event Space genres, that being, those parallel conditions that are very, very similar but not quite similar enough to be considered the same. In this way, the helpers can both observe and action any intervention necessary on a more general basis allowing those redirectional "bombs" to have a "one-size-fits-all" approach for the Event Space genre they are working within. They do this by building in "redirective" redundancy allowing the intervention to cope within certain tolerances of incarnate Aspect response and environmental change based upon the subtle variations in the choices made. As you can imagine, it is hard work to deal with, say, 3,456 versions of an incarnate Aspect they are working with, so this makes the work of the guide and helpers more efficient in the parallel conditions they encounter that their "ward"— the descriptor for the incarnate Aspect they are working with—makes through unlimited choice.

In summary, though, even with the efficiency of working with Event Space genres the guide and helpers work on each parallel version of their ward as if it is the only one in existence, for in real terms, in that Event Space, it is the only one that that particular ward exists within.

Now … I must go for my work here is done. Weep not, though, for I will still be of assistance when required. Think of me, and I will be with you as I always have been and always will be.

Now, though, you need to continue your work, and you have to concentrate on nurturing your relationship with your new partner, Celia, for she is also part of the plan and has much to offer. Look after her, listen to her, and love her, for she is a great asset. And now I go, my love, back to our TES, for I have my work to do as well.

And with that, and more than a few tears from me, the link with Anne dissolved. For a moment I was in bereavement—a bereavement that had been put on various levels of "hold" for nearly three years. I felt lonely for a moment and then thought of Celia, dear, dear Celia. She has really changed my life, my direction, my!!!!!

Mmmm, I thought, was this intervention? A life-changing moment, a "bomb" placed in front of me to make me change direction? I wonder, I just wonder—of course, it is! It's as plain as plain can be. I visualized Celia and smiled. The old adventure, this adventure, had finished but another had just started—one where Celia was at my side, and I hers. The feelings of bereavement left me and were replaced by floods of tears of joy. I was back on track!

17

Afterword

This has been another challenging series of dialogues for a number of reasons, and I feel the need to explain these reasons here and now.

First, although it followed what appeared to be "known" themes on what we are and how we incarnate, there was a much greater level of understanding presented, an understanding which opened the doors to other areas and depths of understanding, areas that were previously unheard of. And, initially they seemed to follow a logical process, and then I noticed that there were a lot of convoluted parallelisms being created. A lot of dichotomies, trichotomies, quadrichotomies—that there are no rules associated with how we experience incarnation, but moreover, only that we do experience incarnation in its various levels of immersion and that we experience it our own way—in general, that is. As long as our incarnations followed a certain level of process and expected experience, that was OK. Anything that was expected to be experienced but was missed out for some reason was added to the next incarnation or negated if this was experienced by another Aspect from the same TES in a way that was similar enough to that which we wanted to experience. This was convolution, random, chaotic convolution—it was beautiful.

Second, that there is no getting away from the fact that what we do "now" not only affects us in the "now," it also affects us later in the downstream functions of what we do. On top of this, it also affects those other incarnate Aspects we have, and will, interact with downstream of the juncture of the event of our action/s, including the fractal versions of ourselves. Our actions should therefore be seriously considered and contemplated before acting, for the statement used by chaos theory stating that *the beat of the wings of a butterfly in one country can create a hurricane in another* is more than a theory—it is FACT. While incarnate in the human form we have the mixed blessing of having individualized free will, which means to me that we can do anything we want to do provided we are willing to pay the price of the downstream consequences. As a result, I now see how important the use of contemplative and mindful thinking/actions are. The details in *Avoiding Karma* on how to be in the physical but not of the physical are essential daily personal practice.

Finally, you, dear reader, will find this dialogue both interesting from the perspective of understanding the details behind incarnation, or at least what we are being allowed to know at this juncture in our existence, which has now been expanded, and that I started this within a few months of Anne's ascension. To say that the energetic contact with my late wife, Anne, helped the human side of me cope with the loss would be a bit of a misnomer. You see, although I experience what I experience could be construed as being a reason not to grieve, because I know and live the truth of what we are from the perspective of the Greater Reality, there is still the need to be "human" while here, and therefore this work, this dialogue, had to some extent delayed my grieving process.

If there is one thing I have learnt from this dialogue, it is that we have to experience the human experience—in all of its aspects—its trials and tribulations, its rises and falls, its loves and hates, its reasons and no reasons. There is no getting away from this. This is a multiversal law associated with incarnation into the physical universe and the Earth-based experience it offers us. This law is as follows: *irrespective of who we are, what we are, and how connected we are, we have to experience being human while being incarnate.* None of us is exempt. ALL the great spiritual leaders have, are, and will experience the limitations and temptations of being human while incarnate in the human vehicle, and others like it. There is no escape; there is only an ability to make the journey easier, should we choose to use this ability. This ability is the ability to see the Greater Reality, the greater meaning of who and what we are—Aspects of our True Energetic Selves experiencing existence in myriad ways to assist in our own evolution, the evolution of The Source and subsequently The Origin. Once we all understand this, we will work with each other in a profoundly enlightened way, making our journey much easier, more fruitful, and more enjoyable, reducing the downstream functions of our decisions in the "now" and reducing our need to incarnate in the process. Only then will we reach heaven on Earth.

I know that I have six more books to channel over the next few years, but at this point I have no feeling as to which one is next— a strange place for me to be as I know the titles of the books and the subjects. Although I think I am being given time to contemplate all of this, I have a niggling feeling that this will be short lived. I feel that I am being pulled toward another function of our existence, one that includes nature. Let's see if this bears fruit!

Guy Steven Needler

19 September 2015

18

Poems for Anne

I wrote a poem for Anne's funeral service. It is, to my memory, the only poem I have ever desired or needed to write *[since I wrote this I have written quite a few to my new partner and future wife, Celia. —GSN]*. It was read out by Giovanni Esposito (Spoz), a previous poet laureate of the city of Birmingham, UK. The poem sums up our physical existence together and my feeling of physical loss—a purely human condition.

I have also, with their permission, included two other poems, one written by Spoz himself, and one from Anne's goddaughter, Sammi-Joy. They all sum up the depth of the incarnate human spirit, Anne's spirit, in different ways.

From Guy ...

I know I should not grieve
For grieving focuses on loss
And loss is such a transient thing
Loss is such a small thing

I know I should not grieve
For grieving brings great sorrow
And sorrow is not a memory
Of that we had between us

Too small a point in time
To warrant its existence
Grieving dominates the joy
We had in OUR existence

I now change my focus
On all those years of joy
Negating the grief and sorrow
In lieu of the joy

Remembering my Anne, I smile and laugh
My tears of sorrow will now depart
And tears of Joy will now apply
For I have years of memories
To wistfully remember
Our life together was such an adventure

Thank you my dear one
You've given me so much
The last thing to do is

JUST STAY IN TOUCH!

From Giovanni "Spoz" Esposito, Birmingham poet laureate, 2006/7 ...

When speaking of Anne
Where should one start?
Her welcoming manner?
Or her gentle heart?

A true friend of Birmingham,
A true caring soul,
Who cared for each fraction,
As well as the whole.

Busy putting smiles
On people's faces,
With no sense of self
And no heirs and graces.

Redressing the balance
Of an unjust lot
She gave what she had ...
to those that had not.

Our world will be poorer
Without our Anne,
Though we'll soldier on
As best as we can,
You'll live long in our memories,
Beyond all measure,
A farewell to Anne ...
Our national treasure.

Spoz x

From Sammi-Joy Lockley ...

Our Gentle Smiler

Lady, first off
I hope you're at peace
Smiling on down at
The absurdity of us
As we mourn and weep for your loss

You can finally say
You beat the beast
You've been set free
Released
Back into The Source entity

Just don't think we'll
Ever forget your gentle ways
That beguiling smile
Your infinite grace

Personally from me to you
I want to say
A huge thank you
No God Daughter could have been prouder
Of the woman who
Introduced me to Pride and Prejudice
Who baked Christmas stars with me
The woman with whom
I could have the most serious in depth
Discussions of Harry Potter

Thanks again for believing in me
I will forever endeavour to make you proud

You just take it easy
We're all winding our way
Back to you, eventually
Just be patient
And know that we'll
Hold your light within us
Eternally

19

What Is the Ego and How Does It Affect Our Spiritual Progression?

In human terms, the ego can be loosely recognized as a state of beingness. That beingness can be described as: if someone is considered to have a "big ego," they are considered to think a lot of themselves and are ambitious. These people are usually highly materialistic and not in control of their thoughts. Conversely, if someone is considered to have little or no ego, they are considered to be introvert or lacking in ambition. They are usually not very materialistic and are generally in control of their thoughts.

In both of these cases the ego is the controlling factor in our daily incarnate lives. The size of the ego alludes to the level of control the ego has on us. So, if the ego has control of us, what is it exactly?

The ego is a creation, a temporary creation. It is created as a result of an Aspect (soul) of our True Energetic Self (TES—sometimes called the Over Soul, Godhead, or Higher Self) being separated out from the TES and projected into the lowest frequencies associated with our multiversal environment, to experience, learn, and evolve in an accelerated way.

To experience this evolutionary acceleration, the Aspect (soul) must enter into the frequencies in the way they are best experienced, as if it were part of them. To do so, it needs to associate itself with a vehicle which it can animate energetically.

This vehicle is, in our instance, the human form. Notice I said "form" and not "body." It is classified as the human form because it uses ten frequency levels to create it. Three gross physical, four spirituo-physical—the partially energetic condition that makes up the semi-physical/energetic components of the human form, sometimes called the "Astral"—and three energetic frequencies that allow the TES to project an Aspect of itself, complete with sentience, in an energetic "step-down" function that allows partial communication between the Aspect and the TES while associated with the lower frequencies that make up the human form.

This condition of being in "partial communication," or even almost "zero communication" is what creates the ego. The ego is therefore a condition where the sentience associated with the energies that are the Aspect (soul) associate themselves in an isolated or individualized way with the gross physical aspect of the human form, the "body." They "are" the human body.

The ego is a temporary or transient condition because it can only exist while the human form is operational (alive), and when we are not self-realized. When the human form demises (dies), it dissolves, although the experiential memories of what we are while incarnate are not lost because they are always transmitted to the TES in parallel with the experience itself. The ego can also be dissolved if we work on our spiritual development and regain contact with our TES or higher self. The ego knows this and does everything in its power to stay in control, in power, "alive" for as long as it can, and so will work hard on arresting our spiritual progression.

As incarnate Aspects of our TES, our main role is to become spiritually self-realized while incarnate, resuming communication with our TES in the process, working in the physical while not being of the physical. In this condition there is no room for the ego and it dissolves. The ego knows this and is patient, sly, and resourceful and can use convoluted methods to trick and fool us into thinking we have mastered it. It infuses us with feelings of self-consciousness, failure, depression, success, materialism, status, and pride. Success and pride are two emotions the ego uses with skill because we can feel these emotions as a result of being pleased with our spiritual progress. And, when it uses these to the best of its ability, we can "think" we are making spiritual progress when in effect we are not. Notice how some of the most spiritual people also have the biggest egos!

The very moment we think that we have mastered the ego, we have lost the battle and the ego is back in control of us and our thoughts, and we lose some of our spiritual progression. So stay aware, stay observant by observing yourself in a passive and nonjudgmental way, and look for the signs of the ego rising within you, then act upon it and continue your spiritual progression and your goal of becoming self-realized while incarnate.

This article, in slightly different format, was previously published by *OM Times* in June 2015, pages 50–52. http://www.editions.omtimes.com/magazine/2015-06-A/

20

Glossary

The Animal Aspect—An Aspect whose TES has a lower sentient content than human TES's. It can evolve beyond its TES. When it does so, it detaches itself from the TES and seeks out a human TES of an evolutionary level (frequency of domicile) that is consistent with its self and negotiates integration and subsequent elevation to human status.

Aspect—An Aspect is a smaller part of the TES that is used to experience the minute detail of the environments within the multiverse. It is used to experience the lowest frequencies of the multiverse presented by the physical universe through the process of incarnation. A maximum of twelve Aspects can be projected by the TES at any one time.

The cart in front of the horse—A way of saying that, for example, the answer to a question is given before the question is asked.

Core Star—Sometimes called the tan tien because it is so close to the nexus, the point of distribution, of the Aspect within the energy network that is the gross physical and spirituo-physical components of the human form.

Dimensiate—An effect of being pan dimensional (across many dimensions simultaneously).

Egress—An alternative word for "exit."

Event Space Horizon—When all events that are concurrently represented in the same space are observed by an entity, the collective images of the environments created by those Event Spaces appear to be a white horizon on a white background. This effect is created when the entity cannot divide the different environments represented by the different Event Spaces into separate images, creating sensory overload and the "white on white" effect. The use of the words Event Horizon to describe the periphery of a black hole, or worm hole as we would call them are therefore no surprise because everything blends into one.

Fits the bill—A way of saying that something does the job.

God Head—The Hindu word/descriptor for the TES.

Hara Line—The energetic link from the True Energetic Self (TES) to the incarnate vehicle. It links the Aspect projected into the human vehicle with the vehicle and the frequencies associated with the physical universe. It is the power and communication source of the human vehicle. The hara line is positioned in the center of the human form from the center of the top of the head, splitting into two at the tan tien and continuing earthward down the legs.

Higher Self—A spiritual word/descriptor for the TES.

In Buckets—A term used to explain when something is in abundance.

Intelliate—Intelligence-based communication.

Lovey Dovey—A term for when one openly and constantly expresses ones love for another by being physically close.

Omniciate—Omniscience-based communication.

Over Soul—The Quantum Healing Hypnosis Technique (QHHT) word/descriptor for the TES. QHHT was a hypnosis-based healing technique taught by Dolores Cannon.

Overdrive—A way of saying that someone or something's performance has increased. The overdrive was a semiautomatic secondary gearbox added on to the manual gearbox of classic sports cars or performance automobiles in the 1960s and 1970s in the UK.

Primary Incarnation—A descriptor for the incarnate functionality of an Aspect if a secondary incarnation is employed.

Secondary Incarnation—A descriptor for the incarnate functionality of an Aspect that uses a significant percentage of its sentient energies to have an incarnation in a lower frequency within the physical universe. This is not a Shard but an incarnation within an incarnation because the Aspect in the primary incarnation continues while the secondary incarnation is in action. In the event that the Primary incarnation is placed in stasis for the duration of the secondary incarnation the primary incarnation will recommence once the secondary incarnation is finished.

Sentiate—Sentience-based communication.

Shard—A Shard is a smaller part of the Aspect that is used to experience the minute detail of the environments within the multiverse. It is also used to experience the lowest frequencies of the multiverse presented by the physical universe through the process of incarnation. As with the TES a maximum of twelve Shards can be projected by the Aspect at any one time.

A silk purse out of a sow's ear—The ability to make something special from something that is considered to be nothing.

The Slinky Effect—The function of projecting a portion of the TES to another frequential level lower than itself to allow it to project Aspects into the lower frequencies of the multiverse. Used if the TES is very highly evolved.

Soul—The Christian and spiritual word/descriptor for the Aspect or Shard. The Soul is considered to be individualized in totality and not part of a larger being. It is also generally related with the human body and no other incarnate vehicles.

Soul Seat—This is where the essence of the Aspect resides. It is the personality of what we are, as a projected Aspect of our TES, while temporarily individualized by association within the human form. Its position is not far from where the front and rear Aspects of the heart chakra join.

Subincarnation—A descriptor for the incarnate functionality of a Shard.

Tan Tien—This is where the Aspect spreads out from the hara line into the energy network that contains the aura and the chakras. It ends up being a focus of tremendous energy. It is positioned two and a half inches below the navel (belly button) and two and a half inches in toward the center of the human vehicle from the navel.

That's about the size of it—A way of saying that something is correct, a statement or other.

True Energetic Self (TES)—What we truly are—an entity of pure sentience with a given or commandeered body of energy.

Walk-In—The swapping in and out (one for another) of Aspects (souls) within a single incarnate vehicle. There are many variations upon this theme.

Where the TES exists—The TES exists in more than one place within the multiverse. It exists in the frequency associated with its evolutionary stasis and under evolutionary tension (see The Origin Speaks). Where it would have been had it not been in evolutionary stasis, and just evolved without using incarnation as an accelerant. And, where it would have been once the evolutionary tension is released.

About the Author

Guy Needler MBA, MSc, CEng, MIET, MCMA initially trained as a mechanical engineer and quickly progressed on to be a chartered electrical and electronics engineer. However, throughout this earthly training he was always aware of the greater reality being around him, catching glimpses of the worlds of spirit. This resulted in a period from his teenage to early twenties where he reveled in the spiritual texts of the day and meditated intensively. Being subsequently told by his guides to focus on his earthly contribution for a period he scaled back the intensity of spiritual work until his late thirties where he was re-awakened to his spiritual roles. The next six years saw him gaining his Reiki Master and a four year commitment to learn energy and vibrational therapy techniques from a direct student of the Barbara Brennan School of HealingTM, which also included a personal development undertaking (including psychotherapy) as a course prerequisite using the PathworkTM methodology described by Susan Thesenga with further methodologies by Donovan Thesenga, John and Eva Pierrakos. His training and experience in energy based therapies have resulted in him being a Member of the Complementary Medical Association (MCMA).

Along with his healing abilities his spiritual associations include being able to channel information from spirit including constant contact with other entities within our multi-verse and his higher self and guides. It is the channeling that has resulted in "The History of God" and is producing further work.

As a method of grounding Guy practices and teaches Aikido. He is a 6th Dan National Coach with 34 years experience and is currently working on the use of spiritual energy within the physical side of the art.

Guy welcomes questions on the subject of spiritual physics and who and what God is.

Books by Guy Steven Needler

The History of God
Published by: Ozark Mountain Publishing

Beyond the Source, Book One & Book Two
Published by: Ozark Mountain Publishing

Avoiding Karma
Published by: Ozark Mountain Publishing

The Origin Speaks
Published by: Ozark Mountain Publishing

The Anne Dialogues
Published by: Ozark Mountain Publishing

For more information about any of the above titles, soon to be released titles,
or other items in our catalog, write, phone or visit our website:
Ozark Mountain Publishing, Inc.
PO Box 754, Huntsville, AR 72740
479-738-2348/800-935-0045
www.ozarkmt.com

OZARK
MOUNTAIN
PUBLISHING

If you liked this book, you might also like:

Dancing Forever with Spirit
by Garnet Schulhauser

Between Death & Life
by Dolores Cannon

The Other Side of Suicide
by Karen Peebles

A Funny Thing Happen on the Way to Heaven
by Grant Pealer

The Dawn Book
by Annie Stillwater Gray

Live from the Other Side
by Maureen McGill & Nola Davis

Holiday in Heaven
by Aron Abrahamsen

For more information about any of the above titles, soon to be released titles,
or other items in our catalog, write, phone or visit our website:
Ozark Mountain Publishing, Inc.
PO Box 754, Huntsville, AR 72740
479-738-2348
www.ozarkmt.com

For more information about any of the titles published by Ozark Mountain Publishing, Inc., soon to be released titles, or other items in our catalog, write, phone or visit our website:

Ozark Mountain Publishing, Inc.

PO Box 754

Huntsville, AR 72740

479-738-2348/800-935-0045

www.ozarkmt.com

Other Books By Ozark Mountain Publishing, Inc.

Dolores Cannon
A Soul Remembers Hiroshima
Between Death and Life
Conversations with Nostradamus,
  Volume I, II, III
The Convoluted Universe -Book One,
  Two, Three, Four, Five
The Custodians
Five Lives Remembered
Jesus and the Essenes
Keepers of the Garden
Legacy from the Stars
The Legend of Starcrash
The Search for Hidden Sacred Knowledge
They Walked with Jesus
The Three Waves of Volunteers and the
  New Earth
Aron Abrahamsen
Holiday in Heaven
Out of the Archives – Earth Changes
Justine Alessi & M. E. McMillan
Rebirth of the Oracle
Kathryn/Patrick Andries
Naked In Public
Kathryn Andries
The Big Desire
Dream Doctor
Soul Choices: Six Paths to Find Your Life
  Purpose
Soul Choices: Six Paths to Fulfilling
  Relationships
Patrick Andries
Owners Manual for the Mind
Tom Arbino
You Were Destined to be Together
Rev. Keith Bender
The Despiritualized Church
Dan Bird
Waking Up in the Spiritual Age
O.T. Bonnett, M.D./Greg Satre
Reincarnation: The View from Eternity
What I Learned After Medical School
Why Healing Happens
Julia Cannon
Soul Speak – The Language of Your Body
Ronald Chapman
Seeing True
Albert Cheung
The Emperor's Stargate
Jack Churchward
Lifting the Veil on the Lost Continent of Mu
The Stone Tablets of Mu
Sherri Cortland
Guide Group Fridays
Raising Our Vibrations for the New Age
Spiritual Tool Box
Windows of Opportunity

Cinnamon Crow
Chakra Zodiac Healing Oracle
Teen Oracle
Michael Dennis
Morning Coffee with God
God's Many Mansions
Claire Doyle Beland
Luck Doesn't Happen by Chance
Jodi Felice
The Enchanted Garden
Max Flindt/Otto Binder
Mankind: Children of the Stars
Arun & Sunanda Gandhi
The Forgotten Woman
Maiya & Geoff Gray-Cobb
Angels -The Guardians of Your Destiny
Seeds of the Soul
Carolyn Greer Daly
Opening to Fullness of Spirit
Julia Hanson
Awakening To Your Creation
Donald L. Hicks
The Divinity Factor
Anita Holmes
Twidders
Antoinette Lee Howard
Journey Through Fear
Vara Humphreys
The Science of Knowledge
Victoria Hunt
Kiss the Wind
James H. Kent
Past Life Memories As A Confederate
  Soldier
Mandeep Khera
Why?
Dorothy Leon
Is Jehovah An E.T
Mary Letorney
Discover The Universe Within You
Sture Lönnerstrand
I Have Lived Before
Irene Lucas
Thirty Miracles in Thirty Days
Susan Mack & Natalia Krawetz
My Teachers Wear Fur Coats
Patrick McNamara
Beauty and the Priest
Maureen McGill
Baby It's You
Maureen McGill & Nola Davis
Live From the Other Side
Henry Michaelson
And Jesus Said – A Conversation
Dennis Milner
Kosmos

Other Books By Ozark Mountain Publishing, Inc.

Guy Needler
Avoiding Karma
Beyond the Source – Book 1, Book 2
The History of God
The Origin Speaks
James Nussbaumer
The Master of Everything
Mastering Your own Spiritual Freedom
Sherry O'Brian
Peaks and Valleys
Riet Okken
The Liberating Power of Emotions
John Panella
The Gnostic Papers
Victor Parachin
Sit a Bit
Nikki Pattillo
A Spiritual Evolution
Children of the Stars
Rev. Grant H. Pealer
A Funny Thing Happened on the
   Way to Heaven
Worlds Beyond Death
Karen Peebles
The Other Side of Suicide
Victoria Pendragon
Born Healers
Feng Shui from the Inside, Out
Sleep Magic
Michael Perlin
Fantastic Adventures in Metaphysics
Walter Pullen
Evolution of the Spirit
Christine Ramos, RN
A Journey Into Being
Debra Rayburn
Let's Get Natural With Herbs
Charmian Redwood
A New Earth Rising
Coming Home to Lemuria
David Rivinus
Always Dreaming

Briceida Ryan
The Ultimate Dictionary of Dream
   Language
M. Don Schorn
Elder Gods of Antiquity
Legacy of the Elder Gods
Gardens of the Elder Gods
Reincarnation...Stepping Stones of Life
Garnet Schulhauser
Dance of Heavenly Bliss
Dancing Forever with Spirit
Dancing on a Stamp
Annie Stillwater Gray
Education of a Guardian Angel
The Dawn Book
Blair Styra
Don't Change the Channel
Natalie Sudman
Application of Impossible Things
L.R. Sumpter
We Are the Creators
Dee Wallace/Jarrad Hewett
The Big E
Dee Wallace
Conscious Creation
James Wawro
Ask Your Inner Voice
Janie Wells
Embracing the Human Journey
Payment for Passage
Dennis Wheatley/ Maria Wheatley
The Essential Dowsing Guide
Jacquelyn Wiersma
The Zodiac Recipe
Sherry Wilde
The Forgotten Promise
Stuart Wilson & Joanna Prentis
Atlantis and the New Consciousness
Beyond Limitations
The Essenes -Children of the Light
The Magdalene Version
Power of the Magdalene
Robert Winterhalter
The Healing Christ

For more information about any of the above titles, soon to be released titles,
or other items in our catalog, write, phone or visit our website:
PO Box 754, Huntsville, AR 72740
479-738-2348/800-935-0045
www.ozarkmt.com